Diary of a Longing Heart

DERICK BINGHAM

AMBASSADOR

AMBASSADOR PRODUCTIONS LTD.
Providence House
16 Hillview Avenue
Belfast, BT5 6JR
United Kingdom

ISBN   0   907927   82   3

D E•D•I•C•A•T•I•O•N

*T*his book is dedicated to my friend Joseph Morrow who, though he went to school bare-footed and knew, like David, great sorrow and poverty in his early life, also found his joy in God. His devoted service to the Lord and sheer kindness to me and to my family has been an inspiration, especially when the going has been rough.

Also by Derick Bingham

RUTH
A Love Story With Secrets For Living

THE EDGE OF DESPAIR
Twelve Psalms That Draw You Back

PROMISES TO KEEP
A Daily Devotional Based On Proverbs

MORE THAN A DREAM
The Story Of Joseph

LORD OF OUR JOURNEY
Devotional Insights

I N·T·R·O·D·U·C·T·I·O·N

*W*riting, for me, has always been a compelling thing. I have always felt "driven" to write, as if I could do no other. Meeting, after twenty years, a former University English tutor of mine I asked him "Why do you think I feel compelled to write?" "Well", he replied, "How can you know what you think until you see what you say?"

So it has been with this biography of David. The life of one of the greatest poets of all time is extremely complex and while studying it over many years of my life I have often wondered what I really thought of David. When David was good, he was very, very good and when David was bad, he was awful. Yet, the more I wrote of this biography of David, based on the words of Scripture, one thing surfaced again and again: here was a man who, despite his faults and huge mistakes, loved God. Not only that, he actually longed for God. From his teenage days to his old age David longed after God like few have ever done.

This book is deliberately written in a daily devotional format and because of that format it must needs be practical in its teaching and inspirational in its aims. I trust that as you read it you will see very clearly that while others went after fame or fortune or whatever, our subject went after God. And he found Him, in the sheepfolds, in the caves, in the mountains and in the palaces of his life. David longed for God's company, God's blessing and, above all, to see God glorified and God always goes where he is wanted.

This book is unquestionably the diary of a longing heart. Not only that, it is the diary of a longing heart that was, in the end, truly satisfied. May David's experience be yours.

Derick Bingham

PSALM 63

O God, thou art my God;
early I will seek thee:
my soul thirsteth for thee, my
flesh longeth for thee in a dry
and thirsty land. where no
water is;

To see thy power and thy
glory, so as I have seen thee in
the sanctuary.

Because thy lovingkindness
is better than life, my lips shall
praise thee.

Thus will I bless thee while
I live: I will lift up my hands
in thy name.

My soul shall be satisfied
as with marrow and fatness;
and my mouth shall praise thee
with joyful lips:

When I remember thee
upon my bed, and meditate on
thee in the night watches.

Because thou hast been my
help, therefore in the shadow
of thy wings I will rejoice.

J·A·N·U·A·R·Y

J·A·N·U·A·R·Y

*T*hose first steps into the assertion of individuality. Babyhood and childhood gone, those days arrive when the young person begins to stand up and argue for what they really believe. Idealism is high, experience is limited, they begin to ask "Why not?" Backed up by a childhood in the nurture of the Lord there is no telling what that youth might accomplish long before manhood. If you doubt me, let's spend January reading about a youth called David. The child was indeed the father of the man.

J·A·N·U·A·R·Y 1ST

"Then the Lord said to Samuel, 'How long will you mourn for Saul seeing I have rejected him from reigning over Israel? Fill your horn with oil, and go; I am sending you to Jesse the Bethlehemite. For I have provided myself a king among his sons'". 1 Samuel 16:1

People like "big" men but "big" is not necessarily great, is it? Robert Maxwell was "big", Howard Hughes was "big", Randolph Hearst was "big", Lenin was "big", but, were they great in their lives?

King Saul was the people's choice but he was not God's. Physically he stood head and shoulders above everyone else. Spiritually, he was an unbeliever. His life proves it again and again. You simply cannot refuse God's Saviour and be a believer and Saul was to blankly refuse the King-Saviour of God's choice, David.

Do you want to be truly great? Bow to the sovereignty of David's greater Son, the Lord Jesus, trust him as Saviour and Lord and He will make you a "king and a priest" in His kingdom. And if you would be truly great in His kingdom, then you must become the "servant of all". That's why God told Samuel to get himself down to Jesse the Bethlehemite's place. A serving lad had just qualified to become a king. So, christian, get into serving this year, it is a mark of true greatness.

J♦A♦N♦U♦A♦R♦Y 2ND

"And Samuel said, 'How can I go? If Saul hears it, he will kill me'. And the Lord said, 'Take a heifer with you, and say I have come to sacrifice to the Lord. Then invite Jesse to the sacrifice, and I will show you what you shall do; you shall anoint for me the one I name to you'". 1 Samuel 16:2-3.

You don't have to tell everything that is in your heart. Samuel knew that he was for it if King Saul found out that he had chosen one of Jesse's sons to be king. So God covered his move with a genuine act of worship.

Are you about to do something that the Lord has guided you to do? Go on your way but don't tell everybody what you are setting out to do. Jane Austen lived in a day when women writers were despised. Yet, Jane wrote her great novels quietly, in private and she had a warning system set up to cover her privacy. She had a door that squeaked and she never oiled it. When she heard the door squeak she knew that someone was coming and she then quickly covered her writing materials with tapestry materials. Take a leaf out of Jane's book. Everybody doesn't have to know everything about you.

J♦A♦N♦U♦A♦R♦Y 3RD

"But the Lord said to Samuel, 'Do not look at his appearance or at the height of his stature, because I have refused him. For the Lord does not see as man sees; for man looks at the outward appearance, but the Lord looks at the heart'". 1 Samuel 16:7.

When Samuel saw Eliab he was sure he was Israel's future king. "Surely the Lords anointed is before him", he said. Yet, he was wrong.

Look around you. How do people judge people? By their weight, clothes, accent, house, educational background, friends, tastes, politics, denomination or where they holiday etc. Image is a big thing in our world. Chic carries clout, possessions speak power. God's view of things is so different. He looks deeper. His chief criterion for picking people for a special purpose is; "Are you willing to do my will?" To be a person "After God's own heart", is to be a person after Gods own will. Can I suggest a motto for the coming New Year? Let it be "The will of God, nothing less, nothing more, nothing else and at all costs".

J•A•N•U•A•R•Y 4TH

"And Samuel said to Jesse, 'Are all the young men here?' Then he said, 'There remains yet the youngest, and there he is, keeping the sheep.' And Samuel said to Jesse, 'Send and bring him. For we will not sit down till he comes here'". 1 Samuel 16:11.

I was travelling in a car once with a friend of mine. Leaning over to the glove compartment he pulled out a piece of paper which he told me his dying father had given him. It read, "I have loved you all equally". My friend treasures that piece of paper but even better he treasures the fact that his father, in reality, actually did love, value and appreciate each of his children, equally, right throughout his life.

To Jesse David was just the lad who kept sheep. He wasn't worthwhile summoning to a religious feast, never to speak of summoning to a throne. It was the biggest mistake Jesse ever made and it is a warning to parents. Don't, whatever you do, play the "you-are-my-favourite" game with any of your children. Making "pecking order" comparisons between your children is odious. We must give our children a clear sense of the fact that they have equal worth in our hearts and plans. They will never hold that against us.

J•A•N•U•A•R•Y 5TH

"So he sent and brought him in. Now he was ruddy, with bright eyes, and good-looking. And the Lord said, 'Arise, anoint him; for this is the one!'" 1 Samuel 16:12.

Much training had gone before the moving moment of David's anointing. Who were his teachers? Solitude. Obscurity. Monotony. Reality. Nature was his nurse and God was his mentor. For one exposed to danger he was not to cower before a nine and a half foot giant because, as he pointed out to Goliath,

"The Lord who delivered me from the paw of the lion and from the paw of the bear, he will deliver me from the hand of the Philistines".

Yet, I think I can detect a mother's hand. David was to say nothing of his father but he refers twice to his mother as "the handmaid of the Lord". His deeply religious character had roots in a good mother. Behind the hand that anointed David lay the hand of Hannah, behind the head anointed lay the love and spiritual fervour of a dedicated woman. Selah.

J♦A♦N♦U♦A♦R♦Y 6TH

"And the Spirit of the Lord came upon David from that day forward". 1 Samuel 16:13.

To watch a baby being born is to experience a great mystery. As a little body is ejected from a warm womb into the much colder air, an agonising moment occurs. The attending surgeon or midwife often takes the baby and slaps it on the back and there comes that piercing, choking, struggling wail that is, in fact, music to the ear; a baby's first cry! What has happened? The baby has first been put into the air, but, just as importantly, the air has just been put into the baby!

When a person becomes a christian they are put into the Spirit of God, but, just as importantly, the Spirit of God is put into them (See 1 Cor 12:13). You can't have one without the other. Only Christ can do this vital work and with you, christian, now in the Spirit and the Spirit in you, great things can be accomplished.

J♦A♦N♦U♦A♦R♦Y 7TH

"So Saul said to his servants, 'Provide me now a man who can play well, and bring him to me'. Then one of his servants answered and said, 'Look, I have seen a son of Jesse the Bethlehemite, who is skilful in playing, a mighty man of valour, a man of war, prudent in speech, and a handsome person; and the Lord is with him'". 1 Samuel 16:17-18.

It is amazing how a call to the Palace comes. David didn't shove and push and pull strings to get himself into Saul's court.

He knew very well that God had great plans for him but consequent to Samuel's confirming God's promises that great things were afoot, David simply went back to keeping his father's sheep. Back to the nitty-gritty. Back to wind and cold and rain and snow and prowling lions and bad-tempered bears.

It was his gift that made room for him. He remained faithful to his few sheep and when the king needed some music to lift his depression he sent for David the skilled musician. So, christian, back to the nitty-gritty and one day, in the midst of it all, the great call to greater things will come. It's guaranteed.

J•A•N•U•A•R•Y 8TH

"For who is this uncircumcised Philistine, that he should defy the armies of the living God?" 1 Samuel 17:26.

It was a question nobody but David thought of asking. While all the army of Israel quaked in their combat boots and King Saul cowered in his tent, the lad from Bethlehem kept on implying "Who does this fellow Goliath think he is in defying God?" God was as real to David as his own breath and it never entered his head to think that anyone who defied God could ultimately succeed. The lad's faith had bred confidence.

Perhaps there is a simple question you need to ask as the giants of worry, fear and pressure come stomping up your valley yelling defiance against the God in whom you have put your trust. Quit heading for the hills or tents of comfort and face those giants head-on with a simple question; "If God be for us, who can be against us?" Measure up the giant against God and he will be a dwarf.

J•A•N•U•A•R•Y 9TH

"Now Eliab his oldest brother heard when he spoke to the men; and Eliab's anger was aroused against David, and he said, 'Why did you come down here? And with whom have you left those few sheep in the wilderness? I know your pride and the insolence of your heart, for you have come down to see the battle'. And David said, 'What have I done now? Is there not a cause?'" 1 Samuel 17:28-29.

The youngest and the oldest are perfectly contrasted in today's text. The youngest, David, had faith, confidence, humility and vision. The oldest, Eliab, could not see beyond his own nose. He sneered at David's faith and with venom despised David's lowly position as a shepherd. Is it any wonder that we never hear of Eliab again?

Mark well the fact that the victory over Goliath was really won by David at this point. If David had thrown up his head and met Eliab's venom with a "How dare you call my faith into question", if he had lost his temper with Eliab he would have underminded the moral high ground which he had taken by God's strength. David simply met Eliab's venom with a soft answer; "Surely", he said, "my father's wish to learn of your welfare was the reason why I came here". Always remember that a victory over your temper in a small matter today will lay the foundation for an even bigger victory in a huge matter tomorrow.

J•A•N•U•A•R•Y 10TH

"David spoke to the men who stood by him ... then he turned ... toward another and said the same thing ... and when the words which David spoke were heard, they repeated them to Saul; and he sent for him."
1 Samuel 17:26

There must have been tens of thousands of men in the valley of Elah, paralysed by fear of Goliath. The sentence, though, spoken by a young shepherd lad spread like wildfire. It even reached the ears of the king and he sent for David.

One sentence spoken by you today could have immense effect in the circumstances that might confront you before the day is out. Even "asides" can have wide repercussions. You can either speak words of dishonesty, unkindness, flattery, impurity, blasphemy, criticism, exaggeration, greed, slander and boasting or you can speak words of encouragement, love, comfort, wisdom, inspiration, praise and blessing. The choice is yours. Repercussions, either way, are certain.

J◆A◆N◆U◆A◆R◆Y 11TH

"You are not able to go against this Philistine to fight with him, for you are but a youth." 1 Samuel 17:33

On the face of it Saul's judgement of David was right. It is a foolish business, though, to get hung up on externals. We must never forget that God has high expectations of young people's spirituality. They do not have to wait until adulthood before they can achieve great things for God.

People who were mightily used by God in their youth include not only David but Joseph, Samuel, Samson, Joash, Uziah, Josiah, Esther, Daniel, Hannah, Mishael, and Paul's nephew. Our God is a God of all ages. Young or old, if God bids you do something; do it. Don't let the Sauls of this world reason you out of it. Because Saul refused to do God's will was no reason for David to refuse to do it just because he was young.

J◆A◆N◆U◆A◆R◆Y 12TH

"Your servant has killed both lion and bear and this uncircumcised Philistine will be like one of them, seeing he has defied the armies of the living God". 1 Samuel 17:36

Some people have very short memories. Did the Lord deliver you from some impossible situations last year? Why would he not do the same this year? Do you really think he has brought you across the Atlantic to drown you in a ditch?

"We write", wrote Spurgeon, "our benefits in dust and our injuries in marble, and it is equally true that we generally inscribe our afflictions upon brass while the records of the deliverances of God are written in water". David knew that the God who helped him in the past was just the same, today. "Jesus Christ is the same, yesterday and today and forever". "The Same", said a Scotsman to me, once, "is a Divine title". Selah.

J✦A✦N✦U✦A✦R✦Y 13TH

"I cannot walk with these, for I have not tested them". *1 Samuel 17:39*

It was a turning point in the history of David when he took Saul's armour off. The thing was as a yoke to him, burdening him down. He had never tested it. A shepherd's bag, a sling and some smooth stones were in David's orbit. Bronze helmets and coats of mail were totally unfamiliar.

It seems to me an awful lot of people go out to fight the Lord's battles burdened down with things other people insist they must carry. Christ said "My yoke is easy and my burden is light". You are called to play the part Christ wrote for you, not the part other people seem to insist on writing. Burn their scripts, cast off their yokes and go for it! I have proved in my life that incredible blessing follows; if not to speak of sheer relief and freedom to go giant-slaying.

J✦A✦N✦U✦A✦R✦Y 14TH

"... that all the earth may know that there is a God in Israel".
1 Samuel 17:46.

Strategy. When you are up to your eyes in problems, pressures and difficulties, think strategy. In modern language, get your eyes on the "big picture". I try to do it all the time. In a city of bomb scares, daily terror and much mayhem, as I climb the pulpit steps to teach God's word to a very hungry and terrorist-weary people each week I try to remind myself that God's word may appear weak and insignificant but it is, in fact, mighty to the pulling down of strongholds.

I remind myself of young David in front of a 9' 6" giant with a spear like a "weavers beam" and his 15 lb iron spearhead and coat of mail weighing 125 lbs, screaming, all the time, blue murder; I think of David's calm, quiet prediction to Goliath that the Lord would deliver him into his hand and the whole earth would know that there was a God in Israel. It's a long way from the valley of Elah to Belfast but David's "big-picture" strategy worked. It will work for you, too.

J·A·N·U·A·R·Y 15TH

"Now the men of Israel and Judah arose and shouted, and pursued the Philistines as far as the entrance of the valley and to the gates of Ekron". 1 Samuel 17:52

Sure, they shouted. The enemy fled when Goliath was slain and now the shouts of excitement could be heard all over the ranks of Israel's massed army. But where were the shouts of encouragement and excitement when young David went down the valley to meet the giant? There were none. Did anybody think to go with him down that valley of death? Nobody moved.

Some little boys were playing war. When an onlooker asked why they were so quiet, one boy replied, "We are all Generals, we can't get anybody to do the fighting". Selah.

J·A·N·U·A·R·Y 16TH

"... but he put his armour in his tent". 1 Samuel 17:54

All of us are human. We need re-assurance. We need things to remind us that God cares and that God does intervene in human affairs. David shows his very human side when he comes back from his victory over Goliath; he collects the heavy armour of the giant and puts it in his tent. I think he meant to preserve it as a keepsake.

Maybe I am too sentimental but I like keepsakes. I like things that remind me of good times, even great times when I'm having bad times. Why do you think christians are commanded by God to break bread and drink wine in memory of his Son's death at Calvary, regularly? It is to remind them of the greatest battle ever fought, the greatest victory ever gained. It reminds meditators that Christ was forsaken of God for them. It brings gratitude, worship and humility surging into their hearts. I can understand David keeping Goliath's armour, can't you? Every time he saw it there in the corner he was reminded that the battle belongs to the Lord.

"And it was so ... that the soul of Jonathan was knit to the soul of David and Jonathan loved him as his own soul." 1 Samuel 18:1

The character of a person indwelt and controlled by the Spirit of God will soon become apparent to all. The key to God's choice of David was the condition of his heart before God and it was this that drew Jonathan, a prince in Israel, to David.

It was this principle which drew a lonely shepherd called Moses before the full blaze of the courts of Pharoah. It brought a Ruth out of obscurity to be put in the royal line. It brought the ploughman Elisha to a place of immense blessing. It took the fig-picker of Tekoa and made him the great court-preaching prophet, Amos. It plucked the Locust-eating, honey fed child of the dessert, John the Baptist from obscurity and instead of him going to the nation, the nation came to him! It took an obscure peasant girl from the highlands of Israel to Bethlehem to give birth to the Son of God. It will take you to a place of usefulness and incalculable blessing. How then, if you will excuse the expression, does your heart lie?

J✦A✦N✦U✦A✦R✦Y 18TH

"Saul took him that day and would not let him go home to his father's house any more". 1 Samuel 18:2

Gary Inrig points out that if you want to ruin a friendship there are seven rules you can learn from Saul in his treatment of David.

1. Make sure your friendship is based on what the other person can do for you. Be selfish. 2. Do all you can to keep that person as your private property. Be possessive. 3. Keep a firm grasp on what is yours and protect it against all intruders. Cultivate jealousy. 4. Don't sit down and rationally discuss your anger and irritation. Just explode. 5. Avoid the person who threatens and annoys you. Do all you can to stay out of his way. 6. Focus so much on what the other person has that you will do anything to get it. Cultivate envy. 7. Believe that your feeling of

contempt for his or her abilities or person is justified. Harbour hatred in your heart.

Follow these rules and you will never have a deep and true relationship with a friend for the rest of your life.

J•A•N•U•A•R•Y 19TH

" Then Jonathan and David made a covenant, because he loved him as his own soul. And Jonathan took off the robe that was on him and gave it to David, with his armour, even to his sword and his bow and his belt."
1 Samuel 18:3-4

There is absolutely no doubt that there are two levels of teaching in the life of David. There is the historical level of the story and there is the spiritual. The spiritual casts long shadows of David's greater son, Christ, again and again in David's story. In today's text we have one. Saul was soon to sadly reject David and, as we have already said, if you reject God's Saviour you cannot be a believer. Jonathan read what was happening very clearly and with no hesitation took, if you like, his "insignia of office" and gladly gave it to David. He made a covenant with Israel's Saviour and, as Jim Elliot would have said, he was no fool to give what he could not keep to gain what he could not lose.

If you have had an encounter with Jesus Christ and gladly handed over your very heart to him you have made a wise decision. As you see world events hurtling us towards the coming of the Lord it is a reminder that soon you will be glad in the Lord's day of glory that you stood with Him in his day of rejection. He renews His covenant with you, today; it says, "I will never leave you nor forsake you".

J•A•N•U•A•R•Y 20TH

"So David went out wherever Saul sent him and behaved wisely".
1 Samuel 18:5

To behave yourself wisely in our day seems to carry the idea of being clever, of somehow pleasing everybody. To say a person was wise usually means they did not confront prickly issues, did not rock any boats, that they became a diplomat and had the world, the flesh and the Devil as well as the christians all saying "What a wise move!" To be wise in modern society often means to become Mr. or Mrs. Facing-Both-Ways.

What is the biblical definition of wisdom? It is to "fear the Lord". David behaved himself wisely because at this time in his life he held God and his word in awe and reverence and this influenced his every move.

It is said that Sir Isaac Newton would never use the word "God" in conversation without first pausing. Before you do what you are going to do today or tomorrow, first ask "What would the Lord think of it?" If you have His approval then what you are going to do is wise.

J♦A♦N♦U♦A♦R♦Y 21st

"So the women sang as they danced, and said 'Saul has slain his thousands and David his ten thousands'. Then Saul was very angry, and the saying displeased him ... so Saul eyed David from that day forward."
1 Samuel 18:7

What is the difference between jealousy and envy? Envy begins with empty hands mourning for what it doesn't have. Jealousy begins with full hands but is threatened by the loss of its plenty. Jealousy is the pain of losing what I have to someone else, in spite of all my efforts to keep it.

David had no designs on the kingdom. He was willing to wait for God's time and God's way but Saul was very jealous for what was his. Saul, the grasper, couldn't even hear a woman's song giving David praise without being terrified. Don't let jealousy with its severe, suspicious, narrow and negative outlook eat you up in your life. Jealousy is a giant that needs to be slain and can be by a simple truth. The truth is that if God opens a door to you, no person can shut it but yourself. Let jealousy with its squinty eyes take over and you will destroy the work you have been given to do.

"And he said, ' They have ascribed to David ten thousands, and to me they have ascribed but thousands.'" 1 Samuel 18:8

I do not condone Saul's jealousy yet I sometimes feel that the women of Israel provoked it. Saul should have seen it for what it was, enthusiasm for David's huge victory over the mighty Goliath that in turn led to a rout of the Philistines. Yet, we must be careful. Jealousy lies beneath the surface of all our lives. When we are praising someone for something let us be sensitive.

We must not be unfair in praising the attraction and dynamism of youth above the experience and accumulated wisdom of seniority. It applies even in churches, for woe betide the church which does not have the proper balance between young people and older people. A healthy respect for both goes a long way.

"So David played music with his hand, as at other times; but there was a spear in Saul's hand". 1 Samuel 18:10

What a contrast! Saul had a spear in his hand but David's hands moved across his harp and produced calming, soothing, moving music. Music is in everyone's heart, from African tribes to Belfast streets. Even in societies where music is not written down, it is there. No matter how sophisticated our appreciation of music and great musicians may be, let us never forget that everyone appreciates music and has music in their very psyche.

A little boy who played music was bitterly disappointed because he could neither play nor sing. But Amati, the violin-maker, said; "There are many ways of making music. What matters is the song in the heart". So Antonio Stradivarius was encouraged to become the worlds greatest violin-maker. Let the Lord put a song in your heart today. And, put down that spear!

J♦A♦N♦U♦A♦R♦Y 24TH

"And Saul cast the spear, for he said, 'I will pin David to the wall with it'".
1 Samuel 18:11

Life takes some amazing turns. From wanting David to be his court musician, Saul now wants to kill him. What a rotten thing the human heart is! The Bible holds no hope for it, apart from the Lords ability to change it. You simply cannot trust a human heart for it is fickle, changeable, capable of great and inspiring love one moment and despising, threatening, wicked hatred the next. "Who can know it?", asks Scripture.

When Saul eventually committed suicide on Mt. Gilboa the Philistines came, stripped off his armour, put it in the temple of their god and "fastened his body to the wall of Beth-Shan". Are you planning to do something to hurt someone? Saul never dreamt that when he tried to pin David to the wall with his spear that one day some people would come and pin his body to the wall. Be not deceived. God is not mocked. Whatever a person sows, that person will reap.

J♦A♦N♦U♦A♦R♦Y 25TH

"Now Saul was afraid of David, because the Lord was with him".
1 Samuel 18:12

It is a long time ago now, but I'll never forget it. I was young and wide-eyed. With a local church we hired a sports stadium in Grangemouth, Stirlingshire for a Gospel Rally. Everybody worked hard at the preparation and someone mentioned a national Scottish newspaper that carried a column on church affairs written by a Church of Scotland minister. They felt he would gladly give the coming Rally some publicity, so, I rang him up. He asked me for details and I told him we would have a children's choir at the Rally, an adult choir, a well known Scottish evangelist and I would preach the gospel, etc.

"If you had the Holy Spirit with you, that's about all you would need, isn't it?", he replied when I had finished my patter. I deserved it. Strange, though, I was suddenly afraid of that minister. Afraid, that is, in the way Saul was afraid of David. There is something about someone really in touch with God that brings you up against reality. The choirs sang well, the preachers preached the gospel, people found Christ that afternoon in Grangemouth Stadium, but I went home with a vital lesson written on my heart.

J♦A♦N♦U♦A♦R♦Y 26TH

" Therefore Saul removed him from his presence". 1 Samuel 18:13

You never read of David preaching a sermon to Saul. He didn't even send him copies of his psalms, he didn't chip away in criticism at Saul's ridiculous behaviour, yet he had a profound effect upon him. So great was that effect that Saul took steps to make sure he saw David as little as possible by making him captain of one thousand men in his army.

People still behave in the same way with the greatest one who came from "the house and lineage of David". The Lord Jesus has had and continues to have a profound effect upon the world that we live in, yet, people when convicted of their need of him try to put his claims away by ignoring the Bible, getting out of the way of christians, and getting on with doing their own thing. They do it to their own detriment. Don't try to remove christian influences from your life, even if you are in a backsliden condition. If you ascend to space or plunge to the ocean depths the Lord is there. Yield to his influences don't try to remove them.

J♦A♦N♦U♦A♦R♦Y 27TH

"But all Israel and Judah loved David, because he went out and came in before them". 1 Samuel 18:16

The storm had not yet come. The people of Israel in general loved David at this time; his lovely life, his obvious gifts were a delight to them. The fierce hatred of Saul's heart against God's Saviour wasn't yet public knowledge.

So it was with Christ, at the beginning. The common people heard him gladly, they flocked to listen to him in such numbers that his fame spread everywhere. Soon, though, the establishment would turn against him and the people would discover that to be associated with Christ would mean being counted outside the establishment. That would never do. The crowds that hailed Christ soon wanted to kill him. They would soon want to do the same to David. Mark it well, christian, sooner or later it will cost you much to be associated with David's greater Son. Don't be surprised when the moment comes. Let today's text warn you of it.

J◆A◆N◆U◆A◆R◆Y 28TH

" Then Saul said to David, 'Here is my older daughter Merab; I will give her to you as a wife. only be valiant for me, and fight the Lord's battles'. For Saul thought, 'Let my hand not be against him, but let the hand of the Philistines be against him'" . 1 Samuel 18:17

The plot thickens. Saul uses a religious cover to try to kill David. Why, outwardly he seems to be fighting the Lord's battles, if you please, yet all the time he is trying to kill God's Saviour, David.

The lesson is not lost on us, is it? The leaders of Israel were to one day drive nails into the hands of the Saviour of the world, all in the name of fighting the Lord's battles. In coming days christians were to join in the persecution of Jews in the name of fighting the Lord's battles. The lesson from our text is very clear; make sure that it is the Lord's battles you are fighting and not your own battles fuelled by your own prejudices and hatred. Who would ever have imagined that Saul in sending David to fight the Philistines in the name of the Lord was secretly hoping they would succeed where he had failed; namely, to spear him to death? Remember; things are not always as they seem.

J◆A◆N◆U◆A◆R◆Y 29TH

"Who am I and what is my life or my father's family in Israel, that I should be son-in-law to the King?" 1 Samuel 18:18

Humility; it is not a universal quality in our world, is it? David's life was, at this time, marked by deep humility. To be raised to be the king's son-in-law was something that didn't give him a big head. He had the right attitude towards himself.

The world places great emphasis upon self-reliance, on self-confidence, on self-expression. Look at its novels, its films, its videos. If you want to succeed in a profession today the big thing is to give the impression that you are a success. Everywhere we see too much confidence placed in the power of education and knowledge to change lives, with tragic results.

"Blessed are the poor in spirit", said Christ. Humility is the mark of those in His kingdom. God's delight is received upon surrender, not awarded upon conquest, it is born in the parched soil of destitution rather than the fertile ground of achievement. Admission of failure is admission into joy.

J♦A♦N♦U♦A♦R♦Y 30TH

"... now Michal, Saul's daughter, loved David. And they told Saul, and the thing pleased him. So Saul said, 'I will give her to him, that she may be a snare to him, and that the hand of the Philistines may be against him'".
1 Samuel 18:21

I believe in romance. I believe you can fall in love and love grow deeper and better. I believe it can last through a lifetime of commitment and be richer at the end than it was at the beginning. I know statistics are stacked against me but despite the failures, success is possible. One thing, though, when we speak of falling in love it is a metaphor that really describes enchantment. That's how it starts but love, real love, is not something you fall into. It requires sacrifice, giving up of independence, willingness to give and take; it could cost you your very life as Michal was soon to find out.

Saul, of course, gleefully learned of his daughter's love for David and set out to manipulate it to his advantage. There is always somebody to slime your Eden, isn't there? Don't let them worry you. Many waters cannot quench love and even a Saul's trickery cannot wreck the real thing. I know, I've proved it.

J•A•N•U•A•R•Y 31ST

"And David said; 'Does it seem to you a light thing to be a King's son-in-law, seeing I am a poor and lightly esteemed man?'" 1 Samuel 18:23

A pastor once approached the great Bible teacher Dr. Martyn Lloyd-Jones. "Thank you for that teaching you have just given", he said. "Thank you for saying so", said the doctor, "Very few people say such things to me". You might be very surprised to learn that the people you think are getting the most encouragement are the ones who are getting it least. Why, even Abraham Lincoln was asked to speak at the dedication of the National Cemetery at Gettysberg only because he said he intended to attend the ceremony. A silver-tongued orator called Edward Everett had been chosen to speak and when he did, he spoke for one hour and fifty-seven minutes. The crowd roared its approval. Lincoln spoke for two minutes. "Is that all?", said a reporter from the Philadelphia Press. "Is that all?" the President answered, "Yes, that's all".

Gentlemen of the press lightly esteemed Lincoln's Gettysberg address yet it became probably the most memorable two minutes in the history of the United States. Lincoln became America's David. Because the crowd lightly esteems something doesn't make it useless; our readings this month have proved that conclusively.

F E·B·R·U·A·R·Y

F◆E◆B◆R◆U◆A◆R◆Y

*I*t was the winter of David's life. Driven out into the mountains and hills by an establishment that despised him, the young king-elect faced the elements with a loving heart. Blasted by the winds of criticism and discouragement, snowed under by fear and the closeness of constant danger, he refused to get bitter. True, he wavered. True, he wondered what on earth was going on. True, he made mistakes. But the loving way in which he refused to harm his persecutor, King Saul, is as a warm fire on a dark winter's night. Let his example inspire you through February days.

F◆E◆B◆R◆U◆A◆R◆Y 1ST

"And there was war again; and David went out and fought with the Philistines". 1 Samuel 19:8

A new month. The "New Year" is fast becoming "This year" and maybe, for you, a troubled one. You thought old arguments had been resolved but there is "war" again in your circumstances. You were trying to get your life into some sort of settled routine but crisis after crisis has arrived. Money problems have come. Ill health, maybe, is worrying you. Bereavement in your family has stunned you. Relationships have recently soured with one whom you first loved, deeply. A medical doctor friend of mine puts it down as "A conspiracy of things". The truth is, there always will be "war again", no matter how long we live on this present earth. What is the answer?

I have always found in my life that the main cause of discouragement and disappointment is a temporary loss of perspective. David's life shows us the true perspective for living like few other lives. He was, you will remember, training for reigning. So are you, christian. This present trouble that you are experiencing will make you stronger, wiser, better. Learn from it. Experience brings patience and patience, hope. That hope is not "hope so". You will reign with Christ and there will be no more war.

"So David fled and escaped, and went to Samuel at Ramah, and told him all that Saul had done to him. And he and Samuel went and stayed in Naioth".
1 Samuel 19:18

It's good for a David to have a Samuel in his life. What if Samuel had said, "Sorry, David, I'm too busy being a judge to talk to you today". What if Samuel had let the fear of man become a snare to him? The court was anti-David and Samuel took his life into his own hands by identifying with this young man.

Is there a David knocking on your door? Out of favour with the hierarchy, the establishment, the in-set, your association with him will be frowned on. Samuel read the situation clearly. David was putting God first and suffering for it and he must protect him and above all, listen to him. How many a christian could have been inspired to go on for the Lord if only they had had a Samuel to sit and listen to their fears and hopes? How many a person would have become a christian if only somebody had stopped to listen to their questions? Be careful in your busy life today; a David may call.

"Then David fled from Naioth in Ramah". 1 Samuel 20:1

There comes a time in all our lives when God begins to remove all the familiar things we lean on to make us lean on him. Is that happening to you at the moment? It certainly happened to David. Let's trace it.

Take David's job; he had to flee from his work as a trusted officer in Saul's army (19:8-10). Take David's wife; Michal had to persuade David to escape for his life by letting him down through a window and putting a dummy in his bed (19: 11-12). Take David's mentor; Saul discovered where David and Samuel were hiding at Naioth and David had to flee again (20:1).

It is not a pleasant experience to have your props removed but if your props have become a substitute for the Lord you are in trouble. There is, in fact, nothing wrong with leaning if you are leaning on the Lord. Remember, one with God is a majority.

F◆E◆B◆R◆U◆A◆R◆Y 4TH

" Then David ... said to Jonathan, 'What have I done? What is my iniquity, and what is my sin before your father, that he seeks my life?" '
1 Samuel 20:1

I can recall an occasion in my life when I had to tell a lady some tragic news. The lady looked up at me and said in anguish "What have we done wrong?" She was overwhelmed with a feeling of guilt, she felt she had sinned and God was punishing her with the tragic circumstances in her family circle.

David had exactly the same experience. He was so overwhelmed with the pressure of Saul chasing him that he was sure that he had done something wrong. In fact he was being chased for the precise reason that he had done right! It is my experience that a wife whose husband has walked out on her feels the guilty one, the person who is approached for money by one who has squandered his own is almost made to feel the other persons debt is their personal debt etc. Such feelings are a delusion from the pit of Hell! Don't panic, just because you are under pressure does not automatically mean that you have sinned.

F◆E◆B◆R◆U◆A◆R◆Y 5TH

"Truly, as the Lord lives, and as your soul lives, there is but a step between me and death". 1 Samuel 20:3

Where is the spirit of the David of the valley Elah, now? Where is the lad who defied the godless giant in the name of the Lord of Hosts? He never even thought of dying when he faced the Philistine, did he?; now, he is overwhelmed with the thought of death at the hand of an Israelite king! Had not God promised David that he would reign on Israel's throne? Was he not immortal until his work was done? What had gotten into him?

Discouragement; that was the root of his loss of vision. Just like you, christian? You can hear the whirr of the hurled spears of your critics and you have joined Elijah under the juniper tree and said 'I am no better than my fathers; let me die'. Away with discouragement, today, away with it! You too are immortal until your work is done and you must not go around saying " There is but a step between me and death". You must change it to "For me to live is Christ and to die is gain".

F◆E◆B◆R◆U◆A◆R◆Y 6TH

"Nevertheless, if there is iniquity in me, kill me yourself for why should you bring me to your father". 1 Samuel 20:8

David had, momentarily, lost his vision, his sense of security and his confidence. Familiar surroundings of home and family, job and position had been removed. He got his attention off the Lord and he begins to look in, rather than up, and makes an extraordinary request of his friend Jonathan; he says, in effect, if you think I am a bad person, kill me yourself.

To walk through David's life is to touch virtually every mood of human experience. Today's mood is what some folk would call "hitting the self-destruction button". David was so discouraged that he thought if Jonathan killed him Jonathan would be justified in doing so. David had no right to treat his precious life so lightly and neither have you, yours. God has a special purpose for you and you must not put your life exclusively at the mercy of anybody's whim. You know that people just don't have to kill you to ruin your life; you just have to let them take you over. Resist their whims and only be mastered by the Master.

F◆E◆B◆R◆U◆A◆R◆Y 7TH

"And you shall not only show me the kindness of the Lord while I still live, that I may not die; but you shall not cut off your kindness from my house forever, no, not when the Lord has cut off every one of the enemies of David from the face of the earth. So Jonathan made a covenant with the house of David". 1 Samuel 20:14-15

Jonathan had no notion of killing David, he never wavered in his belief that David was Israel's Saviour. Though he knew better than to try to be king himself, he was determined to have a covenant with the one who would be. The covenant he made carried the promise that David would never cut off his kindness to Jonathan's family when he came to power.

The Lord Jesus is certainly in his day of rejection at the moment. Few there are who love Him and honour Him. Millions seek the number one spot for themselves. You, though, are different. Like Jonathan you know who the true Saviour is and have trusted Him as your very own personal Saviour. Be sure of this; he has made a covenant with you. When all his enemies are put down and he rules and reigns, his kindness to you will never be cut off.

F◆E◆B◆R◆U◆A◆R◆Y 8TH

"But if I say thus to the young man, 'Look, the arrows are beyond you' - go your way for the Lord has sent you away". 1 Samuel 20:22

The message of the arrows was a sad one for David. Jonathan arranged with David to try to find out how his father really stood with David. He then arranged to return to a place where David would be hidden and if he shot three arrows to the side of the stone Ezel and shouted to his servant boy "Go find the arrows, they are on this side of you, get them and come" the message would mean David would have to flee from Saul. When Jonathan talked to his father of David, Saul got so angry he tried to kill Jonathan. The arrows eventually said to the hidden David; "The Lord has sent you away".

Is that the message to you today? Is it time to go? Is it time to move out from the familiar to the unfamiliar? Don't be afraid. If the Lord sends you away, then he will go before you. David longed to stay; God had other plans. Remember, we don't give the orders, we just turn up for duty. If we do the results will be out of this world. It's guaranteed.

"For as long as the son of Jesse lives on the earth, you shall not be established, nor your kingdom. Now therefore, send and bring him to me, for he shall surely die". 1 Samuel 20:31

This text is the very heart of King Saul's philosophy. He wanted the kingdom of Israel for himself and for his son, following. No matter that Samuel had distinctly warned him long before that " The Lord has torn the kingdom of Israel from you today and has given it to a neighbour of yours who is better than you". He was now fighting God; he wanted to kill God's anointed.

Saul's argument to Jonathan was that he would never be established as long as David lived. Be careful that such a subtle argument does not creep into your heart. We don't pray "My kingdom come. My will be done", do we? If you want to be truly established in life be established in David's greater Son. "For", says Hebrews 13:9, "It is good that the heart be established by grace". All other kingdoms eventually perish. His is a kingdom that cannot be shaken.

*"Now as soon as the lad had gone, David arose from a place toward the south, fell on his face to the ground, and bowed down three times. And they kissed one another; and they wept together, but David more so" .
1 Samuel 20:41-42*

These last moments together were highly emotional ones for David and Jonathan. David outwept Jonathan because he knew the cost of what Jonathan had done for him. The spear that had been hurled towards him had now been hurled against Jonathan (see 1 Samuel 20:33). It is a costly thing to be associated with God's anointed one.

It still is. Do you not think the Lord knows the price you pay for your association with Him? Your king is touched with the feelings of your infirmities. He knows that people often hate you for his sake. It is called "The fellowship of His sufferings". Yet, remember, he has outwept you. He "Who", says Hebrews 5:7-9, "in the days of his flesh, when he had offered up prayers and supplications, with vehement cries and tears to him who was able to save him from death, and was heard because of his godly fear, though he was his son, yet he learned obedience by the things which he suffered. And having been perfected, he became the author of eternal salvation to all who obey him". Selah

F✦E✦B✦R✦U✦A✦R✦Y 11TH

"So David said to Ahimelech the priest, ' The king has ordered me on some business, and said to me, Do not let anyone know anything about the business on which I send you, or what I have commanded you "'.
1 Samuel 21:2

A lie is always a lie. Sheer panic can make you tell one. David now fled for his life to a place called Nob, a town of the priests in the tribe of Benjamin just north of the city of Jerusalem. The tabernacle stood at Nob and David went there in sheer panic. When asked by Ahimelech the priest why he was alone, David replied he was on a secret errand for the king. It was a lie; it was saying that which was not true with the intention to deceive.

Concealment is not lying. Life would be intolerable if we were required to disclose all the truth we know. Withholding truth is often both necessary and kind but here David told a lie to conceal the truth and that was where he went wrong. Nowhere does the Scripture allow for a lie to be justifiable. It will find us out. I like the story of the shop assistant who took a chicken out of a barrel and weighed it. "5 lbs", he said. "I'll have a bigger one", said his customer. The assistant put the chicken back in the barrel and then pulled out the same chicken again, as that was all he had left. He weighed it. "7 lbs", he said. " That's fine! I'll take both of them", said the customer.

F✦E✦B✦R✦U✦A✦R✦Y 12TH

"So the priest gave him holy bread; for there was no bread there but the showbread which had been taken from before the Lord, in order to put hot bread in its place on the day when it was taken away". 1 Samuel 21:6

David was the Lord's anointed and it was no sin for him to be fed showbread. Showbread was strictly consecrated to God and to the priests to teach Israel the holiness of the Lord, the sacredness of his service and the sanctity of those whom he chose to minister to him in the special ministry of the priesthood.

The Scriptures teach that the showbread was for God and then to be eaten by those dedicated to his service. Does God get hungry? He certainly does. He gets hungry for our worship and fellowship. What else do the words of Revelation 3:20 mean?; "Behold, I stand at the door and knock. If anyone hears my voice and opens the door, I will come in to him and dine with him, and he with me". When we worship, we feed God and he feeds us. Can you think of a higher occupation for your heart and mind? Whither it be on the top of a bus or sitting on an aeroplane, or quietly in a church service; worship.

F♦E♦B♦R♦U♦A♦R♦Y 13TH

"So the priest said 'The sword of Goliath the Philistine, whom you killed in the Valley of Elah, there it is, wrapped in a cloth behind the ephod. If you will take that, take it. For there is no other except that one here'. And David said, 'There is none like it; give it to me"'. 1 Samuel 21:9.

There is something haunting, wistful, even pathetic about this action of David's. The priests of Nob had kept Goliath's sword wrapped in a cloth. Often people must have asked to see it. Can't you hear them? ; "What a sword!" "He must have been some giant!" "To think that David's faith in a wonderful God overcame such an enemy!" "He never even got to using his sword on young David, Praise God!" Now, David whose faith never rested in a sword, takes Goliath's sword, of all swords, to defend himself from Saul. "There is none like it", he says. Are there more haunting words in all of David's life story?

Are you depressed, today? Is your spirit choked by somebody who has risen to criticise you? Are the ungodly laughing at the divisions, even in the ranks of christians, around you? Don't hide behind the defences of the ungodly. The name of the Lord is a strong tower and the righteous run into it and they are safe. Run into that name, today; don't fight the ungodly with their own weapons.

F✦E✦B✦R✦U✦A✦R✦Y 14TH

"And the servants of Achish said to him, 'Is this not David the king of the land? Did they not sing of him to one another in dances, saying ; Saul has slain his thousands, and David his ten thousands?"' 1 Samuel 21:11

Even David's enemies recognised that he was the Lord's anointed. Imagine the Gentiles calling him "The King of the land" when his very own people were hunting him to death! Shades of the coming Lord Jesus are very clear in David's life at this time. All analogies break down, and David as an analogy of Christ certainly breaks down at various stages in his life, but the spiritual teaching from the historical setting at this stage is crystal clear.

Even Pilate, Rome's representative governor in Jerusalem wrote "This is the King of the Jews" above Christ's head as he was crucified by his own people. "Surely this is the Son of God", said the Centurion in charge of Christ's crucifixion.

There is coming a day when the Lord Jesus will be received by the nation of Israel. "They shall look on Him whom they pierced", says Scripture. "All Israel will be saved", writes Paul. Meanwhile Christ, like David, is in the hand's of the Gentiles because more Gentiles believe in him in our day than Jews do. But, " The crowning day is coming". Meanwhile;

"King of my life I crown You now, Yours shall the glory be,
Lest I forget Your thorn crowned brow, Lead me to Calvary."

F✦E✦B✦R✦U✦A✦R✦Y 15TH

"So he changed his behaviour before them, feigned madness in their hands, scratched on the doors of the gate, and let his saliva fall down on his beard. Then Achish said to his servants, 'Look, you see the man is insane. Why have you brought him to me?"' 1 Samuel 21:12-14

I will never forget quietly sitting in my friend Professor Gooding's home talking of David. "Who", he asked me one morning, "had saliva fall down his beard, apart from David? Who was also called a madman?" "Christ", I answered. The Professor smiled. He had given me a key to the life of David.

The older I grow the more I am convinced that just as every lane and alley in the country in which you live will lead you to the road which will lead you to the metropolis, so every part of Scripture, no matter how seemingly obscure, will lead you to the heart of it all which is Christ Himself. Look for Him in it all and you will surely find Him.

F✦E✦B✦R✦U✦A✦R✦Y 16TH

"David therefore departed from there and escaped to the cave of Adullam ... and everyone who was in distress, everyone who was in debt, and everyone who was discontented gathered to him. So he became captain over them". 1 Samuel 22:1-2

How often have I heard certain churches described as "Caves of Adullam"? People who were in debt, discontented and in distress gathered to David at Adullam and so churches that draw such people get dubbed as "Adullams".

Such trite remarks draw away from the beauty of David's character. There was something about him that drew troubled hearts. In our day where do millions of people turn when they are in trouble? They read the Psalms of David! No wonder. Can you find an individual in Scripture or in history whom God used greatly until he first allowed them to be hurt, deeply?

Who flocked to the Saviour; the religious, the comfortable, the established? Certainly not. If the distressed and troubled are heading for your local church it is a great sign.

F✦E✦B✦R✦U✦A✦R✦Y 17TH

"Then David went from there to Mizpah of Moab; and he said to the king of Moab, 'Please let my father and mother come here with you, till I know what God will do for me ... then the prophet Gad said to David 'Do not stay in the stronghold; depart, and go to the land of Judah"'. 1 Samuel 22:3-5

We all have times when we don't know what to do next. David did a very wise thing at this time in his life. He cared for his parents and waited on God for guidance. Often we will find days when we are not called upon to do anything more than the every day duties of caring for our family, waiting all the time for the Lord to show us the next step in his plan for our lives.

Be certain of this; the guidance that you need will come. Just as God sent a prophet to guide David, he will send his messenger to guide you. It may come in the form of a telephone call, a magazine article, simply bumping into a friend on the street, whatever, but come it will. God's prophets come in rare guises. Meantime? "I can say", said Dr. Barnhouse, "from experience that ninety-five per cent of knowing the will of God consists in being prepared to do it before you know what it is".

F•E•B•R•U•A•R•Y 18TH

"Then Saul said ... will the son of Jesse give everyone of you fields and vineyards and make you all captains of thousands? ... all of you have conspired against me and there is not one of you who is sorry for me ... then answered Doeg ... 'I saw the son of Jesse going to Nob, to Ahimelech"'.
1 Samuel 22:7-9

Betrayed! The greatest hero in Israel's history was betrayed by a man who loved property and position. Doeg was as Judas; money and what it could buy made him reveal the haunt of God's anointed to his enemy.

I know that a lot has been said about money. If you run after money, you are materialistic. If you don't get it you are a loser. If you get it and keep it, you are a miser. If you don't try to get it, you lack ambition. If you get it and spend it you are a spendthrift. If you still have it after a lifetime of work, you are a fool who never got any fun out of life! Yet, beware of the Doeg's in life. Money motivates them, prestige inflates them. They would sell your very soul, if it were profitable. The love of money is the root of all kinds of evil.

F•E•B•R•U•A•R•Y 19TH

" Then Saul said to him 'Why have you conspired against me, you and the son of Jesse, in that you have given him bread and a sword, and have enquired of God for him, that he should rise against me, to lie in wait, as it is this day?"' 1 Samuel 22:13

The man was paranoid. Jealousy was blinding his reason, his conscience, his view of everything. Saul could see David lying in wait at every corner ready to take his throne from him by force. Ahimelech the priest desperately tried to persuade him that David was in fact one of his most loyal servants but he would not be persuaded.

Watch jealousy, it is a fiercesome thing. It will make you think your friend an enemy, it will make you believe his talents to be a threat. It will turn even his most innocent act into a flame of suspicion in your heart. Many lovely things pass out of life when jealousy comes in. If only Saul had put out the hell spark of jealousy in a sea of prayer. Selah.

F✦E✦B✦R✦U✦A✦R✦Y 20TH

"And the king said to Doeg, 'You turn and kill the priest!' So Doeg the Edomite turned and struck the priest, and killed him that day eighty-five men who wore a linen ephod. Also Nob, the city of the priest, he struck with the edge of the sword, both men and women, children and nursing infants, oxen and donkeys and sheep - with the edge of the sword".
1 Samuel 22:18-19

Saul's soldiers refused his order to kill the priests of Nob but Doeg was only too ready to do it. Of course, as our verse tells us, he was an Edomite. Edomites were the descendants of Esau who sold his birthright for lentil soup. Lentils are red and Edom means "red", a nickname given to Esau.

Edomites, in the Bible, constantly chose the immediate benefit rather than the long term blessing. Here Doeg, for example, would rather have had the friendship of Saul than wait for the coming reign of God's anointed, David. Herod, the last Edomite mentioned in the Bible, would rather have ruled as king than recognise the little baby of Bethlehem as the King of all Kings. There are a lot of the descendants of Edomites who still choose the immediate pleasures of sin rather than the long term rewards of the righteous. Are you one of them?

F◆E◆B◆R◆U◆A◆R◆Y 21st

"So David said to Abiathar, 'I knew that day, when Doeg the Edomite was there, that he would surely tell Saul. I have caused the death of all the persons of your father's house"'. 1 Samuel 22:22

The older you grow, the more you will discover that your life has an influence far beyond your imagination. David fled in panic to Nob, tried to cover his tracks with a lie and before his action was finished it caused the death of eighty-five priests and the sacking of a city, including the deaths of many women and children.

Be careful, today; a word, a hint, an action, even a telephone conversation could, before it is finished set a church on fire, break a marriage, ruin a relationship, bring a tide of heartbreak in its wake. If only David had trusted the Lord instead of taking things into his own hands the community of Nob would have lived. Trust in the Lord with all your heart, and lean not to your own understanding, in all your ways acknowledge Him and He shall direct your paths.

F◆E◆B◆R◆U◆A◆R◆Y 22nd

"Then David enquired of the Lord, saying, 'Shall I go and attack these Philistines?' And the Lord said to David, 'Go and attack the Philistines, and save Keilah '". 1 Samuel 23:4

Have you really made a terrible mess of things and caused hurt to a lot of people, recently? You, like David, panicked and the result has been catastrophic. Find hope in today's text.

What could have been worse for David than the mayhem he caused at Nob? Yet, he learned from it all. He got to prayer and told the Lord that he needed guidance. God did not refuse guidance on the grounds that David had recently disastrously neglected to ask for it. That is what the love of God does. When Peter denied the Lord he was amazed to discover that the Lord loved him, still. Divine love, unlike human love, is not dependant on its object. God's love is not drawn out by our lovableness. Ask him today for guidance, despite the fact that you recently omitted to do so. He will not fail you.

F✦E✦B✦R✦U✦A✦R✦Y 23RD

"And David stayed in strongholds in the wilderness, and remained in the mountains in the Wilderness of Ziph. Saul sought him every day, but God did not deliver him into his hand". 1 Samuel 23:14

It is that little phrase, "every day" in our text that evokes the pain and the anguish David went through. There was no let up. Everywhere he went David daily expected death to strike. It's like a situation here in Northern Ireland where a friend of mine is on a terrorist hit list and every time I approach his house and ring his doorbell I know it strikes fear into his heart. He is daily expecting death at his very door.

It may not be fear of a terrorist that haunts you every day but some pain, some anguish, some problem that seems to eternally hound you.

Take it from me that no problem lasts forever. It's a long road which has no turning. Catch hold of the little phrase "but God" in our text. Yes, you are in trouble, "but God". Yes, your problem seems eternal, "but God". Yes, all seems hopeless, "but God". Comforting, isn't it!?

F✦E✦B✦R✦U✦A✦R✦Y 24TH

"Then Jonathan, Saul's son, arose and went to David in the woods and strengthened his hand in God". 1 Samuel 23:16

Notice Jonathan's approach to David, just when he needed him most. He didn't try the old "Tighten your belt and get going" approach. He didn't paint an unrealistic picture of what was happening, either, with a "Come on, it's not as bad as you think" approach. Jonathan simply redirected David's perspective on life by focusing his attention upon his Lord, not his enemy. There was David hunted, frightened, weary, panic stricken, and hiding in a forest and Jonathan got up out of his comfortable seat in the palace, found David and strengthened his hand in God.

One thing is certain, if my friendships do not enable me to strengthen my friends in the Lord then I need to deepen my commitment to Christ. If I can urge a friend to be directly dependent on the Lord I can do that friend no greater service. Get out there into the woods of life today and strengthen someone's hand in God.

F◆E◆B◆R◆U◆A◆R◆Y 25TH

"Then the Ziphites came up to Saul at Gibeah, saying, 'Is David not hiding with us in strongholds in the woods ... now therefore, O king, come down according to all the desire of your soul to come down; and our part shall be to deliver him into the king's hand"'. 1 Samuel 23:19-20

Beware of attributing to the Lord actions that are not His. It is so easy to say "The Lord sent me" or "The Lord sent you" and later find that circumstances prove that the Lord was not in the thing at all. God often gets blamed for things He has nothing to do with.

I am reminded that the great John Newton who wrote the hymn "Amazing Grace" once read the verse in the Acts of the Apostles where the Lord had encouraged Paul to serve him in Corinth because he had "Many people in this city". Newton felt this verse was God's guidance to him to go to Cheltenham to serve in the christian ministry. He later wrote, "I very soon discovered that Cheltenham was not Corinth and that I was not Paul". Selah.

F◆E◆B◆R◆U◆A◆R◆Y 26TH

"Then Saul went on one side of the mountain, and David and his men on the other side of the mountain. So David made haste to get away from Saul, for Saul and his men were encircling David and his men to take them. But a messenger came to Saul saying, 'Hasten and come, for the Philistines have invaded the land!' Therefore Saul returned from pursuing David, and went against the Philistines; so they called the place the Rock of Escaping."
1 Samuel 23:26-28

Imagine a king of Israel employing an army to stalk and kill one of his most gifted and loyal subjects out of jealousy while he should have been protecting and guarding God's people from an enemy that threatened the whole nation's security.

The christian church, too, unfortunately, is not backward at in-fighting when it should be concentrating on the big and wider issues. It is very easy to get drawn in amongst a set of christians who are bent on hounding a fellow christian, for whatever reason. May the Lord give us grace to focus our fellow christians attention on issues that are vital and important and to try to encourage them to fight Satan's kingdom and not each other. You wouldn't want to be party to a crowd who shot their own wounded, would you?

F♦E♦B♦R♦U♦A♦R♦Y 27TH

"So he came to the sheepfolds by the road, where there was a cave; and Saul went in to attend to his needs. (David and his men were staying in the recesses of the cave). Then the men of David said to him 'This is the day of which the Lord said to you, 'Behold I will deliver your enemy into your hand, that you may do to him as it seems good to you."' 1 Samuel 24:3-4

If you had been hiding in a cave, hunted by King Saul and three thousand men and King Saul came, alone into the cave to relieve himself and your men said "Let's kill him", would you have let them? I reckon my human nature would have gone into overdrive!

The temptation open to David to kill Saul was all the stronger because David's soldiers excused their desire to get even with Saul by saying it was God's timing, God's will. We must never rationalize wrong behaviour and sin as being part of God's plan for our lives. Not everyone who says to you "This is the day to act" is necessarily in God's will, no matter how spiritual they may appear and no matter how highly you might regard them.

F♦E♦B♦R♦U♦A♦R♦Y 28TH

"Let the Lord judge between you and me, and let the Lord avenge me on you. But my hand shall not be against you. As the proverb of the ancient says 'Wickedness proceeds from the wicked'. But my hand shall not be against you". 1 Samuel 24:12-13

The conversation between David and Saul in the cliffs of En Gedi is full of rich instruction. It really is a very moving example of a young, highly gifted man dealing in a godly way with an older, cantankerous, jealous leader. He did not give Saul a tirade of venom and viciousness but showed him respect and let the Lord judge who was right.

Got a nasty letter, recently? Been badly treated by your boss? Have you been snowed under by false accusations and sheer wickedness on the part of those who do not like you? David reminded Saul that "Wickedness proceeds from the wicked". He decided that joining the ranks of the wicked in order to get even with Saul was a very foolish practice. Why should you stoop to wickedness when you have the Lord to vindicate you?

F♦E♦B♦R♦U♦A♦R♦Y 29TH

"Then he (Saul) said to David; 'You are more righteous than I; for you have rewarded me with good, whereas I have rewarded you with evil. And you have shown this day how you have dealt well with me; for when the Lord delivered me into your hand, you did not kill me."' 1 Samuel 24:17-18

There is nothing more wonderful than to see the love of a woman for her child, the love of a husband for his wife, the love of grandparents for their grandchildren, or the love of a friend for a friend. This kind of love, though, is not the test of our christian life. If you simply love those who love you and are kind to those that are generous to you then you are doing no more than those who act at the prompting of their own human heart. If that is all Christianity does for you it is no better than the religions of the world around you. Our Lord draws us to a higher challenge, by far. "Whoever slaps you on your right cheek, turn the other to him also", he said. He calls us to love those who do not love us. This is the litmus test of our christian lives. It is not a charter for any unscrupulous tyrant, beggar or thug to abuse us. God sets up government law enforcement agencies to deal with such people. In our personal relationships, though, there is not to be a trace of retaliation. David's dealing with Saul is a shining example of such behaviour.

M·A·R·C·H

M✦A✦R✦C✦H

C heer up, they say, "things could be worse". And, sure enough, they often get just that. Worse. The gales of persecution, trouble, disillusionment, and despair now sweep across David's life in ever intensifying gusts. Hard it was for David to see a purpose in it all. He started to get his eyes off the Lord and to take things into his own hands. Disaster loomed. And then came Abigail. It's quite a story to match the often dull, damp days of March.

M✦A✦R✦C✦H 1st

"Then Samuel died; and the Israelites gathered together and lamented for him, and buried him at his home in Ramah." 1 Samuel 25:1

There is nothing like death to unite people. Why, there they are around the graveside, Democrats and Republicans, Communists and Capitalists, Conservatives and Labour supporters, Hindus and Muslims; death has stopped them all in their tracks. Death brings people from the penthouse or the outhouse to stand side by side and silently remember that we are but dust and to dust we shall return.

Have you stood there recently? Then, remember the lesson that you must die before you die for there is no chance afterwards; that is, die to self, die to the world, the flesh and the Devil. If you save your life you will lose it. If you lose your life to Christ and His Kingdom you will save it. Got the lesson? Let me repeat it once more; die, before you die, because there is no chance afterwards. If Saul had only learnt the lesson at Samuel's funeral it would have saved him.

M♦A♦R♦C♦H 2ND

"Now there was a man in Maon whose business was in Carmel, and the man was very rich ... the name of the man was Nabal, and the name of his wife Abigail. She was a woman of good understanding and beautiful appearance; but the man was harsh and evil in his doings."
1 Samuel 25:2-3

How on earth does a beautiful and intelligent woman like Abigail end up with a miserable selfish man like Nabal? Sure, he was an opulent sheep farmer but he was intolerable in prosperity and overbearing to his inferiors. Abigail was to describe him as "Such a son of Belial that one cannot speak to him". That simply meant he was "good for nothing".

I don't want to accuse Abigail of anything she was not guilty of but maybe when she married Nabal he appeared to be as good a "catch" as any around Maon because "he was rich". There was certainly no affection between them, never to speak of love. If you want to marry someone, make sure you have affection for them. Yes, affection. "I do not for a moment question", said C. S. Lewis, "That affection is responsible for nine tenths of whatever solid and durable happiness there is in our natural lives". Affection is not the only form of love, but it is the best foundation.

M♦A♦R♦C♦H 3RD

"Then Nabal answered David's servants and said 'Who is David, and who is the son of Jesse? There are many servants nowadays who break away each one from his master. Shall I then take my bread and my water and my meat that I have killed for my shearers, and give it to men when I do not know where they are from?'" 1 Samuel 25:10-11

David and his men had been very kind to Nabal's shepherds in the Carmel district and now David asks Nabal for some kindness in return. Nabal accused David of raising a revolt and his men of being a lot of outlaws. He blankly refused to help David.

Be very, very careful today what judgment you put on another person's lifestyle. Nabal was totally ignorant of the causes which had forced David into his wandering, cave dwelling, forest hiding lifestyle. You too may be totally ignorant of the causes that are forcing the one you are judging into behaving as they do. As the Indians say "Do not harshly judge anyone until you have walked in their moccasins through a few full moons".

M♦A♦R♦C♦H 4TH

"So David's young men turned on their heels and went back; and they came and told him all these words. Then David said to his men, 'Every man gird on his sword'. So every man girded on his sword, and David also girded on his sword." 1 Samuel 25:12-13

Jonathan's influence on David was beginning to wear off. David's righteous anger was raised at Nabal's refusal to help. But his anger soon boiled over into murderous intent. He lost his self control and he got his eye off the one who deals with the rude, uncourteous and uncivil Nabals of this world; David decided to kill Nabal. He who had refused to kill Saul when it lay in his power to do so now finds that yesterdays victories become today's temptations.

It takes two to make a successful temptation and you are one of the two. If you hold the stirrup, it is no wonder if Satan gets into the saddle.

M♦A♦R♦C♦H 5TH

"Then Abigail made haste ..." 1 Samuel 25:18

Abigail's name means "whose father is joy". She had two things which do not always go together; beauty and brains. Of course, as far as the Bible is concerned, you can be beautiful without being good looking. God's idea of true beauty is very different to man's idea and it lasts much longer in the person who has it.

The beautiful Abigail immediately read the situation when she was told what David intended to do to her husband and she acted on it. To look is one thing. To see what you look at is another. To understand what you see is a third. To learn from what you understand is still something else. But to act on what you learn is what really matters. Isn't it? "Action", said the British Prime Minister, Disraeli, "does not always bring happiness; but there is no happiness without action".

M♦A♦R♦C♦H 6TH

"Then Abigail made haste and took two hundred loaves of bread, two skins of wine, five sheep already dressed, five seahs of roasted grain, one hundred clusters of raisins, and two hundred cakes of figs, and loaded them on donkeys. And she said to her servants, 'Go on before me; see, I am coming after you"'. 1 Samuel 25:18-19

Abigail did for David what her husband refused to do. She could have said "I knew it, all that talk of giant killing and girls dancing on the streets to songs about David's abilities; it was all bound to be hype. These young fellows who write psalms and preach, they are all the same. He is a hypocrite. He is going to murder my husband".

On the other hand she could have talked to her husband and raised a local militia against David. But no, the Bible does not say she was "A woman of good understanding" for nothing. She followed the principle at this time which we could all do with following when dealing with people, like David, who was at this time acting out of character; she looked beyond David's fault and saw his need. If, by the way, you are looking for faults, use a mirror, not a telescope for the greatest of all faults is to be conscious of none.

M♦A♦R♦C♦H 7TH

"Now therefore, my lord, as the Lord lives and as your soul lives, since the Lord has held you back from coming to bloodshed and from avenging yourself with your own hand, now then, let your enemies and those who seek harm from my lord be as Nabal". 1 Samuel 25:26

It must have been quite a sight. Abigail at David's feet pleading with David not to avenge himself and the angry David and his four hundred men with murder on their minds listening to her. But, she stopped David in his tracks and made him see reason.

All my life I have believed in a principle and it can be summed up very simply; it is that one person can make a difference. In a church, just one person can make a difference (See Revelation 3:20). In a city just one person can make a difference (See Ecc 9:14-15). In a nation just one person can make a difference (See Esther 4:16). I often think of Lydia who, when she became a christian, opened her home to the Apostle Paul and his friends to help them in the preaching of the Gospel and before very long the city of Philippi was opened and soon the whole Continent of Europe was opened. One person can make a difference; will you be that person in your church, in your town , or village, or countryside, or nation? Don't be a drifter; be an influence.

M✦A✦R✦C✦H 8TH

"For the Lord will certainly make for my lord an enduring house, because my lord fights the battles of the Lord, and evil is not found in you throughout your days". 1 Samuel 25:28

Everything around us is so transient. The older you grow, the more you will see it. We have but a short time here upon earth and yet upon this short time our eternity depends. Abigail's word to David was a wise one; when God builds something, it stands.

I saw this so clearly when making a journey through Romania, preaching God's Word. In Bucharest I saw the Palace of the People. Built on the orders of President Ceauaescu it turned out to be a monstrous folly to stupid pride. It had 7,000 rooms including display cases of cocktail shakers that lit up and played tunes. One journalist when he got into the Palace with the revolutionary troops sat down at the grand piano and played a spirited rendition of "As time goes by". It was most appropriate. There was a book there asking visitors to fill in what they thought the building might now be used for!

Yet, all across Romania I found churches strong and Christ exalting, despite everything that Ceausescu had done to them. The Lord had built those christians an enduring house. He will do the same for you. Abigail got it right, didn't she? Live for the things that endure.

M♦A♦R♦C♦H 9TH

"Yet a man has risen to pursue you and seek your life, but the life of my lord shall be bound in the bundle of the living with the Lord your God; and the lives of your enemies he shall sling out, as from the pocket of a sling" .
1 Samuel 25:29

The tongue. It is three inches long and can kill a man six feet tall. It is the only part of the human body that never seems to get tired. It is the only thing by which you can skate on thin ice and get into hot water.

Words. Have you any idea of their power? Satan used tempting words to Eve and plunged the world into ruin. At Babel they started using proud words and God struck the world with languages. Abraham used lying words and Pharaoh threw him out of Egypt. Sarah used manipulating words and today you have the Arab-Israeli conflict. Saul persecuted David with threatening words and ended a suicide. In our text Abigail used encouraging words, wisely chosen, reminding David of his former victories and the words she used prevented him from a wild rush out of God's will. The tongue sits in a wet place and is liable to slip; take a cue from Abigail and use it carefully, today.

M♦A♦R♦C♦H 10TH

"And it shall come to pass, when the Lord has done for my lord according to all the good that he has spoken concerning you, and has appointed you ruler over Israel, that this will be no grief to you, nor offence of heart to my lord, either that you have shed blood without cause, or that my lord has avenged himself." 1 Samuel 25:30-31

Bad temper can have devastating results. "My bad temper", said the lady, "is over in a second or two". "So is a shot from a gun", replied her listener. Abigail pled with David that as God's promises to him would be kept and that he would one day become Israel's King, he would then be very glad that no haunting memory would cast a shadow on the sunlit hills of his life. It was good advice, and remember, there is nothing more difficult as the art of making advice agreeable.

Are you ready to write a nasty letter to someone? Are you planning some act of revenge because of some vindictive behaviour towards you? Are you on the verge of lifting the telephone and "tearing strips" of an individual who has pointlessly hurt you? The day will come when God will put you in a position of wider influence than you now enjoy; what of the nasty letter, the act of revenge, the un-diplomatic phone call, then?

M♦A♦R♦C♦H 11TH

"And blessed is your advice and blessed are you, because you have kept me this day from coming to bloodshed and from avenging myself with my own hand. For indeed as the Lord God of Israel lives, who has kept me back from hurting you, unless you had hastened to come to meet me, surely by morning light no males would have been left to Nabal". 1 Samuel 25:33-34

One word of advice to someone can turn their life around. You may not think you are one to give advice to anyone but that simply is not true. All of us go through experiences which teach us lessons that are worth passing on. Abigail's advice is a shining example of advice wisely and carefully given, backed up by practical action and as a result she actually saved lives. David told her that if she hadn't spoken not a single male in her husbands circle would have been left alive.

My advice to you today is very simple; go, like Abigail, and lay a cool hand on a hot head.

M♦A♦R♦C♦H 12TH

"And when the servants of David had come to Abigail at Carmel, they spoke to her saying, 'David sent us to you, to ask you to become his wife'. Then she arose, bowed her face to the earth and said, 'Here is your maidservant, a servant to wash the feet of the servants of my lord' So Abigail became his wife". 1 Samuel 25:41-42

Abigail went home to find her husband drunk, so she didn't tell him of her action until morning. When she did he had a heart attack and ten days later the Lord struck him dead. David, on hearing of Nabal's death proposed to Abigail and she accepted.

What do we learn, ultimately, from Abigails input to Davids life? We learn, in the words of David's son Solomon that "Open rebuke is better than love carefully concealed" and that "Faithful are the wounds of a friend but the kisses of an enemy are deceitful" (Proverbs 27:5-6). Abigail didn't flatter David, she didn't shrug her shoulders and say "It's none of my business what he does"; she openly and lovingly rebuked him and he was eternally grateful to her. Have you had to lovingly rebuke someone recently? Comfort yourself with the fact that such advice could have eternal repercussions.

M♦A♦R♦C♦H 13TH

"David therefore sent out spies, and understood that Saul had indeed come". 1 Samuel 26:4

It was back to the trenches. Human emotions soon change and Saul had again forgotten David's kindness in sparing his life. He once more leads three thousand specially chosen men to hunt David down. David, though, sent out spies to discover just what was going on. He was not chosing to be ignorant of Saul's devices.

There is a lesson in this. Every christian needs to be on the lookout for what Satan is up to. We must never get to the situation where we moan and say that "I never thought Satan would ever use him or her". "Watch", said Christ, "for in such an hour as you think not, temptation may come upon you and woe to you if you are not found watching". God promises a safe landing but not a calm passage. So, watch.

M♦A♦R♦C♦H 14TH

"'Who will go down with me to Saul in the camp?' And Abishai said, 'I will go down with you'". 1 Samuel 26:6

David wanted to know who would accompany him on a special mission into dangerous territory. It was hazardous to sneak into Saul's camp at night, especially if you were accompanying the man Saul specifically wanted to kill! Abishai proved to be the man.

Son of David's sister, Zeruiah, Abishai was always intensely loyal to David. When Absalom and Sheba were later to revolt, Abishai stood firm and was also to later rescue David in the fight with Ishhibinob, the Philistine giant. Loyalty is a very decent quality and it applies to writers just as much as anyone else because some writers sacrifice their loyalties for their royalties! Abishai reminds me of what the British Prime Minister Pitt said about a certain MP called Dundas. "Dundas", said Pitt, "was no orator but he would go out with you in any kind of weather". Be loyal to your friends, even when the going gets rough. Let Abishai's example inspire you today.

M✦A✦R✦C✦H 15TH

"So David took the spear and the jug of water by Saul's head, and they got away; and no man saw it or knew it or awoke. For they were all asleep, because a deep sleep from the Lord had fallen on them". 1 Samuel 26:12

God cares about detail. The very hairs of your head are numbered. If you could only see the angels that are ministering spirits in your life, if you could only see the myriad ways in which God is opening and shutting doors for you and using different circumstances around you to guide you through; then you would cease worrying and fretting.

As David and Abishai slipped through Saul's camp and took Saul's spear and jug of water from under his very nose, Saul or his three thousand sleeping men never stirred. Why? "Because a deep sleep from the Lord had fallen on them". "That night the king could not sleep", we read of the king in Esther's day. As a result a nation was saved. This night the king in David's day, slept and David was spared. It is obvious, then, that kings, asleep or awake are in God's hands. So, stop your fretting; all things that happen to you are not necessarily good but they work together for good. Always.

M✦A✦R✦C✦H 16TH

"Then David went over to the other side, and stood on the top of a hill afar off, a great distance being between them". 1 Samuel 26:13

I find this one of the most haunting of all verses in David's life. Lift your eyes to the bigger scenario and see David, again, as Israel's immediate Saviour and Saul as the one he is trying to save. Time after time David had spared Saul, shown him amazing grace and kindness and time and again he had spurned it all. Now, says Scripture, there was "a great distance between them".

Could someone be reading this book who has long been shown the kindness of the Saviour of the world? Again and again you have been spared to know the long-suffering grace of the Lord Jesus. Be warned. Do not trifle with such love and grace for soon, if you are not careful, you may cross over the line and a great gulf be fixed between you and him (See Luke 16:26), over which there is no bridge. Choose you this day who you will serve. If you, like Saul, choose to serve yourself you will be left to yourself, forever. The Gospel message says to you, today, that the greatest barrier to Hell is the cross of Calvary. Pass it at your peril.

M✦A✦R✦C✦H 17TH

"So David said to Abner, 'Are you not a man? And who is like you in Israel? Why then have you not guarded your lord the king? For one of the people came in to destroy your lord the king. This thing that you have done is not good'". 1 Samuel 26:15-16

It must have been a rude awakening from sleep for Abner, Saul's cousin. Abner was the commander in chief of Saul's army and it was he who had first brought David to Saul following the slaying of Goliath. Now David berates him across the night-time divide for not guarding his master. David always had a high regard for Abner and even here tells him there is no one like him in all Israel.

There is a message for us all in David's night-time rebuke. We have all be given something to guard and cherish. Children, for example, are a heritage from the Lord. Parent, are you guarding those supple minds in your care from the sneaking invasion of Satan's pollution?

I think of my late and good friend Mrs. Isobel Johnston. I visited her when she was dying. "Derick", she said, "I used to pour spiritual truths into my children's ears when they were young and I was criticised for it. My answer was that I had decided it was better to pour spiritual truth into their minds as soon as possible because soon the Devil would be pouring his rubbish into their ears and I wanted to get in first!" As I see her children rise up across Northern Ireland and each one of them deeply involved in christian things I am reminded that Isobel was no Abner. Guard the treasure God has given you. Guard it, I say, for many will try to steal it.

M♦A♦R♦C♦H 18TH

"For the king of Israel has come out to seek a flea, as when one hunts a partridge in the mountains" . 1 Samuel 26:20

David never rose higher than the night he gave this amazing speech in the hill of Hachilah. Did ever the stars shine on such a scene as David taking the moral high ground before thousands of waking men, speaking out of inky blackness? Ah! Right is might and David had it. One with God was a majority that night as he humbly exposed the stupidity of Saul and his army wasting their time hunting one of God's own servants.

Has some young person exposed your folly recently? Like a young lad I know who stumbled drunk into his father's home, one night. His father told me that he scolded him for his drunkenness until the young lad said, "But it was you, Dad, who bought me my first shandy". Selah.

M♦A♦R♦C♦H 19TH

"Indeed I have played the fool and erred exceedingly" . 1 Samuel 26:21

What an obituary! Saul began so promisingly yet he deteriorated so dismally and ended so ignominiously. His decline started when he committed an act of irreverent presumption. He was expressly told to wait seven days in Gilgal for Samuel but he was wilfully impatient and violated the priests prerogative and presumed to offer up with his own hand pre-arranged sacrifices to the Lord. He did it to impress the people. Samuel's final word to him was in the form of a haunting question; "When you were little in your own eyes were you not head of the tribes of Israel?"

Beware of pride. Humility ousted by arrogance and pride can lead to disaster. Advantages are not in themselves a guarantee of success. The greatest opportunities which can come to us are not in themselves enough to give life its highest fulfilment. Not even special gifts from God certify ultimate achievement. Saul let self get the upper hand in his life and he missed the best and courted the worst. May God give us grace not to follow him.

M♦A♦R♦C♦H 20TH

"You shall both do great things and also still prevail". 1 Samuel 26:25

God has great things in store for you. Far greater than you imagine. You will find he is a God who gives and gives and when you think, "That's it, God has brought me to the zenith", He then gives again. Because of who you are associated with, great things will be accomplished through you. Be assured of that. God will never make you blush because of His word, or because of any errand He sends you on. You will have your down days and up days but God will see to it that, if you obey Him, you will prevail.

Our text was spoken by Saul and he, even though he was a fool, could see that David's close association and walk with God was going to make him prevail in life. Be encouraged, christian, you shall both do great things and also still prevail.

M♦A♦R♦C♦H 21ST

"And David said in his heart ..." 1 Samuel 27:1

Watch what you say when you talk to yourself. Your heart does not always tell you the right things. I have followed my heart on occasions and have been sobered when what it has told me came up against reality.

After all the victories of his recent life, David was just as wide open to self's seductive voice as any of us. Sadly David did not seek the Lord as to what he should do next and he was to almost end up fighting for Israel's enemy. Watch the voice of self for if we could see ourselves as others see us, we would probably have our eyes examined!

M♦A♦R♦C♦H 22ND

" There is nothing better for me than that I should speedily escape to the land of the Philistines; and Saul will despair of me, to seek me anymore in any part of Israel. So I shall escape out of his hand". 1 Samuel 27:1

Does today's text find you in a corner with your back to the wall? You are not thinking straight because your appraisal of your situation is overwhelmed by fear of somebody or something. Listen to David's reasoning; he says "There is nothing better" for him but that he flee to Israel's enemy for help because Saul is still after him.

Are you tempted to leave the path of christian service for something less demanding? Are you sick with fear because you are afraid? We in Northern Ireland face such fear every day as we go out; terrorists are all around us bombing and killing and trying to wreck any normality in our society. We have had twenty consecutive years of it, now. For christians in this society it is a great temptation to say "There is nothing better for me" than to emigrate, or to forget the Sermon on the Mount's teaching and do something very stupid. Steady up. Geographical moves don't take you away from thugs, they are everywhere. If the Lord guides you to leave your present situation, leave. If you have no clear guide it is better for you to wait until you have. Remember that, ultimately, no opposition can finally crush you as a christian. No good thing will finally be withheld from you. If it is good for you, you will get it, if it's not, you won't. No accusation can ever finally disinherit you. Nothing can separate you from the love of God which is in Christ Jesus our Lord. Isn't that enough to be getting on with?

M♦A♦R♦C♦H 23RD

*" Then David arose and went over with six hundred men who were with him
to Achish the son of Maoch, king of Gath". 1 Samuel 27:2*

There is no such thing as a person without influence. The
Lord Jesus distinctly taught that those who follow him are the
"salt of the earth". Put a little salt in something and you will
influence it. Christians have a far greater influence in the world
than their numbers indicate.

Example is not the main thing in influencing others; it is the
only thing. David did not, you will notice, go over into Philistia
alone, six hundred of his men followed him. His example was
followed and now six hundred and one Israelites were living in
their enemies lap. Be careful of what you do, very careful. Others
are watching. Ask yourself a simple question; "If everybody was
like me, what kind of a world would it be?"

M♦A♦R♦C♦H 24TH

*"And it was told Saul that David had fled to Gath; so he sought him no
more" . 1 Samuel 27:4*

Beware of lulls; they can throw you off your guard. They can
give you a false sense of security. It was in a lull that Peter denied
the Lord. It was in a lull that Samson fell. It was in a lull that
Solomon became an effeminate fool. It was even a longing for a
lull that drew Demas off the track.

This problem was to surface in David's life again and was to
lead to the darkest sin in his life, for it was in a lull he was to stoop
to adultery and murder. Saul now left David alone, there was a
welcome lull in all the pressure David had experienced for years,
but, look at the price he paid. It was to lead to compromise with
the enemy. You will notice that during his sixteen month resi-
dence in Gath no psalms emerge for this period in his life. "If you
can't beat them join them", they tell me, but such a philosophy
will not wear in the christian life. Goliath's Gath was still Gath.
Too far East is West.

M♦A♦R♦C♦H 25TH

"And so was his behaviour all the time he dwelt in the country of the Philistines". 1 Samuel 27:11

What was David's behaviour all the time he was resident in Philistia? It was marked by hypocrisy, deceit and cruelty. David was no Philistine but he had to act as though he were one for there is a price to pay if you would have security from your enemy. He turned his sword on the smaller tribes of the south country, who were in alliance with the Philistines but who were the foes of Israel. Among these were Nomad tribes who lived by plunder. When asked by king Achish, under whose protection David was now living, to give an account of himself David gave very vague replies, which turned firmly into downright lies. He implied to Achish that he had been raiding Israel and to cover his tracks David cruelly killed every member of the tribes he attacked.

What is the lesson from this cruel period in David's life? It is that we must beware of having a fit of mistrust in God. Had God not sworn to put David on the throne of Israel? What of that "sure house" he had promised him? David began to live on his wits alone. He was soon to come to Wits-End Corner.

M♦A♦R♦C♦H 26TH

"Then the princes of the Philistines said, 'What are these Hebrews doing here ... make this fellow return, that he may go back to the place which you have appointed for him, and do not let him go down with us to battle, lest in the battle he become our adversary. For with what could he reconcile himself to his master, if not with the heads of these men?"' Samuel 29:3-4

It is in the nature of things that we are forced to take sides. King Achish was fooled by David's deceit but the commanders of the Philistine army weren't. David was dismissed from his post as bodyguard to Achish, despite the pleas of Achish.

One thing is for sure; if you are the Lord's you can never truly be the world's. You may play at it but once you have tasted of Christ, nothing else compares. You will be disillusioned with the world as David was with Philistia. He had put everything into

Achish's protection but the flimsy protection was eventually withdrawn. Put not your trust in Princes for expediency and public opinion can draw away their championing and sponsorship of you and your cause. No one who ever trusted in God was disappointed.

M✦A✦R✦C✦H 27TH

"So David and his men came to the city, and there it was, burned with fire; and their wives, their sons and their daughters had been taken captive".
1 Samuel 30:3

David had been given the town of Ziklag by king Achish. As he and his men trudged a long three day journey, home, it was to find their town burnt to the ground by the Amalekites and their families taken captives. Everything was now in ashes; David's trust in the Philistines was misplaced.

It is a long way from the ashes of Ziklag to the promiscuity of the dying years of the 20th Century, but, just the other day I noticed a headline in " The Times" which read "High priests of love fall out of bed". The article pointed out that America's postwar generation now faced fresh disillusion as William Masters and Virginia Johnston, the apostles of the sexual revolution were applying for divorce. The "first family of sexology" who used surrogates and other controversial methods in their therapy have long been denounced as the authors of the notion of sex as irresponsible recreation, "An approach which has fallen from favour in the age of AIDS".

It should never have been in favour! Now, the pair who took multitudes with them in their unbiblical theories can't even get along with each other! Sad it was that David listened to the seductive voice of self and went to the world for help. David was later to write in the first psalm that the person who is truly happy is the one who does not walk in the "counsel of the ungodly". He had to learn the hard way; let his words save you from the same experience.

Then David and the people who were with him lifted up their voices and wept, until they had no more power to weep". 1 Samuel 30:4

Displaced. Disillusioned. Distrusted. Distressed. David at Ziklag reached one of the lowest points of his life. He cried until he could cry no more.

Recently, I watched on television a young christian teenager lifting her head to the skies and crying almost beyond human comfort as they carried away the coffin of her christian boyfriend, who had been heartlessly shot by terrorists in the North of Belfast. My heart was wrenched by what I saw. There are, in our city, many people who are on the edge of severe spiritual doubt over all the murderous darkness around us. They would not be the first.

Back in the 1880's the young and blind Scottish minister of Inellan was driven to consider himself "an absolute atheist". His name was George Matheson and out of the pit of his deep depression he wrote one of the loveliest of all christian hymns entitled "Oh, love that will not let me go". As he wrestled with his doubts his gloom was dispelled and central to his restoration was the reminder that Calvary was older than Eden.

"Stand where Job stood under the shadow of Gethsemane for remember that the patience of Job is the patience of hope", preached Matheson to Queen Victoria at Balmoral in 1885. She asked for the sermon to be printed and distributed. "I lay in dust lifes glory dead, and from the ground there blossoms red, life that shall endless be", says Matheson's hymn. There is a message there for a heartbroken city like mine and for you, wherever you are. As David was able to find out, there truly is a love that will not let us go.

M✦A✦R✦C✦H 29TH

"Then David was greatly distressed, for the people spoke of stoning him". 1 Samuel 30:6

Yes, they will sing of David when he leads them to victory but they will speak of stoning him when he leads them to disaster.

There is a driving reason why I chose to write this study of the life of David. I wanted us to walk for a year through his amazing life together, in order to see that the life, even of a man after God's own heart, is not dissimilar to ours. God penned the story in order that we might understand that even God's greatest heroes fall upon days when their very friends turn against them, and, for good reason. As one has put it, "The loyalty and devotion he had never failed to receive from his followers was suddenly changed to vinegar and gall". Yet, when even your friends are justified in finding no good in you, the Lord will continue to take you up. Why? Because he didn't take you up in the first place because you were good, he took you up because he loved you.

M♦A♦R♦C♦H 30TH

"But David encouraged himself in the Lord his God" . *1 Samuel 30:6*

Hope in darkness. Blues skies amid ashes. Surging new strength for a tired heart. Forgiveness for time wasted. Guidance for the future. David took a pair of shears, if you like, and cut the meshes of the net that was holding him down. He got himself out of the false position into which he had drifted.

What brought this great change? Committees? Money? Personal influence? His wits? A reinforced army? A new public image? None of these things could have got David out of the net that he had enmeshed himself in. No. The answer lay in the fact that David returned to God. He suddenly, amid overwhelming circumstances, as F. B. Meyer put it, "Sprang back to his old resting place in the bosom of God". It was to be a well spring of blessing with far reaching repercussion. Within seconds he was his old noble self once more.

So, leave off moaning to your friends. Leave the fireside chat of "What he said to you", or " They" criticised you for. Stop pulling strings and manipulating moves. Turn to the Lord with your burden and leave it there. The circumstances around you might remain the same but you won't. That will make all the difference.

M♦A♦R♦C♦H 31ST

"But as his part is who goes down to the battle, so shall his part be who stays by the supplies; they shall be alike" . *1 Samuel 30:24*

It is a new David who swoops upon on the marauding troops holding his family and those of his men. Notice the fairness that pervades his life at this time. He certainly fights the enemy but he stands against the greed of some of his followers who propose to withhold the plunder they had from those who had stayed behind to protect their supplies. David would have none of it. He certainly believed that "They also serve who stand and wait". The two hundred men who had protected his supplies were to receive an equal share of the reward.

As we leave March days behind let us never forget that in christian service God thinks as much of seemingly obscure service as of that which is up-front. Schubert would have made a poor show of it if the piano tuner hadn't turned up. The brilliant surgeon can't do without the help of ambulance drivers. The Q.E.2 would never have sailed if the riveters hadn't riveted. We all need each other and no service, honestly done, is insignificant. Find out where you can render a service; then, render it. The rest is up to the Lord.

A P·R·I·L

A◆P◆R◆I◆L

*T*he promises of God are the key to our hope. If God says He will do something, He delivers. Despite all the labyrinth of ways David had to traverse, God's promise was that David would become King of Israel. Ziklag might burn, the daughter's of the Philistines might rejoice at Israel's dilemmas but slowly and surely the springtime of David's life burst out. Yes, the thorns and nettles were there too but God's Word came true. As springtime comes let's be assured that not one word of God to us will fail, either.

A◆P◆R◆I◆L 1ST

"On the third day, behold, it happened that a man came from Saul's camp with his clothes torn and dust on his head. So it was, when he came to David, that he fell to the ground and prostrated himself". 2 Samuel 1:2

David's life was about to turn a new corner. The charred remains of Ziklag might still have been smouldering at his feet but the hunted, despised, out-on-a-limb David was about to see God's promises to him, fulfilled.

Imagine David at this crossroads in his life. Where would he turn to now? Would he rebuild his life at Ziklag or look for a new place to live with his family? He may have just defeated the Amalekites but he was still hemmed in by enemies all around him. Returning to Israel seemed out of the question, living at Gath was barred. But, suddenly, a young man arrived in his camp and though dishevelled, the news he brought was to change David's life forever.

So it will be for you. God has more for you in His programme for your life. That is certain. Learn one thing as you ponder what to do, next. Remember that in this life things do not remain the same very long. It is a very long road which has no turning. Mark my word; your road will turn, soon.

A♦P♦R♦I♦L 2ND

"And Saul and Jonathan his son are dead also". 2 Samuel 1:4

How would you respond if someone told you that your greatest enemy was dead? If that enemy had tried to kill you time after time, how would you have reacted to his death, especially, if that death had been suicide? Would you gloat? Would you say that it served him right?

The news the young Amalekite brought to David confirmed that Saul had died albeit that the young man lied about the circumstances. David's reaction was quite extraordinary; he "Mourned and wept and fasted until evening for Saul and for Jonathan his son". Wasn't David glad he had kept his mouth shut all those provoking years? Wasn't he glad he had not retaliated in kind? There was not a word he had to regret.

If a wicked word is on the tip of your tongue today against your enemy, leave it there. If your enemy died tonight you will have no regrets this week, should you stand by his graveside.

A♦P♦R♦I♦L 3RD

"And he told them to teach the children of Judah the Song of the Bow; indeed it is written in the Book of Jasher". 2 Samuel 1:18

From the great Mausoleums of the Pharaoh's to the tiniest memorial stones of the obscure, people leave their mark. There is something truly majestic about David writing his Song of the Bow to mark Saul and Jonathan's passing and ordering it to be taught to the children of Judah. David's treatment of Saul's memory was more than kind, it was downright majestic. How can we account for it?

I remember a christian I once knew who argued and disputed with every church in town. When he died and we came to bury him, I took a friend with me to swell the crowd. In all, there were about seven of us. "You can't fight with your fellow christians and expect them to turn up at your funeral", quipped one of the seven to me, quietly, as we entered the graveyard. A gentleman prayed. "We remember, Lord, all that was good about our brother", he said. It was, in the circumstances, the most gracious prayer I ever heard. It was also the best practical exposition I have ever heard of David's Song of the Bow. David remembered the good in Saul and drew a curtain of silence around the bad. Let's sing and practice the Song of the Bow, more often.

A◆P◆R◆I◆L 4TH

" The beauty of Israel is slain on your high places! How the mighty have fallen! Tell it not in Gath, proclaim it not in the streets of Ashkelon -lest the daughters of the Philistines rejoice". 2 Samuel 1:19-20

Suicide; what images the word raises! The word might come very close to home in your family where, maybe, someone you love has seen it as an answer. Saul's suicide is surrounded by silence in Scripture. David in his Song of the Bow, his funeral dirge to Saul's memory, urges that what happened to Saul is not talked of lest it cause rejoicing in the enemies camp.

Is there anything more sickening than the faults of the people of God being the glee of the unconverted? In recent years certain TV evangelists have provided abundant fodder for hungry journalists and stand-up comics. Their behaviour has not been lost on the general public, either. Let's live so that no enemy of the Cross will ever have the chance to do the same over us.

A◆P◆R◆I◆L 5TH

"I am distressed for you, my brother Jonathan, you have been very pleasant to me; your love to me was wonderful, surpassing the love of women".
2 Samuel 1:26

Few friendships have had the depth that Jonathan and David's reached. Jonathan was a friend in God to David. Nobody in David's life ever moved him from fear to faith like Jonathan did. It is now over thirty centuries since David lost Jonathan and yet our hearts are still wrenched when we sense David's grief in the words of our text.

It is worth asking the question "What would David have been without Jonathan?" The answer is that Jonathan was one of God's tools for making David the man after God's own heart. David could never have been what he was without Jonathan. Jonathan's role in life was different from David's but he served the purpose of God every bit as much as David did by being David's friend.

The most practical lesson that comes out of Jonathan's life for us is that if we are prepared to be a Jonathan in someone else's life we can have a spiritual impact for God in this generation that only eternity will reveal. Jonathan found that friendship with David was costly but it was eternally worth the price.

A♦P♦R♦I♦L 6TH

"David enquired of the Lord, saying, 'Shall I go up to any of the cities of Judah?' And the Lord said to him, 'Go up'. David said, 'Where shall I go up?' And he said, 'To Hebron'". 2 Samuel 2:1

There is something majestic about David at this time in his life. It marks the mid-way point, for, on one side lay the years of being hunted by Saul and soon, on the other side, were to lie his years as Israel's great king. What he did at this great crisis in his life as a thirty year old is an inspiration for all who suffer from fits of impatience. David could have taken an army and marched on Saul's supporters who were in disarray at Saul's suicide and taken Israel's throne by force. Instead he enquired of the Lord what he should do. David had ended in too many cul-de-sacs in his life by failing to talk to God before taking journeys the Lord had not ordered. This time David prayed about it and was directed to live in the city of Hebron.

Are you in a so-near-so-far situation today? Patience, christian, patience. If God is holding up on giving you full directions go as far as His light has shown. Then, wait. David was to wait in Hebron for seven and a half years but he was not to be sorry. Waiting for an answer to prayer is often part of the answer.

A✦P✦R✦I✦L 7TH

"Then the men of Judah came, and there they anointed David king over the house of Judah. And they told David, saying, 'The men of Jabesh Gilead were the ones who buried Saul'". 2 Samuel 2:4

If ever anyone went the second mile in kindness to an enemy, David was that person. Saul was dead, his son Ishbosheth was trying to thwart David as king over Israel at every turn and still David refused to degrade even Saul's memory!

The men of Judah now crowned David king over the house of Judah and in conversation with him tell him how the men of Jabesh Gilead had gone into Philistine territory at the dead of night and had brought back the body of Saul and buried him. David immediately says he will reward them for their action. To put it plainly, if somebody had tried to kill you and bury you dozens of times would you have rewarded the people who buried him saying "You are blessed of the Lord for you have shown this kindness to your lord"?

The other day I was travelling through a Scottish town with an elder of a church. He told me that trouble had risen in his local church and he was under great pressure to be vindictive towards a certain man. This man had done nothing wrong but a person in his family circle had and many tarred him with the same brush. The elder told me the thing that held him back from being unfair was the example of David's behaviour towards Saul. The man the people wanted to wrong held high office in the local church and the elder told me that because this man was "The Lord's anointed", he refused to harm him. The lesson should not be lost on any of us.

A✦P✦R✦I✦L 8TH

"Sons were born to David in Hebron; his firstborn was Amnon by Ahinoam the Jezraelitess; his second, Chileab by Abigail the widow of Nabal the Carmelite; the third, Absalom the son of Maacah the daughter of Talmai, king of Geshur; the fourth, Adonijah the son of Haggith; the fifth, Shepatiah the son of Abital; and the sixth, Ithream, by David's wife Eglah. These were born to David in Hebron". 1 Samuel 3:2-5

I warn you, if you do not already know, the latter half of David's life is going to shock you. It makes, often, pathetic and tragic reading. David was to later experience social and domestic trials as few men have ever done. Why? God hangs the key of explanation on the door that opens 2 Samuel to us. Today's text is that key; David, unfortunately, practised polygamy when he got to Hebron.

God's original creation of only one man and one woman shows very clearly that monogamy was God's intention for the human race. Nowhere, repeat nowhere, did the law of Moses sanction a plurality of wives. Proverbs 5:18, for example, plainly indicates the joy and health to be gained by monogamy. The law warned that any king whom he Lord choose was not to "multiply wives for himself, lest his heart turn away" (Deut 17:15-17). David deliberately disobeyed the law as our text shows.

There is no question that sexual indulgence was the besetting sin of David's adult life. It was to sear through his family life and at a later stage was to wrest almost the very nation out of his hand. The reaping of his sowing was to be disastrous. It is worth remembering that if we sow a thought, we reap an action. If we sow an action, we reap a character. If we sow a character, we reap a destiny.

Be warned by Jeremiah who said "Your iniquities have turned these things away, and your sins have withheld good things from you". Jeremiah 5:25.

A♦P♦R♦I♦L 9TH

"And David said, 'Good, I will make a covenant with you. But one thing I require of you; you shall not see my face unless you bring Michal, Saul's daughter, when you come to see my face'. So David sent messengers to Ishbosheth, Saul's son saying, 'Give me my wife Michal' ... and Ishbosheth sent and took her from her husband, from Phaltiel the son of Laish. Then her husband went along with her to Bahurim, weeping behind her. So Abner said to him, 'Go, return!' And he returned." 2 Samuel 3:13-16

Matthew Henry has a very concise word on David's recovery of his first wife, Michal. He writes, "David enters into a treaty with Abner but upon condition that he shall procure him the restitution of Michal his wife. (1) David showed the sincerity of his conjugal affection to his first and most rightful wife; neither

her marrying another, nor his, had alienated him from her. Many waters could not quench that love. (2) He testified to his respect to the house of Saul. He cannot be pleased with the honours of the throne unless he have Michal, Saul's daughter, to share with him in them, so far as he is from bearing any malice to the family of the enemy....Her latter husband was loth to part with her, but there was no remedy: he must thank himself; for when he took her he knew that another had a right to her. If any disagreement has separated husband and wife, as they expect the blessing of God let them be reconciled, and come together again: let all former quarrels be forgotten, and let them live together in love, according to God's holy ordinance". Good advice, for sure.

A♦P♦R♦I♦L 10TH

"Should Abner die as a fool dies? Your hands were not bound nor your feet put into fetters; as a man falls before wicked men, so you fell".
2 Samuel 3:34

If David had a besetting sin, he also had a superb gift. He was able, through his pen to turn the drab into a jewel. Time after time as life rolled its experiences over his head David lifted his pen and wrote about them. The death of Abner is a perfect example.

Abner was a man of war, a soldier, held in deep suspicion by Joab, David's captain. Abner knew Joab's attitude very well, yet, one day, Abner came too close and Joab knifed him to death. Even in the midst of foul murder David could draw a lesson for us all with his pen. He tells us Abner need not have died; he was a free man, yet he walked straight into a trap with his eyes wide open. Just apply today's text to your life. Are your feet in fetters? Are your hands, bound? No? Then don't be a fool and walk into trouble. Walk away from it, not into it.

A♦P♦R♦I♦L 11TH

"For all the people and all Israel understood that day that it had not been the kings intent to kill Abner the son of Ner". 2 Samuel 3:37

David's intentions towards Abner may not have appeared to be good because outward circumstances are not always trustworthy as a gauge of people's intentions. Truth, though, has a habit of surfacing for it is incontrovertible. As Churchill said of truth; "Panic may resent it; ignorance may deride it; malice may distort it; but there it is". Before long everybody knew David never had any evil intention toward Abner, despite what outward circumstances may have indicated.

There is a popular singer from Co. Donegal called Daniel O'Donnell. Appearing on local television recently he said that his mother had once given him some advice in the form of a poem. It was good advice and in the light of today's text I would share it with you.

"Your future lies before you like a field of driven snow,

Be careful where you place your feet for every step will show."

A♦P♦R♦I♦L 12TH

"When someone told me, saying, 'Look, Saul is dead', thinking to have brought good news, I arrested him and had him executed in Ziklag - the one who thought I would give him a reward for his news. How much more, when wicked men have killed a righteous person in his own house on his bed? Therefore, shall I not now require his blood at your hand and remove you from the earth?" 2 Samuel 4:10-11

Rechab and Baanah thought they would do David a good turn. They murdered Saul's son Ishbosheth on his bed, one day at noon, and thought David would be delighted. They reminded David that Ishbosheth had tried to kill him and now "The Lord has revenged my lord the king this day of Saul and his descendants". They were not prepared for David's reaction. He had them executed. David had long established the fact that he would not take the throne by force and that he would not harm any of Saul's family .

Some people misread what is going on in other people's hearts and minds. I do it all the time, don't you? Why, Peter thought his Lord would be delighted when he used his sword to defend him in the Garden of Gethsemane. He made a grave mistake. Just remember;

A Doctor's mistake is buried.
A Lawyer's mistake is imprisoned.
An Accountant's mistake is jailed.
A Dentist's mistake is pulled.
A Pharmacist's mistake is dead.
A Plumber's mistake is stopped.
An Electrician's mistake is shocking.
A Teacher's mistake is failed.
A Printer's mistake is repeated. And yours?

A✦P✦R✦I✦L 13TH

Then all the tribes of Israel came to David at Hebron and spoke, saying,
'Indeed we are your bone in your flesh' ... and they anointed David king
over Israel" 2 Samuel 5:1-3

People are often a long time in submitting to God's way,
aren't they? Think of the long years that led to this huge multitude
making their way to Hebron to make David king of Israel, at last.
For seven and a half years the tribes of Israel had fought David
knowing all the time that he was God's man to rule Israel.
Happily they now submitted saying, "We are your bone and
your flesh".

A christian who has submitted to the Lord Jesus can also say
He became "Bone of their bone and flesh of their flesh", sin apart.
Here is no Christ who merely cries to us from the heavens to
repent or gives us a tract on the street, at arms length. He actually
became one of us to win us. He was incarnational. He can be
touched with the feelings of our infirmities. He suffered and
died for us. I have stood in a Buddhist temple and watched
people burn their prayer sticks to the wry smiling figure of the
Buddha. Yet, you will find no scars on him. We worship David's
greater son as our king because of His scars. All Israel came to
Hebron to recognise David as king. One day all Israel will do the
same to the Lord Jesus. "They shall look on Him whom they
pierced" and acknowledge Him as Lord. The scars on His hands
and feet are our passport to eternal joy. Has your god got scars?

"Also, in time past, when Saul was king over us, you were the one who led Israel out and brought them in; and the Lord said to you, 'You shall shepherd my people Israel and be ruler over Israel '". 2 Samuel 5:2

David's place was now carved in history; he was the king. No, he was not just head man in a village or head of a tribe, he was now king of all Israel. He was king of Judah and of the Moabite, the Hittite, the Edomite, the Ammorite and more. But he was, according to our text, a shepherd-king. The people did not forget what David had been originally and they wanted to put themselves under his protection, under his tender, comforting care. The boy who was faithful with a few sheep now had a nation of sheep to care for. He faced adversity in the past and was now found faithful to lead a nation through coming adversity.

As Ted Engstrom wrote; "Cripple him, and you have a Sir Walter Scott. Lock him in a prison cell, and you have a John Bunyan. Bury him in the snows of Valley Forge and you have a George Washington. Raise him in abject poverty and you have an Abraham Lincoln. Strike him down with infantile paralysis, and he becomes Franklin Roosevelt. Deafen him and you have a Ludwig von Beethoven. Call him a slow learner, 'retarded', and write him off as uneducatable, and you have an Albert Einstein".

Greatness awaits those who refuse to run scared and are faithful, first, in the little things.

"All these men of war, who could keep ranks, came to Hebron with a loyal heart, to make David king over all Israel; and all the rest of Israel were of one mind to make David king. And they were there with David three days, eating and drinking, for their brethren had prepared for them."
1 Chronicles 12:38

There were at least 303,822 armed men who came to Hebron to make David king, apart from hundreds of thousands who were civilians. For three days they feasted. But what if David had refused them? What if he had listed their crimes against him and refused to be their shepherd-king?

Often, in ancient times, a nation would send an emissary to test how the king of another nation would react to them. How the king treated the emissary would indicate his opinion of those the emissary represented. When for example, God sent his emissary, John the Baptist, king Herod had John beheaded. When God sent His son, the Lord Jesus, they crucified him. All christians believe that Christ is their representative at God's right hand. He has gone up from earth to heaven as our emissary and what we want to know is "How is he getting on?" Has he been accepted? God's view of us will show up in how Christ, our representative, is being treated.

Isn't it wonderful to know that Christ has been fully accepted by God because of His Calvary work? Because of that all who rest in that work and in that Christ are accepted by God the Father. David's kingly feast is a picnic compared to the coming Marriage Supper of the Lamb.

A♦P♦R♦I♦L 16TH

"For there was joy in Israel". 1 Chronicles 12:40

Israel had, at last, chosen God's king and there was joy in Israel. So it is when you give God's king the rightful place in your life; the inevitable result is joy. I can testify that through all of my christian life, no matter how difficult the circumstances, the joy of the Lord has been my strength. Always, everywhere, overriding all depressing thoughts and failures, the joy of being accepted in Christ, of being forgiven by God, of being commissioned by him to his service, grips me.

Thomas Watson said, "There is as much difference between spiritual joys and earthly as between a banquet that is eaten and one that is painted on the wall"! As Billy Sunday put it "If you have no joy in your religion, there's a leak in your Christianity somewhere!" If the joy has gone out of your christian living, christian, you must be flirting with another god. Selah.

A✦P✦R✦I✦L 17TH

"Now when the Philistines heard that they had anointed David king over Israel, all the Philistines went up to search for David. And David heard of it and went down to the stronghold. The Philistines also went and deployed themselves in the Valley of Rephaim". 2 Samuel 5:17-18

Sudden reversals. Have you had a few recently? Redundancy, maybe? A broken engagement? Sudden illness? One day you are enjoying life at full tilt, and the next, you are looking at four walls. One day, joy, the next chaos and sorrow.

Take David's sudden reversal. Yesterday he was at the centre of national acclaim, loved, feted, exalted to the highest office in Israel; today the Philistines pour over into Judah in vast numbers to kill him. It was a startling, frightening reversal of David's fortunes. He had to go back to the cave of Adullam for protection.

Don't be surprised if God makes your circumstances tremble now and again if only to remind you that he is Lord. It has been pointed out that the bright light of popularity can be too strong and searching for the perfect development of christian character. Pressure, loneliness, solitude, temptation, conflict, trouble are the flames that burn off the dross and bring out the gold in the christian's life. Then, and only then, can you be a help to people going through the same thing. It was, after all, sudden reversal days that brought out David's greatest psalms.

A✦P✦R✦I✦L 18TH

"Then David went on and became great and the Lord of hosts was with him". 1 Chronicles 11:9

I commend to you, today, a poem, written by my late friend Mr. R. J. Wright, christian missionary to Japan. It reads:

"Go on. Go on. Go on. Go on.
Go on. Go on. Go on.
Go on. Go on. Go on. Go on.
Go on. Go on. Go on.

Go on. Go on. Go on. Go on.
Go on. Go on. Go on.
Go on. Go on. Go on. Go on.
Go on. Go on. Go on.

Go on. Go on. Go on. Go on.
Go on. Go on. Go on.
Go on. Go on. Go on. Go on.
Go on. Go on. Go on."

A♦P♦R♦I♦L 19TH

"And David said with longing, 'Oh, that someone would give me a drink of water from the well of Bethlehem, which is by the gate!' So the three broke through the camp of the Philistines, drew water from the well of Bethlehem that was by the gate, and took it and brought it to David. Nevertheless David would not to drink it, but poured it out to the Lord".
1 Chronicles 11:17-18

Who of us, at some wistful moment in our lives have not expressed the desire for something and, maybe, weeks later have had it handed to us? Imagine David stuck in the narrow circumstance of the Cave of Adullam and one sultry day, on a whim, he expresses a longing for a drink of water from his favourite well in Bethlehem. The only problem was that Bethlehem was occupied by the Philistines.

Soon, though, a cup brimming with David's favourite mineral water from his favourite well was in his hand. Three of his men risked their necks, broke through the enemy lines and brought it to him. To his eternal credit David didn't drink it for he realised that his whim could have caused his men their lives. He poured it out as a sacrifice before God. Beware of expressing your whims because someone you love might take them seriously and be jeopardised in trying to get them for you. Watch the "All-because-the-lady-loved-Milk-Tray" syndrome!

A♦P♦R♦I♦L 20TH

"And David enquired of the Lord, saying, 'Shall I go up against the Philistines? Will you deliver them into my hand?' And the Lord said to David, 'Go up, for I will doubtless deliver the Philistines into your hand'. So David went to Baal Perazim, and David defeated them there; and he said, 'The Lord has broken through my enemies before me, like a breakthrough of water'. Therefore he called the name of the place Baal Perazim". 2 Samuel 5:19-20

Baal Perazim means "Master of Breakthroughs". There are many titles for the Lord in Scripture but this one, though tucked away in a corner of David's life, is one of the most graphic.

Your Lord is certainly a master of breakthroughs. The Red Sea was a breakthrough, if ever there was one. Jericho and its wall breaching was a very dramatic breakthrough. What shall we say of Gideon and his 300 men and the enemy "lying in the valley as numerous as locusts"? Soon their pitchers were broken and the enemy fled as God's breakthrough came. King David, too, knew very well where the secret of his strength lay; his Master was the master of breakthroughs.

And you? Hemmed in? Frightened? Little blessing? Despised for your work? Discouraged? Ready to quit? Lift your eyes to the master of breakthroughs. The Lord who got Peter through iron gates, Paul out of murdering hands, John out of Patmos blues, is your Lord. His breakthroughs are by no means over.

A♦P♦R♦I♦L 21ST

"And they left their images there and David and his men carried them away". 2 Samuel 5:21

A good idol scattering would do our modern-day world a power of good. Would to God you and I could be used, like David, to carry some idols away in our community.

How could we best do this? One of the best ways is to refuse to bow to idols ourselves. Refuse to chase the idol of fame which brings with it the urge to be popular, to be liked, the hunger to be known, to make a name for oneself. Let's refuse to give in to the idol of pleasure, that dictates that everything we do must be judged by the amount of pleasure we get out of it. Let's repudiate the idol of fortune that demands we get rich materially or else we will never know success.

The eye is a better teacher than the ear. People are watching us. If we preach that all idols are wrong then let's not be found worshipping or even flirting with them. Remember that an idol of the mind is as offensive to God as an idol of the hand. Let's scatter a few today, by God's grace.

A◆P◆R◆I◆L 22ND

"The Lord will go out before you". 2 Samuel 5:24

How often have we discovered, in life, that the Lord has gone out before us? Years ago I knew a great christian lady called Mrs. McCarthy. When I was a lad she once said to me "Don't be afraid to go around the corner, God is already there!" He certainly is.

The Lord always goes before us when he calls us to do something. You will be amazed how the way is prepared for you. Ninety-five per cent of knowing the will of God, though, consists in being prepared to do it before you know what it is. Wasn't that David's secret in the great things he did in life? He was prepared for Goliath long before he ever met him. On the occasion of the source of today's text he had enquired of the Lord what he should do, fully prepared to obey him. On a former occasion God had said "Go up for I will doubtless deliver the Philistines into your hand". David had obeyed, implicitly. This time God said "Circle behind them and when you hear the sound of marching in the tops of the mulberry trees, then you will advance quickly". He obeyed. Forward, backward, or around, David was willing, at this time in his life to obey God. Such obedience opens up your way like nothing else.

A♦P♦R♦I♦L 23RD

"Again David gathered all the choice men of Israel, thirty thousand. And David arose and went with all the people who were with him from Baale Judah to bring up from there the ark of God, whose name is called by the Name, the Lord of Hosts, who dwells between the cherubims".
2 Samuel 6:1-2

The ark. It was a symbol of God's presence. Made of acacia wood and covered with gold, the lid of the ark was of solid gold and on the gold lid were carvings of two cherubim that faced each other. Placed in the Holy of Holies in the tabernacle, there was no greater symbol to Israel that God was their God and that they were His people.

Saul had long forgotten about the ark's importance but David hadn't. Determined to restore it to a place of importance he took thirty thousand men to the house of Abinadab to bring the ark to Jerusalem. Worship, which had become virtually meaningless in Israel, was now going to be central in King David's Israel. And, shouldn't it be in ours?

As Tozer said; "We are here to be worshippers first and workers only, second. We take a convert and immediately make a worker out of him. God never meant it to be so ... out of enraptured, admiring, adoring, worshipping souls, then, God does his work. The work done by a worshipper will have eternity in it". You will certainly find that there is nothing drier and more boring than work for God without worship of God.

A♦P♦R♦I♦L 24TH

"So they set the ark of God on a new cart, and brought it out of the house of Abinadab, which was on the hill". 2 Samuel 6:3

In his zeal to bring the ark to Jerusalem, David overlooked God's instructions on how to transport it and brought it, instead, on the wheels of haste and convenience. The instructions were that the ark was to be carried only on the shoulders of the Levites, and was to be covered over, during transportation, from the gaze of the curious.

Where did the captains who advised David on the ark's transportation get the idea of moving it on wheels? They got it from the Philistines who, to the subsequent wrath of God, had originally taken it from the Israelites using wheels for transportation (See 1 Samuel 5:2-11).

The message is loud and clear. Don't despise God's detailed instructions. No amount of haste or convenience can see something through the onslaught of time and circumstance if God has not given it His favour. To use a modern example; a sail board may be convenient and let you go where you want on water but it was never built to last the Atlantic. Follow God's blueprint and your work for Him will weather every storm.

A✦P✦R✦I✦L 25TH

"And when they came to Nachon's threshing floor, Uzzah put out his hand to the ark of God and took hold of it, for the oxen stumbled. Then the anger of the Lord was aroused against Uzzah, and God struck him there for his error; and he died there by the ark of God". 2 Samuel 6:6-7

Many people object to the punishment of Uzzah as excessive. They say if his intention was good, why did he have to die? They say he had "a zeal for God". That is true, but it was not according to knowledge. God had warned in His word "Provoke me not and I will do you no harm" (Jeremiah 25:6). Uzzah put out his hand and touched the ark albeit to steady it, as the oxen stumbled, but in touching it he desecrated its holiness and died as a result.

Of course, you might say, the New Testament christian is not open to such sudden reaction from God. Who told you that? Paul warned the christian church not to provoke the Lord to jealousy, but they did. Some of them got drunk at their own supper before they partook of the Lord's supper and treated the act of remembrance of their Lord lightly. The result? Listen to the warning; "For he who eats and drinks in an unworthy manner eats and drinks judgment to himself, not discerning the Lord's body. For this reason many are weak and sick among you, and many are dead". Selah.

A✦P✦R✦I✦L 26TH

*"And David became angry because of the Lord's outbreak against Uzzah;
and he called the name of the place Perez Uzzah to this day".*
2 Samuel 6:8-9

Here is a side of David we have not seen before; David's
anger burned against God as Uzzah's body lay alongside the
ark. A fear of the Lord now gripped David's heart but it was not
a healthy fear.

Could it be that you are angry at God? What, with all those
people praying for you as you faced your trial, how could God
have allowed you to suffer so much? Is that your kind of
thinking? Do not have such hard thoughts of God because
following in their train comes a slavish fear of God. This kind of
fear is very different to the healthy and holy fear of God that
comes from worshipful and high thoughts of God. A. W. Pink
defines the two kinds of fear, perfectly. "One is the fear of wrath,
as Adam had in Eden, the other is a fear of displeasing one who
is gracious. The one is our treasure, the other our torment; the
one draws from God, the other draws to God".

When we entertain hard thoughts of God we dread His anger.
When we accept God's perfect will in that acceptance lies peace,
not burning anger and unhealthy fear.

A✦P✦R✦I✦L 27TH

*"So David would not move the ark of the Lord with him into the City of
David; but took it aside into the house of Obed-Edom the Gittite. The ark of
the Lord remained in the house of Obed-Edom the Gittite three months.
And the Lord blessed Obed-Edom and all his household".*
2 Samuel 6:10-11

David's refusal to have anything to do with the ark as a result
of Uzzah's death was understandable in human terms but it was
foolish. Because David had not heeded the law of God on the
matter of the ark's transportation and was chastened for it was
no reason for him to refuse to have anything to do with the ark
at all. All he had to do was to obey God's instructions and he
would have had the blessing.

Instead, David left the ark at the house of a Philistine called Obed-Edom for three months and the Philistine and his family got the blessing. Obed means "servant" and it soon became obvious to the whole countryside that this most unlikely person was rendering God a great service and was being blessed as a result. Be careful that by plain stubbornness you are not missing God's blessing on you and your household. Don't let somebody else, in the words of Scripture, "steal your crown". By simple obedience, the blessing could be yours, this very day.

A♦P♦R♦I♦L 28TH

"So David went and brought up the ark of God from the house of Obed-Edom to the City of David with gladness ... then David danced before the Lord with all his might". 2 Samuel. 6:12-14

So, you thought that following every detail of God's law would make you unbending and stern, morbid and stilted? It certainly wasn't the case with David. At last, he obeyed the law of God regarding the ark and inspired by God's blessing on the Philistine family who had kept it for three months, he returned the ark to Jerusalem. As it neared Jerusalem David, released from his remorse, restored to the joy of his Lord, liberated from raw fear of God's anger, danced with all his might before the Lord.

People are embarrassed by this, and, as we shall soon see, so was David's wife. Yet, why should we be embarrassed? After preaching one morning in Portrush, Co. Antrim I was standing below the pulpit as the congregation moved out when a man came literally running up the aisle. He wanted to become a christian, there and then. And he did. What was wrong with his running? I wouldn't expect everybody to run around a church building as he did. It would be downright dangerous, apart from anything else! Yet, in the circumstances, what he did was entirely appropriate and in order. So was David's dancing. Excited and thrilled at the return of the ark David danced with joy.

As we watch footballers hug each other and dance up and down excitedly after one of their number has put a bag of wind between two posts, who would criticise David for dancing with joy that the greatest symbol of God's presence with His people had returned to Jerusalem? There would have been something wrong if he hadn't. I heard a lady shriek with joy in a prayer meeting one morning as her husband, the subject of at least twenty years of her prayers, rose and publicly received Christ as his Saviour in quiet, audible prayer. The rest of us never heard a sweeter sound.

A✦P✦R✦I✦L 29TH

"And when David had finished offering burnt offerings and peace offerings, he blessed the people in the name of the Lord of Hosts. Then he distributed among the whole multitude of Israel, both the women and the men, to everyone a loaf of bread, a piece of meat, and a cake of raisins. So all the people departed, everyone to his house" . 2 Samuel 6:18-19

I well remember a friend of mine speaking on worship. "Now", he said, "If I had been asked to speak to you on humour would I have told you to put your lips or cheeks in a certain way? No. I would have told you funny stories and you would have laughed. If I want you to worship would I say raise your hands this way or walk around in that way? No. I would show you God and you would worship, without any instruction from me".

So it was that when David returned with the ark he worshipped the Lord, offering sacrifices to God with a grateful heart. But it didn't stop there. He was so grateful he gave a loaf of bread, a piece of meat and a cake of raisins to the whole multitude of Israel. Worship and giving are closely related. When your heart wells up in praise to God the inevitable result is blessing to others. We need more people who are more interested in what they can contribute than in what they can collect. Worship is the key.

" Then David returned to bless his household. And Michal, the daughter of Saul came out to meet David, and said, 'How glorious was the king of Israel today, uncovering himself today in the eyes of the maids of his servants, as one of the base fellows shamelessly uncovers himself!' So David said to Michal, 'It was before the Lord, who chose me instead of your father and all his house, to appoint me ruler over the people of the Lord, over Israel. Therefore I will play music before the Lord. And I will be even more undignified than this, and will be humble in my own sight. But as for the maidservants of whom you have spoken, by them I will be held in honour'. Therefore Michal the daughter of Saul had no children to the day of her death". 2 Samuel 6:20-23

There is always somebody to slime any person's Eden. To put it another way, whenever you are truly free, someone in the bondage of disobedience will envy your freedom and will try to destroy your joy. Michal, David's wife was David's wet blanket. She despised him for his exuberance.

David's response is an inspiration to all who are despised within or without their family for devotion to the Lord. He simply refused to let Michal's sarcastic, carnal gibes sink his joy. Why should he? Hadn't the Lord brought him all this way, given him the Children of Israel to rule over, restored the ark to the centre of worship, and brought revival to the people of God? Why let Michal spoil it all because she wanted a life of ease? I'm glad David didn't live in a truce with Michal on spiritual matters. God has no favourites but He does have intimates. David was one of them and he was determined not to lose such intimacy. Are you?

MAY

M♦A♦Y

Let's pause, at this stage in David's life, to spend a month with one of his most magnificent psalms. It was written at the time when David brought the ark to Jerusalem and there is no question that few match it for the honour, praise, glory, power and majesty that it pours out upon God. Here is a real zenith in David's life; let's share its thrilling, exuberant theme. It was delivered into the hand of Asaph, the leader of Israel's praise, the day the ark was "set in the midst of the tabernacle that David had erected for it". It is as fresh today as the day it was delivered.

M♦A♦Y 1ST

"Oh give thanks to the Lord!" 1 Chronicles 16:8

David's first theme is a good start for this month. Thankfulness. To have a thankful spirit can make a great difference to any day. Do you have a happy spirit of thankfulness in your life? It's like the minister who was always praising the Lord and his congregation wondered one wet, windy, miserable morning what on earth he had to praise the Lord for on such a day. "Thank you, Lord", he said in prayer, "That every day is not like today!"

I'm always moved by the story of the young lieutenant who died while saving the life of one of his soldiers in Vietnam. His parents invited the soldier he had saved to dinner, after he had returned to the United States. He arrived for dinner, drunk. He spent the meal telling filthy stories and using blasphemous language. Mercifully he left. The mother of the dead lieutenant fell into her husband's arms and said "To think that our darling son had to die for that!" It is certain that God the Father will never say that about you. Yet, can there be in all the world a sin more grievous to the heart of the Father, if, after Him giving His Son for us, we in turn show little gratitude?

M♦A♦Y 2ND

"Glory in His holy name". 1 Chronicles 16:10

As I quietly walked around a synagogue in Manchester, which is now a museum, a Jewish gentleman pointed out a stain glass window in the building which contained the name of God. "We put a picture of that window on a brochure", he said "To advertise this museum but the orthodox Jews wouldn't let us use it in case the brochure would fall on the ground and the name of God would be desecrated by someone stepping on it".

Such a high view of God's name is not the average view in our western world. The two top swear words in the United Kingdom at this time are, sadly, "God" and "Christ". Let those of us who know the Lord be different. Let's glory in His holy name.

The story is told of a famous leader of an American baseball team who was attending a meeting to negotiate a contract for professional football in New York. Suddenly he threw down his pencil, pushed back his chair and said " The deal is off". Surprised, the other man asked why there had been such an abrupt break-off when all seemed to be going well on a deal involving big money on both sides. "Because", said the leader, staring at one of the football representatives, "I don't like the way you've been talking about a friend of mine". "But what friend? I haven't been talking about anyone, let alone a friend of yours". "Oh, yes you have", countered the leader, "You mentioned him in almost every sentence". Then he pointed out the man's repeated profane use of the name of Jesus Christ. "I get you", the other man said quietly, "I won't do it again. You can count on it". May the time never come when our ears no longer negatively tingle to hear the Lord's name flippantly juggled in virtually every other sentence by thoughtless people.

M♦A♦Y 3RD

"Talk about his wondrous works". 2 Chronicles 16:9

So many people waste words. According to the New York Academy of Sciences, the average man speaks 12,500 words a day and the average woman more than 25,000. How many of those words are positive, helpful and inspiring? How many are negative, sarcastic, hurtful, and a real put-down? Words have igniting power, for good or bad. "Life and death are in the power of the tongue", says the Bible. Some of the most damaging individuals have never fired a gun or incited a riot. They have simply used the power of words to break down and destroy marriages, families, friendships and businesses.

Those who use words to benefit others are such a breath of fresh air. Those who talk of God in a positive and healthy way can bring enormous comfort and hope to those in need. Let the words of William Cowper inspire us to healthy talk;

"Have you no words? Ah! Think again, words flow apace when you complain, and fill your fellow creature's ear, with a sad tale of all your care. Were half the breath thus vainly spent, to Heaven in supplication sent, your cheerful song would oftener be; Hear what the Lord has done for me!"

M♦A♦Y 4TH

"Seek the Lord and His strength". 1 Chronicles 16:11

My friend John Merson, a worker in the oil industry in the North Sea was called by God to full time christian service. I shall never forget his valedictory service in Aberdeen. It was quite a night and I felt somewhat embarrassed in carrying a large box onto the platform with me. I got quite a few "looks". Still, I bore them for I had method in my seeming madness.

What can you give a young fellow about to give his life to christian service? There are no Oscars or Emmy's or Nobel Prizes for such heroes, so, while preaching I opened my box and drew out a pair of scales. "See", I said, "On this pan of the scale is the word 'AS' and on the other the word 'SO'. As your day gets going the pressures mount". I tipped the scale down on the 'AS' side. "Yet", God has said, "As your day so shall your strength be". Down on the 'SO' side comes "God's strength", I rebalanced the scales, dead even. "God's balance is always perfect. As your day, so His strength will match it".

I expressed the wish that maybe one day God might bring to my friend John, a scale-polisher. Months and many letters later,

I received a wedding invitation to Copenhagen where John told me a lovely Danish scale-polisher would begin work on a certain date!

(P.S. It is worth noting that Mr. Stephen Cordiner, Senior, and I, hunted shops in Aberdeen that morning for a pair of scales. In the end he and his good wife Carol gave me a pair of scales from their home as a present to John. Mr. Cordiner always notes that when I arrived at his home "His scales fell off!")

M♦A♦Y 5TH

"Remember ... the judgments of his mouth". *1 Chronicles 16:12*

David wants us to think about the way God judges things. I listened to Lord Tebitt, a former Conservative Party chairman, and Member of Parliament, in the British House of Commons, recently attempt to answer the question "Do you believe in a benevolent God?" He replied that he was an agnostic and explained that if there was a God then if we could explain him or analyse him he would no longer be God.

I was immediately reminded that, in fact, the Bible claims from beginning to end that God has explained himself, and has actually revealed his thinking and his motivation. He has particularly explained himself regarding judgment. We all deserve the judgment of God, but, nevertheless, the very wrath of God that should have fallen on us, fell on the very God it came from. Christ died for our sins! That God, incarnate, should bare the punishment of his own wrath and set those free who accept Christ's death as enough to atone for their sins, is the best news on earth. What was God's judgment on Calvary's work?; Christ expressed it perfectly when He cried just before his death "It is finished". Nothing more needs to be done. Rest, then, where God rests.

"The other gods were strong; but Thou wast weak;
They rode, but Thou didst stumble to a throne;
But to our wounds only God's wounds can speak,
And not a god has wounds, but Thou alone."

(Edward Shillito)

M✦A✦Y 6TH

"Remember his covenant always, the word which he commanded, for a thousand generations". 1 Chronicles 16:15

"There are", said Vance Havner, "Sickly christians living on crackers and cheese when they have a standing invitation to feast of the grace of God. His promises are cheques to be cashed, not mere mottos to hang on the wall!"

David had proved right through his life that when God makes a promise (a covenant), he delivers. No amount of skullduggery on Saul's part or the Philistines part, or even on the part of traitors within his own camp, could turn around the promise God had made to make David, king of Israel. In David's lowest moments that promise held.

You cannot starve a person who is feeding on God's promises. Take God's promises, boldly, and say "These are mine". You will never pray better than when you plead the promises of God. You will never behave better than when you are motivated by the promises of God. You will even sleep better when you lay your head down on the promises of God. Your future is as bright as the promises of God.

"His every word of grace is strong,
As that which built the skies;
The voice that rolls the stars along,
Speaks all the promises." (Isaac Watts)

M✦A✦Y 7TH

"And confirmed it to Jacob for a statute". 1 Chronicles 16:17

My friend, Dr. R. T. Kendal says that there was a time when he identified most with Joseph but that the older he gets the more he identifies with his father, Jacob. He says the older you get the more you can see the mistakes you have made and the more there is to feel guilty about. Jacob provides a classic study in the problem of guilt.

Too right. Even when Jacob was presented to Pharoah, all he could say was "Few and evil have been the days of the years of my life". Goodness, what a summary! Do you, like Jacob, feel overwhelmed with guilt? Take heart, christian. Where does Jacob end? We read in Hebrews chapter 11 that "Jacob when he was dying, blessed each of the son's of Joseph and worshipped, leaning on the top of his staff". Surely his final reflection was to understand, to quote my friend "R. T." again, "That which once gave him the great sense of guilt now gave him the greatest sense of gratitude. God sanctified to him his deepest distress. All that was wrong in his relationship with Joseph became the very springboard of the good he had seen". God confirmed even to guilty Jacob all his promises.

"Depth of mercy - can there be Mercy still reserved for me?
Can my God his wrath forebear? Me the chief of sinners, spare?
There for me the Saviour stands, shows his wounds and spreads his hands,
God is love, I know, I feel,
Jesus lives and loves me still." (Charles Wesley)

M♦A♦Y 8TH

"To you I will give the land of Canaan as the allotment of your inheritance'. 1 Chronicles 16:18

"It is", said an Arab recently on BBC's Radio 4, "Difficult to negotiate with the Bible". The Arab was right; the Bible is not filled with "ifs" and "buts" and "perhaps" or "on the other hands". David knew Gods promises regarding the land of Canaan and today, although millions in the world would want to wipe Israel out, she still has that special protection from God.

Just the other day I took a friend to see the house in Belfast where C. S. Lewis lived as a boy. He writes of that time when, as a schoolboy of 13, he was "Soon altering 'I believe' to 'one does feel'. And oh the relief of it? From the tyrannous noon of Revelation I passed into the cool evening of Higher Thought, where there was nothing to be obeyed and nothing to be believed except what was either comforting or exciting".

Are you tempted to live in such a world? Thank God C. S. Lewis came out of it to the blessing of millions. God's word is fixed. It is not negotiable. Whither it is God's promises to Israel or God's promises to you, no one can sell them, re-write them, undermine them, or alter them. As they are, so they stand. From promised land, to promising heaven, there will never be a heavenly voice to say "But, on the other hand".

M♦A♦Y 9TH

"When you were but few in number, indeed very few, and strangers ...He permitted no man to do them wrong" 1. Chronicles 20:19-21

David reminds Israel that because they were few in number their numerical position did not affect God's promises to them. David's reminder is a timely reminder for all of us. Don't you think 20th Century Christianity needs to recover from its love affair with bigness? After Christ's ascension the disciples must have looked a sorry bunch as they made their way towards Jerusalem.

There were no computers, no fax machines, no aircraft, no portable phones, no huge stadiums or tents, no media campaigns, no big choirs or recording equipment, no video or audio recordings, no celebrity guests in those days. What was there? A lot of tramping about in one's and two's or three's and four's, conversing and preaching in homes and synagogues and market places and prisons. Why did the Gospel spread so far, so fast? Because average christians lived out their faith and took it with them as they moved around the empire. The result? They moved an empire for God until the very Roman Emperor himself fell in line.

We are often into big events, big projects, big budgets, big personalities, big institutions. Are we getting big results? Often, the answer is "No". Are you few in number down at your place? Don't get discouraged. Little is much if God is in it.

"When they went from one nation to another, and from one kingdom to another he permitted no man to do them wrong". 1 Chronicles 16:20-21

You do not need to know key men in order to know true success; you need to know the keeper of the keys. When God opens a door no man can shut it. As Israel were on the move across the nations, he preserved their identity, their ultimate safety as a nation. David reminds Israel of God's preserving care, for few knew it as intimately as he did, whether from a javelin throwing Saul or the warring, threatening nations around him.

You can know it, too, for you are immortal until your work is done. Listen to Paul; "For a great effective door is open to me, and there are many adversaries" or "Furthermore, when I came to Troas to preach Christ's gospel ... a door was opened to me by the Lord". What better word could come to any of us than the word given by the angel of the church in Philadelphia, in Revelation 3:7, "These things says He who is holy, He who is true. He who has the key of David, He who opens and no one shuts, and shuts and no one opens"? The key of David, indeed. The key that opened the door of victory in the valley of Elah, the key that sent Abigial across David's path, the key that brought all Israel to Hebron to make David king, the key that opened the flow of Psalms from David's pen, like the one we are now studying to bring untold help, comfort and inspiration to millions, was the same key!

He who has the key of David is the same one who holds the keys to your life. When He opens, no one shuts, and when He shuts, no one opens. With such a key holder, what are you worried about?

"Yes, he reproved kings for their sakes". 1 Chronicles 16:21

There is no earthly power structure which is impenetrable to God's power. There is no mistake too great that God cannot, despite it, make all things work together for good. Our text proves it. David is referring to an incident at the beginning of the life of the Hebrew people when Abraham panicked in a time of famine in Canaan and went down to live in Egypt. He knew that there could be a threat to his life because of his beautiful wife Sarah because they might kill him and keep her. So, Abraham persuaded Sarah to say that she was his sister.

Pharoah was actually attracted to Sarah and had her brought to his house and he treated her "brother" right royally. Suddenly great plagues began to sweep across Pharoah's life and the life of his family "Because", says the Bible, "Of Sarah his wife". When Pharoah discovered the truth he threw Abraham and Sarah and all that they had out of Egypt.

Think of it! Abraham makes a great mistake and God reproves a king for his sake and pulls Abraham out of the mess he had gotten his life into. Now if that isn't commitment, I don't know what is. Scripture shows us a string of saints making great and grievous mistakes; Moses murdering the Eygptian, Peter boycotting Gentile believers, Elijah running away from Jezebel. Yet, none became incurably second class. They were, as Abraham was, forgiven and restored. God does not condone wrongdoing and even Abraham smarted for it but wrongdoing on the part of a believer does not change God's commitment to that believer. Comforting, isn't it?

M♦A♦Y 12TH

"Do not touch my anointed ones, and do my prophets no harm".
1 Chronicles 16:22

"I made a vow", wrote J. Sidlow Baxter, "Over 30 years ago, now, never to criticise another evangelical minister behind his back. That vow has not spared me from being criticised - often wrongfully, cruelly, and with no chance to reply but it has spared me those wretched feelings of self-despising which follow after we have jealously or hurtfully defamed others; and it has saved me from one of those leading faults which becloud or completely fog divine guidance".

David writes our text about God's warning against those who would seek by tongue, pen or sword to wrongfully harm those he has called to serve him or to deliver his word. David himself was anointed of God to service and few have suffered within a lifetime as much as he did from those who wrongfully opposed that service; they, not he, lived to regret the day they lifted their hand against him.

Voltaire, the French atheist dedicated a lot of energy in trying to destroy the christian faith. The maid in his house told of him screaming on his deathbed two haunting words; "The Nazerene! The Nazerene! The Nazerene!". She said "Not for all the wealth in Europe do I ever want to see another infidel die". Be careful that you don't lift your tongue or anything else against God's anointed. Selah

M♦A♦Y 13TH

"Sing to the Lord, all the earth". *1 Chronicles 16:23*

Do you remember when you fell in love with your husband or wife, first? Your's was an unselfish, ardent, humble love. No low motive lurked. Your love was bright with the promise of hope. First love is the abandonment of all for a love that has abandoned all. You cannot put it into a mathematical formula. It forgets calculation. It is the crowning consciousnes of life.

Such was the love of the Ephesian church for Christ. But something had happened. Christ confronted the great church and told them that he missed their first love. They were, it seems,"Faultily faultless, icily regular, Splendidly dull".

I like what Dr. G. C. Morgan said about the Ephesian church. He said he reckoned the Lord did not hear from the christians at Ephesus a song "At the unusual hour". You know what he meant, don't you? It's easy to sing at the usual time of worship, when it is expected, but, what about first-love-to-Christ singing? In the car as you travel, about the house as you work, a quiet hum as you walk on a city street? Is there no "unusual hour" singing to the Lord in your life, anymore? "Sing to the Lord, all the earth", wrote David. Never were you busier for the Lord, but activity in the king's business will not make up for the neglect of the king. You will even do more harm by your defence of the faith if you have left your first love. Christ told the Ephesian church "I will come to you quickly and remove your lampstand

- unless you repent" (Rev 2:5). Without first love we may retain ceaseless activity, doctrinal purity, severest orthodoxy, and even have a great christian reputation but there will be no light shining in a dark place and certainly no song at the unusual hour. Without it we are but as sounding brass or a clanging cymbal.

M♦A♦Y 14TH

"Proclaim the good news of his salvation from day to day".
1 Chronicles 16:23

I was on a plane between San Francisco and Chicago and a young lady, about eighteen years of age sat beside me. She was in no mood for talking and any attempt I made to be friendly was rebuffed, so I gave up.

About half way through the flight she suddenly turned round to me and asked "What is your job, sir?" I thought if she didn't talk to me when she didn't know what my work was, she would never talk to me once she discovered it! Still, I said, quietly, "I preach the Gospel". "I am a Roman Catholic", she said. "I'm pleased to meet you", I said. "Tell me", she asked, "When you go preaching do you tell people they need to be born again?" "What interests you in such a subject?", I asked. "Well there was this fellow in my class at school. He was the dirtiest tongued, filthiest minded individual in the class. His mind was like a sewerpipe and the girls detested his stories and his language. One day he walked into class and there was no more filthy talk or bad language. I couldn't believe it. I watched and listened to him for three days and then I could stick it no longer. I walked up to him and asked him what on earth had happened to him. He told me that he had been born again. Is that what you preach each, sir?" "I do indeed", I replied. "And, if we heed David's good advice we'll do it every day".

M♦A♦Y 15TH

"Declare his glory among the nations". *1 Chronicles 16:24*

In Mineralogy there are perfusions of precious gems and all sorts of shapes in the forms of prisms, cubes and pyramids. But our Lord is the precious Living Stone (1 Peter 2:4,6). In Botany who could amply define the variety of the fabulous colours, nectars, aromas and odours of plants? But our Lord is the tender plant (Isaiah 53:2), and is the plant of renown (Ezekiel 34:29).

In Ornithology the eagle is unhindered by obstacles and can soar as no other. As with the eagle, so with the Lord (Deut 32:11). In Philology, the science of language, the alphabet is indispensable. Our Lord is the Alpha and Omega (Rev 1:8). In Biology, the origin of life is a huge question. Our Lord is the answer to it for He is "The fountain of life".

Get out there today and declare His glory.

M♦A♦Y 16TH

"Declare ... his wonders among all peoples". *1 Chronicles 16:24*

The wonders of nature, even in its most intricate actions are amazing. For example the time of incubation for a canary is fourteen days, for a chicken, twenty-one, and the eagle is, forty-two days. All the gestation periods in bird life are in periods of seven; the kitten is born on the fifty-sixth day, the pup on the sixty-third and right up to the whale on the three hundred and first. All, again, in periods of sevens.

Our Lord Jesus was the one who inaugurated time. And so it was in the exact fullness of time God sent His Son, born of a woman (Gal 4:4). It was "In due time Christ died" (Rom 5:6). As Christ inaugurated time so it will be Christ who will consummate it. And He has your times in His hand. Nothing comes from Him too late or too early. But remember; there is no way on earth to save time, all you can do is spend it.

"Give the Lord the glory due his name". 1 Chronicles 16:29

Recently, I met a Jewish doctor, and, over a cup of tea and some delicious scones we fell to talking about the name of God. I asked her a question I have always wanted to ask a Jew; "What do you call God in general conversation".

The doctor answered, immediately. In prayer she said "I say 'Baruch ata adonai' meaning 'Blessed art Thou O Lord'. When I have to refer to God in general conversation I say 'Baruch ata adoshem', which, roughly translated means 'Blessed art Thou of the name'". She told me that she would not even write the name of God in a letter but would simply put G-d. Such is the sacredness of the name of God with orthodox Jews.

What a name, God's name is! From Genesis 1:1-2:4 he is called "Elohim" thirty-five times. Elohim expresses the idea of greatness and glory and contains the idea of creative and governing powers. He is called "Jehovah", the one who is absolutely self-existent 6,823 times in the Old Testament. Jehovah means the one who always exists, who is eternal, unchangeable, the one who is a God of moral and spiritual attributes.

He is called "El-Shaddai", the one who nourishes, supplies, and satisfies; the all-sufficient one. He is "Jehovah-Jireh"; the God who provides. He is "Jehovah-Rophe"; meaning, Jehovah heals. He is "Jehovah-Nissi"; the Lord is my banner. He is "Jehovah-Mckaddish"; the Lord who sanctifies. He is "Jehovah-Shalom"; the Lord is peace. He is "Jehovah-Tsidkenu"; the Lord our righteousness. He is "Jehovah-Rohi"; the Lord is my shepherd. He is Jehovah-Shammah; the Lord is there. Let's heed David's advice and give to the Lord the glory due his name.

M♦A♦Y 18TH

"For the Lord is great and greatly to be praised. He is also to be feared above all gods". 1 Chronicles 16:25

There is very little of the fear of God around. Swearing is all too common and it is lack of the fear of God that makes it so sadly prevalent in our world. What is the difference between swearing and cursing? Swearing involves the irreverent use of God's name as a witness or party to some statement and cursing implicates God's name with another's damnation. Often, in anger, people swear or curse. It is so pointless because it neither honours God nor brings honour to the person swearing or cursing.

A travelling salesman was once asked "Are you paid anything for swearing?" "No", he replied. "Well", came the answer, "You certainly work cheap. You lay aside your character as a gentleman, inflict pain on your friends, break a commandment, lose your soul and all for nothing!" Let's, then, control our anger and cultivate a sense of reverence. Let us remember how very serious swearing and cursing are. If there were only two sins in the world and those two sins were swearing and cursing Jesus Christ would still have died to pay for them. May the fear of God above all gods rule our tongues.

M✦A✦Y 19TH

"For all gods of the peoples are idols but the Lord made the heavens".
1 Chronicles 16:26

It must have been a great moment when the smitten children of Israel looked to the serpent on the pole and were healed (See Numbers 21). But do you know what happened to that metalic snake? If you don't you are in for a big surprise. In 2 Kings 18:4 we learn that for eight hundred years the children of Israel had kept it. They preserved it, protected it, and polished it and finally made an idol out of it. They called it Nehushtan meaning "A piece of bronze". That's all it was but they worshipped it, none the less. Crazy, isn't it? Yet, sadly true.

Such things happen, even today. Your child, your partner, your business, your house, your education, your holidays, your ambitions can so grip your heart that they can become your Nehushtan. Consumer religion all around us shows that the service of Mammon outstrips the service of the Master. "In ten hours we fly you to where Jesus walked" runs the El Al advertisment over a shot of the Lake of Galilee with the text "Come ye after me and I will make you to become fishers of men". If you take that one seriously you have come a long way but the El Al "Pilgrimage Department" winks all the way to the bank. Is it any wonder that Kierkegaard the atheistic Dane wrote; "In every way it has come to this that what one now calls Christianity is precisely what Christ came to abolish"? Could you blame him? The preacher Jim Jones, who led so many of his congregation to commit suicide, once held up a Bible and said "Too many people are looking at this instead of looking at me!" Nehushtan, indeed.

"Happiness, what is it?", said Greta Garbo. "I have never known it. I have messed up my life and it's too late to change that". She once said to a friend; "Promise me that you'll never let money or glory rule your life". Good advice, for as David tells us "All the gods of the peoples are idols (worthless things) but the Lord made the heavens". Happy is the person who worships Him.

M♦A♦Y 20TH

"Honour and majesty are before Him; strength and gladness are in His place". 1 Chronicles 16:27

God has not got any strong points for the simple reason that He does not have any weak ones. He is, in his character, perfectly balanced. When the Lord Jesus came to earth he was the exact image of his Father's person; all that his Father is, he displayed it.

David pinpoints four attributes of God in today's text. Did the Lord Jesus show these four attributes anywhere in his earthly life? He certainly did? Take the attributes of honour and majesty. Honour means personal integrity, a sense of what is right; majesty, a sense of stateliness and true grandeur. Taken by Satan to a high hill Christ was shown the kingdoms of this world and their glory. Notice Satan didn't say "Sing me a few choruses to my glory". No, he told Christ if he would bow down and worship him he would give him those kingdoms. It was a very subtle temptation but honour was before Christ and true majesty; "Away with you Satan. For it is written, 'You shall worship the Lord your God and him only shall you serve'", said Christ.

David also highlights strength and gladness as two further attributes of God. These lovely attributes are seen perfectly in the way the Lord Jesus dealt with the woman who had been bent over for eighteen years. "Woman", said Christ, "you are loosed from your infirmity". She was made straight immediately. The ruler of the synagogue protested that this was work on the sabbath day but, with strength, Christ said to him "Hypocrite. Does not each of you on the Sabbath loose his ox or his donkey from the stall and lead it away to water it? So ought not this woman being a daughter of Abraham whom Satan has bound - think of it - for eighteen years be loosed on the Sabbath"?

The Sabbath was set up to commemorate freedom from slavery (See Deut 5:14-15 ; Lev 26:13) and the stance of the slave was to be bent over (See Luke 26:13). God had set his people free then and he still sets them free, now. If ever there was a day for setting folk free the Sabbath was that day. The result of Christ's action was sheer gladness on the part of the woman who had been straightened. Honour, majesty, strength and gladness. What a place, to borrow from today's text, is His place!

M✦A✦Y 21ST

"Give to the Lord, O kindreds of the peoples". 1 Chronicles 16:28

David certainly gave to the Lord. He gave Him his time, his energy, his pen, his very heart. Did he lose? He got back everything, one hundredfold.

"I gave God spoonfuls", said John Wesley, "And he gave me back shovelfuls". Are you giving God what is right, or what is left? We certainly make a living by what we get but we make a life by what we give. The best thing, though, which you can give to the Lord is your self. There is only one you. Your face, your features, voice, style, characteristics, abilities, walk, handshake, manner of expression, everything about you is found in only one individual since man first began - you!

Amos, the fig picker from Tekoa was called to bring messages in the king's sanctuary up at the palace. The problem was the image keepers of Israel didn't like his rugged style. That didn't stop him giving himself to the Lord's will for his life. Just because Amos was outnumbered didn't mean he had to change, did it?

"I was neither a prophet nor a prophet's son but I was a shepherd and I also took care of sycamore-fig trees. But the Lord took me from tending the flock and said to me 'Go, prophecy to my people Israel'". Amos gave himself to the Lord in his work no matter what the king's image builders, or spin doctors as they are now called, said or thought. Is it any wonder we are still reading his book, today? In this world it is not what we take up but what we give up that makes us rich. So give.

M✦A✦Y 22ND

"O worship the Lord in beauty of holiness!" 1 Chronicles 16:29

Mark well what David is saying. He is saying that holiness is beautiful. We somehow imagine that holiness is drab, colourless, stern, critical, and cold; we forget that God is holy and being that is in every way, beautiful. Look around the tabernacle from the colourful gate of entry to the curtains of the inner sanctuary, to the gold and silver and the shining candlesticks. Every facet of these things speak of the holiness of God but it is anything but colourless; it is breathtakingly beautiful. Why, even the very top of the pillars that held up the white linen surround of the tabernacle were made of ornamented silver. The white linen certainly spoke of holiness but that which held it up was also beautiful in its intricacy.

Christians are to hold up the white linen of holy living as a testimony to the God they have trusted, but they need ornamentation too; the ornamentation of joy and gladness, of wholesome and happy marriages, and the obvious qualities of integrity, truthfulness and dependability. Their words should be their bond. Such lives attract. If our worship is backed up by holy living its potent force in the world cannot be underestimated.

M✦A✦Y 23RD

" The world is firmly established, it shall not be moved".
1 Chronicles 16:30

Some would find our text a contradiction. They would refer to Peter's affirmation that " The elements will melt with fervent

heat; both the earth and the works that are in it will be burnt up"
(2 Peter 3:10). A little reflection will show that both David and
Peter are right.

Any secondary school child will tell you that if you burn a
table you cannot destroy its atoms. So it is with the earth. In a
coming day it will be burnt up for sure and there will be, the Bible
assures us, a new earth. But there will be something of the old
earth in the new one. You cannot redeem something if there is
not something of the original there. God is not going to say "I
made a terrible mistake in creating the earth, Satan got the better
of me, now away with it all". No, He is going to redeem the earth
just as He is going to redeem our very bodies. That implies that
there will be something of you, the original you, christian, that
will remain when you reach Heaven in a glorified state. It also
implies that we will know one another in Heaven. Quietly study
Romans 8:18-28 and if it doesn't cheer your day, what will?

M♦A♦Y 24TH

"Let them say among the nations, 'The Lord reigns'". 1 Chronicles 16:31

Do you think the nations recognise the truth of our text?
David is urging that they should, but sadly, few do. Recently in
a study of the book of Daniel I was intrigued by the two great
images of the governments of the world that are given there. One
was an image of government as being like a beautiful statue with
a head of gold and the other was the image of nations as being
like animals. This is not a contradiction; government can
sometimes behave like animals and take just what they want
when they are threatened, at other times they can behave well
and do very intelligent and useful things.

The great image of Nebuchadnezzar's dream in Daniel 2
telling of coming world empires had an outstanding feature; it
had feet of clay, it was unstable. This tells us a plain fact about
all nations and all governments; they are basically unstable.
Whether it be democracy, or communism, feudalism or dicta-
torships, all make great promises but cannot entirely deliver.
The book of Daniel tells us that one day the Anti-Christ will rise

and his government would destroy everything, even life itself, if God did not intervene (See Dan 2:34-35 ; Dan 11:36-12:3 ; 2 Thess 2:3-12). So, don't put your trust in princes, or governments, or nations; put your trust in the Lord.

M♦A♦Y 25TH

"Let the sea roar and all its fulness". *1 Chronicles 16:32*

I'm not often in Buckie. The truth is, I am not often in Findochty either - Banffshire on the Moray Firth is a jewel of a place where I came across a rather haunting thing, recently. Church of Scotland minister Bill Ross took me on a tour of the little fishing village of Findochty where the church building, set high on a rock overlooking the cove, is a guiding point for boats coming home, just as they have done for decades.

Bill greeted an old man walking by the sheltered side of the building. "Aye", he said. "Aye", said the other, (Local talk for "Hello"!). "Watch him, Derick", said Bill, "He'll come back". Sure enough, he came back on his tracks. "Now he'll continue the same pattern", said Bill. Sure enough, back and forward, back and forward, he went.

"It has to do with a lifetime at sea", explained Bill. "He is walking the width of his boat". Soon another man joined him, and then a third, all of them looking out every now and again to sea. It was haunting to watch them. I have to confess that I have never understood why Revelation 21:1 says that in the new heaven and earth "there shall be no more sea". The men of Findochty have at last explained it for me. The absence of sea is a God-given symbol telling us that in Heaven there will be no more restlessness. Those old salts of Banffshire cannot rest because they have spent the best part of their lives heaving up and down on the sea. Similarly, millions cannot rest because of the continuing pressure and problems that living in a sinful world brings. In Heaven there will be, perfect rest. Men of Findochty, I thank you.

M♦A♦Y 26TH

"He is coming to judge the earth". 1 Chronicles 16:33

For months an image has been playing over and over again on television, worldwide. It has been a eighty-one second video tape of a blackman called Rodney King writhing on a pavement in Los Angeles being kicked by uniformed policemen, jolted with a stern gun and hit with night sticks fifty-six times. Yet, seeing for the jurors was not believing. A superior court jury in Sinni Valley, north west of Los Angeles had acquitted on all but one count the four white Los Angeles policemen on trial for mistreating black motorist Rodney King. That judgment sparked the worst race riots in the United States this century. More than 3,700 fires were started and fifty people died.

David tells us in this Psalm that when God comes to judge the earth, things will be different. It will be some Judgment Day. No riots will be started, no voice will be raised in protest, no murmur will be heard when the judge of all the earth gives his verdict. No judge on earth ever gave a judgment, yet, that wasn't criticised. When God judges the earth every mouth will be stopped. When that great day comes will you be found in Christ?

"When as a child I laughed and wept,
Time crept,
When as a youth I grew more bold,
Time strolled,
When I became a full grown man,
Time ran,
Soon I shall find as I journey on,
Time gone,
Wilt Thou O Christ have saved me then?
Amen."

M♦A♦Y 27TH

"O give thanks to the Lord for He is good". 2 Chronicles 16:34

When you are disappointed, when circumstances do not work out for you, the Bible reminds you that the Lord still preserves your going out and your coming in. The Lord is not controlled by circumstances but reminds you that circumstances are controlled by Him. When you are worried, He reminds you not to let your heart be troubled, that He will not leave you, comfortless. He is not ignorant of your needs. You are told to cast all your care upon Him for He cares about you. That word means to turn over to somebody else, to take your hand off it and let somebody else bear it for you.

When you doubt, you are reminded of Thomas who at the end of a very long day, doubted. What changed Thomas from being a practising atheist to one who looked into Christ's face and said "My Lord and my God"?; the personal intimate presence of Jesus Christ. You can't keep doubts from coming into your mind but you can bring them into the living presence of Christ and the light of his countenance will cause the darkness of doubt to disappear. When your mind is subjected to the mind of Christ, darkness will be dissipated.

When you are discouraged, when you have lost heart, when you have lost the will to fight, you are asked to look to Jesus, the author and finisher of your faith and He will inspire you to keep going. You are reminded that you are in God's hands, that He will fulfil His purpose and provide, direct, and accomplish His perfect will in and through you.

There is not a circumstance that the Lord will not meet you in and pull you through. David, of all men, proved it. No wonder he calls us to give thanks to the Lord, for He is good.

M◆A◆Y 28TH

"His mercy endures for ever". 1 Chronicles 16:34

Mercy means two things. It first of all means forebearance from inflicting punishment upon an adversary or a lawbreaker and secondly it means compassion to help the weak, the sick or the poor.

Of all the truths in the Bible the one that moves me most is the truth of the self-substitution of God. There is a fundamental difference between penitent substitution in which the substitute offers what we could not offer and penal substitution in which the substitute bears what we could not bear. Let Dr. Packer define the latter from his book "What did the Cross Achieve?"; "That Jesus Christ our Lord, moved by a love that was determined to do everything necessary to save us, endured and exhausted the destructive divine judgment for which we were otherwise in escapably destined and so won us forgiveness, adoption and glory. To affirm penal substitution is to say that believers are in debt to Christ specifically for this and this is the mainspring of all their joy, peace and praise both now and for eternity". What mercy we have been shown and the great thing is, as David reminds us, that mercy endures for ever.

M✦A✦Y 29TH

"Save us, O God of our salvation". 1 Chronicles 16:35

What are the great images of salvation in the Bible? There are four major images. There is "propitiation" which means to appease or pacify someone's anger. The death of the Lord Jesus has averted God's wrath against us, so that as far as the person who has received Christ as Saviour is concerned, God can look upon them without displeasure and they can look on God without fear. There is "redemption" which means that through his death Christ has bought us at a huge price, the price of His blood, and set us free from slavery to sin. We are now the slaves of Christ and find in His service perfect freedom.

There is "justification" whereby the believer is no longer condemned, but now has, given to them, a righteous standing before God. What a relief! But more, there is "reconciliation". It is the most popular of the four great images of salvation in the Bible because it is so personal. An original relationship with God had been broken, alienation and enmity had come, but Christ came, as the agent of reconciliation and brought the two parties together.

Find some quiet spot today, christian, and thank God for His salvation for though in creation God has shown us His hand; in salvation He has shown us His heart.

M♦A♦Y 30TH

"To triumph in your praise'. 1 Chronicles 16:35

There was once a very serious situation facing the people of God. The people of Moab with the people of Ammon came to battle against the children of Israel. The king of Israel, at the time was Jehoshaphat and he "Set himself to seek the Lord". He got an amazing answer; "You will not need to fight in this battle", said the Lord, "Position yourselves, stand still and see the salvation of the Lord, who is with you".

The next day the whole army of Israel moved out to face the enemy but Jehoshaphat did a fascinating thing. We are told that "He appointed those who should sing to the Lord, and who should praise the beauty of holiness as they went out before the army and were saying 'Praise the Lord for his mercy endures forever'". A miracle occurred and as the singer sang Israel's enemies were defeated through the power of praise! (See 2 Chronicles 20:14-25).

There is no calculating what might happen when humbly and joyfully the people of God enter His gates with psalms and hymns and spiritual songs, singing and making melody in their hearts to the Lord. Vance Havner once said that "When God's people repent and give themselves to God they will have a song. It will be spontaneous, for what is down in the well will come up in the bucket". Say, how is it down in your well?

M♦A♦Y 31ST

"Blessed be the Lord God of Israel, from everlasting to everlasting".
2 Chronicles 16:36

In March 1972 the persecuted writer Alexander Solzhenitsyn invited the Moscow correspondents of the New York Times and the Washington Post to interview him. This was a rare occurence, indeed no journalist had observed him closely for five years. He was enduring the full wrath of the Soviet leadership of the time and he talked about the fact that he and his family were "a kind of contaminated zone" in the eyes of that leadership.

It was a most graphic and pained interview but one thing deeply impressed me when I read of it. Asked for his opinion of two young Russian writers who had aroused interest in the late 1950's, Solzhenitsyn pointed out that writers who deal with highly topical questions as opposed to "Themes of eternal significance" naturally fade from the limelight together with the issues they have treated.

I read, the other day, of the Solzhenitsyn's looking for a new home in Moscow. Their long exile from their native land is over and the Soviet Union is no more. Solzhenitsyn's statement in 1972 was true, wasn't it? He dipped his pen in a theme of eternal significance and it outlasted the very regimes that had tried to rub out what he had written.

David, in the beautiful psalm we have studied together this month, would bear out the truth of Solzhenitsyn's statement. He too wrote of themes of eternal significance. In fact he wrote of that which is most eternally significant of all; the God who is from everlasting to everlasting. Worship Him! Give your heart to Him! Be ambitious for His truth! Live for the immediate and soon it will be gone. Serve the everlasting God and the results will be as everlasting as the one you serve. It is the best gilt edged security available.

J U • N • E

J♦U♦N♦E

*D*avid was so sure-footed in his walk with God when first he settled into his reign as King. God gave him rest from all his enemies and his time of recreation became a time of re-creation. He initiates the whole concept of a temple in Jerusalem and at every turn he seeks to glorify God. And then, he shows kindness to Mephibosheth; it proves to be one of the loveliest actions of his life. We'll find our June days with David are amongst his best.

J♦U♦N♦E 1ST

"The king was dwelling in his house, and the Lord had given him rest from all his enemies all around". 2 Samuel 7:1

I notice with young people that the "in" word at the moment is, "Give me some space". Isn't it good, though, at times that God gives His children special "space"? There are few days in a christian's experience when Satan does not stir things up and the battle against him and the flesh gives precious few moments of respite. You no sooner see a victory than Satan's onslaught is pouring in through another hole which he has found in your defences. Yet, there come those delicious moments when the battle eases and the much needed rest is given.

Just today, as I was writing this, I experienced one of those. Last night I flew across the Atlantic on a long and tiring journey to get to this particular city where I am now preaching God's Word and I woke this morning feeling a wonderful sense of having been deeply rested and with a lovely sense of assurance that "If the Lord cares for sparrows he cares for me".

It is not that the birds of the air don't work. They may not "toil" in the fields like men do or "spin" in houses like women do, but they work. They have enemies, they suffer from the cold, wind and rain. They often face starvation. They have accidents. They die. but, they are without anxious care. So it should be with us. The Lord, at times gives us much needed respite from our enemies but He can give us at all times constant freedom from anxious care. Trust Him for it, today.

J◆U◆N◆E 2ND

" The king said to Nathan, the prophet." 2 Samuel 7:2

Nathan was always a good friend to David; in a time of great spiritual crisis that was soon to burst on David's head he was to prove an invaluable friend. Always wise, always out for David's spiritual welfare, he was unselfish and unstinting with his time and energy. He had a gift from God because he was a prophet but he used his gift wisely. Not everyone who is gifted from God is necessarily the best behaved. Samson, for example, was highly gifted but he behaved disgracefully at times.

There can be no doubt that our time of greatest temptation is not when we are busy and occupied; it is when we are at leisure. It was good for David that he had a good companion like Nathan for his leisure time. Be careful who you team up with in your leisure time for if you have only yourself you could have problems;

An enemy I had who is mean,
I slowly strove to know,
For hard he dogged my steps, unseen,
Wherever I might go.

My plans he bulked, my aims he foiled,
He blocked my onward way,
When for some lofty goal I toiled,
He grimly said me nay.

"Come forth!", I cried, "Lay bear thy guise!,
Thy features I would see!"
But always to my straining eyes,
He dwelt in mystery.

One night I seized and held him fast,
The veil from him did draw,
I gazed upon his face at last,
And lo! myself I saw.

(E. L. Sabin)

J♦U♦N♦E 3RD

"See now, I dwell in a house of cedar, but the ark of God dwells inside tent curtains". 2 Samuel 7:2

I have long wrestled, while writing this book, with the sadness of David's behaviour when he stepped out of the will of God for his life. To put it bluntly, when David was bad he was awful. But today's text reveals, for me, the great redeeming feature which had God calling David a man after his own heart.

David now lived in a beautiful cedar palace erected on Mount Zion with the assistance of Hiram, King of Tyre, but in a quiet moment be began to contrast his house with the temporary structure which served as a house for the Ark. David longed that God's Ark should be placed in a splendid temple. Notice how David's time of recreation actually became a time of re-creation. David's desire was as precious as Mary's when she lavished her costly ointment upon the Saviour.

Let the impact of David's desire challenge us. Do we spend more on ourselves than we do on furthering God's Kingdom? Do we put more energy, more planning, more strategy and more time into furthering our own business than into furthering God's work? I cringe when I often see penny-pinching in christian churches while the same penny-pinchers spend a small fortune on holiday! Not so, David.

J♦U♦N♦E 4TH

"Then Nathan said to the king, 'Go do all that is in your heart, for the Lord is with you"'. 2 Samuel 7:3

Nathan often comes in for commentators stick for his reaction to David's desire to re-house the Ark of God. It is said that Nathan "At first approved, apparently because he acted without consulting the Lord". I like what A. W. Pink says; "Nothing is said in the record here that David actually proposed to build

Jerusalem a temple, but only that he was troubled because one was not yet erected. Whatever conclusion Nathan may have drawn therefrom, he was careful to say nothing to modify David's godly concern, but rather sought to encourage his spiritual aspirations".

I heard of a young person who once rose and gave out a hymn in a local church at a time of open worship. He asked for someone to help him find the number. Afterwards an older person approached him and said "If the Holy Spirit gave you a hymn don't you think he could give you the number as well?" That young man never gave out a hymn in public again. Selah.

J•U•N•E 5TH

"But it happened that night that the word of the Lord came to Nathan, saying, 'Go and tell my servant David, thus says the Lord; would you build a house for me to dwell in? ... In all the places where I have walked with all the children of Israel, have I ever spoken a word to anyone from the tribes of Israel, whom I commanded to shepherd my people Israel, saying 'Why have you not built me a house of cedar"'. 2 Samuel 7:5-7

Quietly and gently in the darkness of the night God's word came to Nathan, a word of guidance and instruction for David; at its heart God was saying he had not yet instructed anyone to build him a temple to live in. That time would come and in the meantime "A tent of his own appointing was better than a temple of man's devising". It was not yet time for David's dream, though let it never be forgotten, God said "Whereas it was in your heart to build a house for my name, you did well that it was in your heart". (1 Kings 8:18)

Every dream we have of doing great things for God is not necessarily a dream from God, is it? Have you been given an assignment by God in some obscure situation, though you dream of greater things? Be content. If God wants to open a wider door to you, He will. Meantime, let me repeat, "A tent of his appointing was better than a temple of man's devising". One, with God, is a majority.

J✦U✦N✦E 6TH

*"When you days are fulfilled and you rest with your fathers, I will set up
your seed after you, who will come from your body, and I will establish his
kingdom. He shall build a house for my name, and I will establish the
throne of his kingdom for ever ... and your house and your kingdom shall be
established for ever before you. Your throne shall be established for ever."*
2 Samuel 7:12-16

God said, "No" to David's dream, but notice how balanced
God's answer was. As Nathan broke the news to David the next
day you would be hard pushed to find a direct negative in the
whole message. Certainly it was a message of refusal but it was
wrapped up in so many assurances of blessing, in so much
promise and benediction that the king was hardly sensible of the
disappointment amid the rush of intense and overwhelming
gladness which Nathan's words aroused.

So what if God has said "No" to your dream? If he is to be
glorified by your staying where you are isn't that what really
matters? His promises to you if you are working in Tillycoultry
Post Office are just as powerful as to a chief executive of a multi-
million pound corporation in Toronto, are they not? God's
"No's" are infinitely better than man's "No's" because there is
the safety net of his promises to fall into. David may not have
gotten to build a temple but God built him a sure house, so sure
that even Israeli jets carry his star on their wings to this very day.
Your house will be established for ever, too, for you too, christian,
will dwell in the house of the Lord, for ever. Comforting, isn't it?

J✦U✦N✦E 7TH

*"Then David went in and sat before the Lord; and he said; 'Who am I, O
Lord God? And what is my house, that you have brought me this far? And
yet this was a small thing in your sight, O Lord God; and you have also
spoken of your servants house for a great while to come. Is this the manner
of man, O Lord God? Now what more can David say to you? For you, Lord
God, know your servant. For your Word's sake, and according to your own
heart, you have done all these great things, to make your servant know
them."' 2 Samuel 7:18-21*

David certainly didn't go into a huff with God because God had said "No" to his plan to re-house the Ark, nor did he get carried away with the position of greatness promised to his dynasty. Instead he went in to the humble tent where the Ark was presently housed and sat and adored God.

Stop today and think about David. Here he was, settled, rich, prosperous, possessing the highest position in Israel, but see him quietly sitting before God pouring out his heart in worship and praise and adoration. Instead of choking with disappointment at not being able to build a grand place of worship, he goes and actually worships. What may have been a drab day for someone else, David turns it into a jewel of a day. What God had done for him so far, he reckons to be far out-weighed by what is coming. Are you disappointed? Then meditate on the only verse in the Bible where a believer is said to be seated in prayer. Go and get in the same position and get David's perspective. If that doesn't turn the drab into the jewel, I don't know what will.

J✦U✦N✦E 8TH

"So let your name be magnified for ever". 2 Samuel 7:26

Never ever be ashamed of the name of the Lord. Slip it into your every day conversation with people, naturally, but with purpose. You will be surprised how very seldom most people ever hear the Lord's name spoken of reverently by people who hold it in awe. David was a king but he had a higher king in mind whose name he wanted to magnify. What kind of a king is the Lord?

He is the King of Israel (John 1:49). He is the King of the Saints (Rev 15:3). He is the King of the Ages (1 Tim 1:17). He is the King of Righteousness (Heb 7:1-3). He is the King of Heaven (Dan 4:37). He is the King of Glory (Psalm 24:7). He is the King of Kings (Rev 19:12). As C. R. Rolls has said; "We cannot enrich him, for in him are hid all the treasures of wisdom and knowledge. We cannot engrace him, for he is full of grace and truth. We cannot instruct him, for he is omniscient, we cannot improve him, for he is perfect in kingliness and kindliness, in greatness and goodness, in holiness and helpfulness. We cannot enlighten him, for he is true light. We cannot confine him, for the Heaven of heavens cannot contain him". So, why be ashamed of his name?

e, let it please you to bless the house of your servant, that it
for ever before you; for you, O Lord God, have spoken it, and
r blessing let the house of your servant be blessed for ever".
2 Samuel 7:29

you wish in the world to advance,
Your merits you're bound to enhance,
You must stir it and stump it,
And blow your own trumpet,
Or, trust me, you haven't a chance."

So wrote W. S. Gilbert, satirically. The Bible is dead set against such procedure. It was David himself who wrote "Humble yourselves before the Lord and He will lift you up". In today's text David was not blowing his own trumpet but he is applying the principle old Matthew Henry described perfectly when he said "It is by turning God's promises into petitions that they are turned into performances". God promised David that he would establish his house and David turned God's promise to a petition and God certainly performed it. We are to read the promises of God in Scripture and then we may lift up our souls, our heads, our eyes, our heart, our hands, our voices to God; but the one thing we must not do is to lift up ourselves. On the contrary, we are to lower ourselves and lift up the Lord Jesus. Go then and turn a promise of God into a petition and watch him perform it. If you doubt the relevance of such a procedure, remember David.

J◆U◆N◆E 10TH

"After this it came to pass that David attacked the Philistines and subdued them". 2 Samuel 8:1.

It is always important to remember that the Gates of Hell are defensive weapons, not offensive. We are inclined to think that Satan must, always necessarily, overwhelm us from time to time. This is not so. We can, by Christ's power, drive back the

Gates of Hell in our town, or district, or city, or village. Greater is he that is in us than he that is in the world. We do not need to always be in a defensive position but we can surge out on the offensive for the Lord.

Take David at this period in his life. Today's text tells us that David went on the offensive for the Lord against the Philistines. Up until this time they had been the aggressors, searching for David to kill him, hassling the Israelites and thwarting their progress. Now David takes the offensive and subdues them. The lesson for us, spiritually, is that this offensive of David's comes directly after a time of prayer and meditation on God's promises. Be strengthened in your inner self by the power of prayer and Scripture, today, and then go on the offensive. "Seize the day", taught Lord Byron. Only problem was he seized it without God and as he put it later, "The worm, the canker and the grief are mine alone". David's activity at this time was borne out of communion with God. Is yours? Is mine?

J◆U◆N◆E 11TH

"And David took Metheg Ammah from the hand of the Philistines".
2 Samuel 8:1

Methog Ammah means "The bridle of the mother city". For many a long day Metheg Ammah had curbed Israel in her progress, held her back from possessing her possessions. David as a strategist knew if he would subdue the Philistines he must first take this fortified city on a high hill.

Is there something in your life holding you back from progress in christian things? You must deal with it if you are to possess your possessions. (See Obadiah 17). The Lord Jesus put it this way, "Therefore if you have not been faithful in the righteous mammon, who will commit to your trust the true riches? And if you have not been faithful in what is another mans, who will give you what is your own?" (Luke 16: 11-12). All who repent and trust the Saviour will enter Heaven, that is abundantly clear, but all will not possess the same positions of responsibility and reward. All christians are heirs of a great inheritance but there is a world of difference between being born heirs to an estate and actually possessing the estate. So it is with God's inheritance.

You must possess that which is your own. So, storm, by God's grace, the citadel that is holding up your progress and you will break through to new days. David certainly did.

J◆U◆N◆E 12TH

"Then he defeated Moab". 2 Samuel 8:2

Moab was the incestuous son of Lot and the Moabites had long been a thorn in the side of God's people. There can be no doubt that Scripture represents Moab as the epitomy of the flesh. In the book of Judges their leader Eglon was, we are told, in detail, "A very fat man". That was Moab; self indulgent to the last and, in fact, particularly in the area of immorality. Moab hired Balaam to curse Israel and even the daughters of Moab snared Israel's sons (See Numbers 25:1).

As Ehud, the left handed judge, just as well as David, knew, Moab was not to be parleyed with. She must be defeated. And so must the flesh. You must not say "Now flesh, I am sorry this is going to hurt", you must crucify it or it will have you. But how? The best advice I ever came across in this connection was from Jim Elliot, missionary to the Auca's. He wrote that when he was overwhelmed by the sinful thoughts of immorality, particularly when travelling by train across the United States, he used to think about Calvary. He found the two lines of thought couldn't live together. Try it and you will be amazed at the power of Calvary thoughts over Moabitish thoughts.

J◆U◆N◆E 13TH

"And the Lord preserved David wherever he went". 2 Samuel 8:6

Twice in 2 Samuel 8 we read the words of our text. It is as though God would emphasise to us once more that without his preserving care we can do nothing. All the great heroes of Scripture knew this and were not afraid to say so. When Joseph stood before Pharaoh he was greeted with outstanding praise; "I have heard it said of you that you can understand a dream, to interpret it". So Joseph answered Pharaoh; "It is not in me, God will give Pharaoh an answer". So it was when Daniel stood before Nebuchadnezzar. "There is a God", he declared fearlessly, "who can reveal secrets ... but as for me, this secret has not been revealed to me because I have more wisdom than anyone living".

"Not in me to lift the weary spirit,
Not in me to save a precious soul,
Not in me to make a day seem brighter,
Not in me to set a nation's goal.

Not in me to move a congregation,
Not in me to heal a broken land,
Not in me to tell secrets of the future,
Not in me to turn the tide upon life's sand.

Not in me to bring about repentance,
Not in me to put life into bones,
Not in me to bring about revival,
Not in me to calm ten thousand moans.

Not in me to be a new trail blazer,
Not in me to write the inspiring song,
Not in me to stop the gossips story,
Not in me to halt the critic's tongue.

But Christ in me, the power to change a nation,
Christ in me to break the Satanic sword,
Christ in me for love and life and future,
Jesus Christ, my Master, King and Lord."
                                                    (D.B.)

J•U•N•E 14TH

"King David dedicated these to the Lord, along with the silver and gold that he had dedicated from all the nations which he had subdued".
2 Samuel 8:11

The Lord Jesus once told a parable about a strong man who held all his treasures under tight security. One day a stronger man came and overpowered him and took all his possessions and distributed them to others. David was such a man and it is to his eternal credit that his spoils of war were given to the service of the Lord.

The Lord Jesus, of course, did the very same thing. At the cross he overcame Satan and "led captivity captive" and gave gifts to men. He is still doing this wonderful work. All over the world people who are in the grip of Satan are being freed by Christ and the gifts they once used in Satan's service they are now using in God's service. Don't think that gifts you had before your conversion are useless, they can now become very useful in your new Master's hand. When God wants a worker he calls a worker. Selah.

J◆U◆N◆E 15TH

"And David said, 'Is there still anyone who is left of the house of Saul, that I may show him kindness for Jonathans sake?'" 2 Samuel 9:1

Grace. What is it? Donald Barnhouse caught it perfectly when he said "Love that goes upward is worship; love that goes outward is affection; love that stoops is grace". In Eastern dynasties when a new king took over it was common for him to kill every member of his predecessor's family. But David had a covenant with Jonathan that he would spare Jonathan's descendants. He now stoops to show grace.

Notice that little word "anyone" in our text. Not "Is there a rich, or clever, or gifted, or scholarly" member of Saul's family left to show kindness to, but, "Is there anyone?". Grace is to extend favour or kindness to one who doesn't deserve it and can never earn it. David's grace, as is God's, was unconditional and free.

Just last evening one sat before me who was being tortured in mind and heart because of past sins. I listened to the story and then asked the person if they were apologising for actually breathing! The person had been forgiven and cleansed in Christ but was far from living in the enjoyment of God's grace. There are millions, like that person. God's grace turns lions into lambs, wolves into sheep, monsters into men, weakness into strength and wants into abundance. God is for you, that is the essence of grace. Is that not enough?

J✦U✦N✦E 16TH

*"And there was a servant of the house of Saul whose name was Ziba. So
when they had called him to David the king said to him, 'Are you Ziba?'
and he said, 'At your service!' Then the king said, 'Is there not still
someone of the house of Saul, to whom I may show the kindness of God?'
And Jiba said to the king, 'There is still a son of Jonathan who is lame in
his feet"'. 2 Samuel 9:2-3*

Reading between the lines it seems pretty obvious that
David was finding it hard to find anyone who could answer his
question. There were few in his household who knew, or even
cared, whether any of Saul's family still existed.

All around you are people who are in need. They lurk in
corners of all kinds, broken, hurt, frightened. Like Jonathan's
son, many are even unable to walk to you for help. If you don't
care for them, few others will. Even Paul was to later write to
Timothy and say "All seek their own".

We must go and find those who need help, and, believe me,
they are there. And grace isn't picky. Even if Jonathan's de-
scendant was badly handicapped it made no difference to
David; the kindness of God must be shown and David was
determined to find his man and show it to him. Just think;
somewhere today you will come across someone and you will be
able to show the kindness of God to them. Is there any greater
privilege? When the opportunity comes, don't miss it, for it may
not come again.

J✦U✦N✦E 17TH

*"So the king said to him, 'Where is he?' and Ziba said to the king, 'Indeed
he is in the house of Machir the son of Ammiel, in Lo Debar'".
2 Samuel 9:4*

An acquaintance of mine once went to an Open Air Service
in the Scottish town of Kilburnie. The preacher was waxing
eloquent on the condition of the people of the town. "See you
people in Kilburnie!", he asked rhetorically, "You are all doon
in Lo Debar!".

My friend told me he didn't know whether to laugh or cry, as he was sure the people didn't have a clue as to what the preacher was on about. He reckoned they must have been puzzled as to the fact that the preacher had them in two places at the one time! The preacher, of course, meant that folks even in Kilburnie could be in a place like Lo Debar, spiritually. Lo Debar means "The place of no pasture". Jonathan's son lived in the barren fields of Israel where he was hiding from the king's sword. Raised on the false premise that if David ever got near him he would kill him, Jonathan's son, Mephibosheth had a totally discoloured picture of what David was really like.

So it is with many people. They think God hates them when, in fact, he loves them. They think if they got near him he would spoil everything in their lives whereas, in fact, he would do the very opposite. It's like all those irreligious swindlers and sinners who crowded around Christ at mealtimes. They couldn't believe God was so available, so loving and so amazingly full of grace and truth. If you have a false view of God may your eyes be opened, today. (And if you live in Kilburnie, you need never be in Lo Debar at the same time!)

J•U•N•E 18TH

"Then David sent and brought him out of the house of Machir the son of Ammiel, from Lo Debar". 2 Samuel 9:5

The invitation to the king's palace was gladly accepted by Mephibosheth. I can think of another king's invitation to visit his palace for a banquet which was mentioned by our Lord. There were many excuses given regarding the invitation. One fellow had land he had bought, a second had oxen he had to test and a third had a wife, so he said he couldn't possibly come. Notice how God dealt with them. He sent his servant, the Holy Spirit, to invite blind folk who had never seen land, lame folk who could never walk behind oxen to test them and others whom no girl would ever marry. The banquet was filled with the most unexpected people. So it will be at the marriage supper of the Lamb.

As David brought Mephibosheth to his palace, so the Holy Spirit draws you after Christ. Have you responded or are you still filled with excuses? There is not a better evangelist in all the world than the Holy Spirit. Listen to him.

J♦U♦N♦E 19TH

"Now when Mephibosheth the son of Jonathan, the son of Saul, had come to David, he fell on his face and prostrated himself". *2 Samuel 9:6*

Who took the initiative to bring Mephibosheth to David's palace? David. Who took the initiative, christian, to bring you into all the riches you have in Christ? Christ. Before you ever thought of reaching up to the Lord, he was already reaching down to you. Long before the stars of the sky, the mighty oceans of the world and the great ranges of mountains were formed, God thought of you. David himself knew it well for he wrote "My frame was not hidden from you, when I was made in secret and skilfully wrought in the lowest parts of the earth. Your eyes saw my substance, being yet unformed, and in your book they all were written when as yet there were none of them. How precious also are your thoughts to me, O God! How great is the sum of them! If I should count them they would be more in number than the sand!"

Walk today, christian, in the conscious knowledge that you are beloved of the Lord. As Mephibosheth fell before David's incredible kindness, may we too bow down and worship in the face of his love that first loved us, long before we ever loved him.

J♦U♦N♦E 20TH

"Then David said, 'Mephibosheth!' and he answered 'Here is your servant!'" *2 Samuel 9:6*

There were no long speeches. No past sins of Mephibosheth or his family were dragged up to condemn him. No details of "Did you know your grandfather tried to pin me to the wall with his javelin, once?", were heard. Not a word of condemnation fell from David's lips. Mephibosheth was Jonathan's son and that was enough for David. "Mephibosheth", he said. That was all. One word. What emotion was packed into it! What pathos!

So it will be, christian, on that great day when you enter glory. It will not be that God has forgotten your sins. He will not be saying, "I see those nail prints in Christ's hands and I cannot for the life of me remember how they came to be there". He will remember very well. But there will be no remembrancer as in the court of King Ahasuerus, in Esther's day. The remembrancer would call up wrongdoings to the king about those in his kingdom. There will be no remembrancer of sins to be brought up to condemn you to penal judgment. That is the meaning and background to the words of Scripture which say "Your sins and your iniquities I will remember no more". You will then learn as never before that " There is therefore now no condemnation to those who are in Christ Jesus". As Mephibosheth was accepted by David because of the beloved Jonathan, so you will be accepted because of the beloved Christ. Your name will be called out in glory without rancour or condemnation. What a moment!

J◆U◆N◆E 21ST

" Then he bowed himself, and said, 'What is your servant, that you should look upon such a dead dog as I?"' 2 Samuel 9:8

Mephibosheth well knew his position. The long history of his grandfather's hounding of David was no secret in Israel or to him. To be treated with such kindness, such grace, such magnanimity, certainly did not give Mephibosheth any sense of personal pride or inflate him with self importance. He was just filled with amazement that David should ever consider him at all.

Does the kindness of God in saving us, inflate us? Does it give us a sense of spiritual one-upmanship on others? If it does there is something seriously wrong. Have we forgotten our Hell deserving position and our wretched sins that bar us from fellowship with God? Have we forgotten that what we are getting is in no way what we deserve? Have we forgotten the frightful cost of our redemption in the death of our Lord and Saviour Jesus Christ? Even at its highest point christian joy is always tinged with sorrow. Sorrow at the fact that our sins put those nailprints in those precious hands and feet. Let's never forget it. That is why we are commanded in Scripture to remember our Lord's death; sitting at the Lord's Table is good for our pride. If, like Mephibosheth, we learn humility it might spare us humiliation.

J✦U✦N✦E 22ND

"And the king called to Ziba, Saul's servant, and said to him, 'I have given to your master's son all that belonged to Saul and to all his house'". 2 Samuel 9:9

There are, obviously, a multitude of lessons which we can learn from David's relationship with Mephibosheth which are applicable to our christian position. The question of Mephibosheth's inheritance is one of them. All that Saul had lost through sin, Mephibosheth gained through his connection with Jonathan. Wasn't it a wise decision that Jonathan made those long years back when he took the insignia of his office and laid them at David's feet? Jonathan read very clearly that David was Israel's Saviour. Poor Jonathan was despised for his decision at the time, mocked, even. Yet, the day came when all that was lost was restored. His son regained "All that belonged to Saul and to all in his house".

Think of what we had lost because of Satan and sin; our relationship with God, our innocence, our spiritual blessings and inheritance. There was a time when sin even shocked people. Indeed people used to blush when they were ashamed. Now they are ashamed if they blush. It takes a lot to shock people, these days. We have only to look around us in the areas of abortion, homosexuality, integrity and authority to see what this generation has lost because of sin. Yet, despite the devastation, when the Lord Jesus comes into a person's life he can restore the years that the locusts have eaten. We can regain through Him the inheritance that we lost through Adam. Even the earth we stand on, marked now by the fall, will one day be redeemed because of Christ. Of all the themes in the Bible one of the most exciting and most contemporary is the theme of God's restoration programme through Christ. Are you part of it?

"'As for Mephibosheth', said the King, 'He shall eat at my table like one of the king's sons'". 2 Samuel 9:11

No courtier barred Mephibosheth's passage to the king's table. No special ticket gained him entrance to the cedar palace at Jerusalem. No protocol had him sit below the king's son. No special occasion, or special guest ousted his privileges. The king said, "He shall eat at my table like one of the king's sons", and the king's word was final.

Let this beautiful action of David's remind you, christian, of where the Lord has placed you. Don't let anyone rob you of the joy of your privileges as one of God's children. Believe me there are plenty of apparently clean-living, nice-looking, Bible-carrying people who would kill your freedom, spontaneity and creativity in Christ by their words and their looks. Don't let their bullying tactics continue unchecked. Mephibosheth no longer lived in shame, fear and intimidation. The king had set him free and he never forgot it. I see and counsel too many christians burdened down with yokes other christians put on them. Christ said, "My yoke is easy and my burden is light". If that is so, prove it.

J◆U◆N◆E 24TH

"And it happened after this that the king of the people of Ammon died and Hanun his son reigned in his place. Then David said 'I will show kindness to Hanun the son of Nahash, as his father showed kindness to me'. So David sent by the hand of his servants to comfort him concerning his father. And David's servants came into the land of the people of Ammon".
2 Samuel 10:1-2

David might show kindness to a Hebrew like Mephibosheth, but the same David was not beyond showing kindness to those outside his own people. The king of the Ammonites died and he had shown in the past a kindness to David and David did not forget a kindness, easily.

Do you? It's easy to forget those who have shown us kindness in the past. Even children sometimes thoughtlessly forget the very parents who raised them. Perhaps you have recently forgotten that spiritual leader who once helped you or a friend who stood by you. Did not the butler forget Joseph? Are we not told constantly in Scripture that Israel even forgot the God who saved her from slavery? Why, they were only a few days out of Egypt when they forgot where they were going and who was leading them and worshipped the golden calf. People have such short memories. There are even some christians who set out for Heaven and they no sooner start out than they have forgotten their destiny and settle in heart and spirit in a place where the Bible says we have "no continuing city".

Let's be like David at this stage in his life, let's keep long memories of whose we are and whom we serve and of those who have shown us kindness along the way. Let us particularly never treat God like some people treat the doctor. When they need the doctor he has their full attention and affection but when they are well they would hardly take time to greet him on the street.

J◆U◆N◆E 25TH

"Then the princes of the people of Ammon said to Hanun their lord, 'Do you think that David really honours your father because he has sent comforters to you? Has David not rather sent his servants to you to search the city, to spy it out, and to overthrow it?' Therefore Hanun took David's servants, shaved off half of their beards, cut off their garments in the middle, at their buttocks, and sent them away". 2 Samuel 10:3-4

Not everyone will understand your motivation in life. The Ammonites certainly didn't understand David's. His single-hearted purpose of sending his men to sympathise was interpreted as a spying mission. His men were taken and humiliated.

People can be desperately wrong in their appraisal of motivation and situations. There was once a man who was travelling in his carriage with his children. His children were restless and crying. "Parents these days", said a lady at the other end of the carriage to her friend, "They can't control their children". "The mother is probably divorced from her husband, I should imagine", grumbled the other. They twittered on and on until the father, overhearing, interrupted. "Actually", he said, "their mother's body is in a coffin in the guard's van and we are going home to bury her". There was an immediate silence from the two know-alls up the carriage. Selah

J♦U♦N♦E 26TH

"When they told David, he sent to meet them, because the men were greatly ashamed. And the king said, 'Wait at Jericho until your beards have grown, and then return"'. 2 Samuel 10:5

This verse was mightily used by God in the life of one of my greatest heroes. He was nineteen at the time and was asked to give an address at the annual meeting of the Cambridge Sunday School Union. He spoke first and was followed by two other older ministers. One of them savagely insulted him saying it was a pity that boys did not adopt the Scriptural practise of tarrying at Jericho till their beards were grown before they had tried to instruct their seniors.

He was given the right of reply and reminded the audience that those who were bidden to tarry at Jericho were not boys, but full-grown men, whose beards had been shaved off by their enemies at the greatest indignity they could be made to suffer and who were ashamed to return home until their beards had grown again. He added that the true parallel to their case could be found in a minister who, though falling into open sin had disgraced his sacred calling and so needed to go into seclusion until his character had been to some extent restored. Unknowingly he had given the exact description of the man who had attacked him! A gentleman present felt sorry for the young fellow and recommended him as a supply for a vacant pulpit in London. He filled it as no other. His name? Charles Haddon Spurgeon.

J♦U♦N♦E 27TH

"When Joab saw that the battle line was against him before and behind, he chose some of the choice men of Israel and put them in battle array against the Syrians". 2 Samuel 10:9

I once read a translation of one of Christ's statements which read "Many are called but few are choice". When Joab, king David's commander in chief saw the tens of thousands of men arrayed in battle against him it was time to call in "The choice men of Israel". Do choice people come up overnight? No. I think home is where life makes up its mind. Show me choice people and I'll show you, more times than not, a choice home background. Take me back to a person's roots. You may think it a long way from Joab's choice men to the Cosby Show, but let me show you the connection.

I am a Bill Cosby fan. He is apart from anything else, spontaneously funny. He once described fatherhood as "Pretending that the present you love most is soap-on-a-rope or thinking that the height of fashion is matching socks!" He also said that it doesn't make any difference how much money a father earns, his name is always Dad-Can-I? Voices keep saying "Dad can I get? ..., Dad can I go? ..., Dad can I buy?"

It must be a remarkable feat in the area of race relations when millions watch the Cosby Show and find it transcending colour and representing a role model for how families should behave, no matter what their colour, class or creed. It was a seering irony that the final episode of the Cosby Show went out on American television on the second night of the recent Los Angeles riots. At the end of the last episode Bill Cosby and Phylicia Rashad walked off the stage set and out into reality; the reality where blacks make demons of whites and whites make demons of blacks. We are going to miss Dr. Huxtable. Bill Cosby once said something we should all listen to. He said that if a father ever gets to saying to his wife "Get these kids out of here; I'm trying to watch T.V." he is liable to end up watching one of those kids on the 6 o'clock news. I have a feeling that we, never to speak of the citizens of Los Angeles, are seeing precious little else on the 6 o'clock news.

The message is clear; we need to build loving, God fearing families. God put families together before he put churches together. The longer I live the more I am convinced that choice people come from choice homes. If you didn't come from one, don't panic. God can still use you and make you a choice person. You then, in turn, can set up a choice home.

J♦U♦N♦E 28TH

"Then he said, 'If the Syrians are too strong for me, then you shall help me. But if the people of Ammon are too strong for you, then I will come and help you '". 2 Samuel 10:11

Strategy. Joab was a strategist. It is the way to win wars and it is the way to win in christian warfare, too. How many christian churches do you know who rush to help another when things are under pressure? I fly to many a corner of earth visiting christian churches and I am appalled at how most want to see their own local fellowship filled with people but have precious little interest in seeing the one down the road in the same state.

It doesn't only apply to churches, it applies to hospitals, schools, communities, government departments, businesses. Would the world fall apart if we came to each others aid? Would our communities be harmed if the one-upmanship of one hospital over another, one university or school over another were to be toned down for each praising the qualities of the other? Joab's "If I need help, you come to me, and, if you need help I'll come to you", is a very healthy attitude for life's battles, never to speak of Israel's. No wonder the Syrians fled. "Share one anothers burdens", says the Scripture, "And so fulfil the law of Christ". If we did so our world would be a better place. Get out there and share someone's burden, today. You might find that they will share your burden, tomorrow.

J♦U♦N♦E 29TH

"Be of good courage, and let us be strong for our people and for the cities of our God". 2 Samuel 10:12

Joab urged his army to be strong, not just for themselves but for others. There are times when we need to be strong for others. We often forget that the decisions we make in the privacy of our own hearts have huge repercussions for others.

I remember, one day, a christian asking me if he thought he should smoke cigarettes. He happened to have a family who were deeply involved in christian work and I simply said that I thought his smoking would embarrass them. I can see him looking at me, yet. Much later he told me that if I had scolded him, that afternoon, he would have reacted negatively but when I mentioned his influence on his family, it really made him think. Smoking never kept anyone out of Heaven, any more than overeating, but we have got to remember that what we do, even in our habits, influences others.

Suzanna Wesley had 19 children and used to throw her apron over her head when praying; it was the only way to get a place to pray. Her children knew not to approach her when her apron was over her head! I often reflect on what came out, in terms of influence, from behind that apron. The great hymns of her son Charles Wesley are hymns that millions of christians love today and the gospel that her son John Wesley preached, saved, apart from other things, England from the French Revolution.

John Stackhouse once wrote, "Renewal movements wax and wane, denominations come and go, and institutions of all sorts will not outlast the earth itself, but we will - we, and all of those whom we influence every day, right around us. The importance of our daily faithfulness within our families, with our friends, and in our occupations, cannot be measured by human reckoning. But one thing seems sure; it is not little."

J✦U✦N✦E 30TH

"And may the Lord do what seems good to him". 2 Samuel 10:12

There are three wills of God. There is God's sovereign will. This is God's overall purpose throughout eternity whereby he determines all that should take place. As Ephesians 1:11 puts it "Who works all things according to the counsel of his will". History is God's story and he writes the storylines. Much of God's sovereign will is hidden from us, shrouded in mystery and majesty. Then there is God's moral will. The Scripture tells us what God wants us to believe and how God wants us to behave. The moral will of God is very clear.

Then there is God's individual will. You need not know all of God's will for your life in order to make choices in your life. In fact, we are called upon to make individual choices based upon God's revealed moral will. If we were never allowed to decide anything but were always controlled by constant interventions of direct guidance, we would remain moral and mental infants all our days. God can, at times, intervene in our lives with special direct guidance, but that never bypasses or supresses our personal judgments.

The greatest guiding line to follow when faced with a decision as a christian, I have found, is to shut your door. Get the influences of life out of the way and explain everything in secret to your heavenly Father. Acknowledge him. Then go and act in a commonsense manner according to your abilities and limitations. When you acknowledge him he then directs your paths. Ask two simple questions, "Is it right?", and, "Is it necessary?" If there is no cloud between you and your Lord, go ahead, and as Joab puts it in today's text, "May the Lord do what seems good to him".

J U·L·Y

J♦U♦L♦Y

*T*he greater a man, the greater his fall. We must now face the reality of the sin of David's life. Many people think that the Bible is an escape from reality whereas the plain fact is that it represents ultimate reality, itself. David certainly lost a lot of credit through his sin but the way the Holy Spirit has insured that his sin and repentance has been recorded for us far outweighs, for all penitents, the loss. David's moral collapse is sad but searching reading. For summer days it is also a warning.

J♦U♦L♦Y 1ST

"Now it came to pass in the spring of the year, at the time when kings go out to battle, that David sent Joab and his servants with him, and all Israel; and they destroyed the people of Ammon and besieged Rabbah. But David remained at Jerusalem". 2 Samuel 11:1

Who of us doesn't need rest, from time to time? A lot of life suffers from overloading. We all know our capacity, and, suddenly, we find load and capacity are clashing. We need a safety valve and certainly rest was designed to be our safety valve.

So, after leading many exhausting military campaigns, David remains in Jerusalem. For seventeen years he had enjoyed an unbroken spell of prosperity; he had been successful in every war. But is there not a warning in our text? While his famous army was out facing the enemy, David was cushioned by royal comforts. Little did he know that in the warm springtime evening there lurked an arrow that would pierce his life and character far more furiously than any arrow in the walls of Rabbah which his army was now besieging. It was to plunge David's life into adultery, murder, civil war and heartache that was to burden him to his dying day.

Leisure time is a million times more fraught with danger than those times when the mind and imagination are concentrated on work. Watch your leisure time. Watch those times when you are

138

yawning and stretching with boredom. The Holy Spirit has placed on record this account of David's fearful fall because if He hadn't, no human compiler would have included it on the pages of the Bible. The details are put there to warn us and the first warning is "Watch your leisure time". Heed it.

J♦U♦L♦Y 2ND

"Then it happened ..." 1 Samuel 11:2

It happened. Many would have said it couldn't have happened. The shepherd boy who defeated Goliath, the psalmist who wrote the psalms enjoyed by millions, the man who longed for God's glory more than anything else, the trusting fugitive from Saul's court who refused to harm a hair of the head of King Saul who had so often tried to kill him; such a man, surely, would never steal another man's wife and arrange his murder. "Then it happened ..."; David fell, morally, and committed the sin of his life.

I remember so well preaching one evening with Dr. Alan Redpath in Co. Wicklow in Ireland. The aged servant of God was nearing the end of his long and tremendously successful ministry for the Lord. Lifting his head he looked at that audience and said something I have never forgotten. "There is", said the great Bible teacher of long experience, "No sin that I'm not capable of committing, five minutes after this service is over"'. We must remember that the awful conduct of David shows clearly that it is not only the unbeliever than can sin but the believer is also fully capable of sinning grievously if his eye is taken off his Lord. Let these words burn into your mind and heart today ... "Then, it happened". Only by God's grace and a humble walk with God will you avoid such things happening to you.

J♦U♦L♦Y 3RD

" Then it happened one evening that David arose from his bed and walked on the roof of the king's house. And from the roof he saw a woman bathing, and the woman was very beautiful to behold" . 2 Samuel 11:2

Should Bathsheba have pulled the curtain a little closer? If she had would things have been very different? I don't know, except that the Scripture lays the burden of David's sin on David alone. Nowhere is Bathsheba blamed for what happened.

Sadly, too sadly, many christian men in our generation are falling, morally, and the Bible does not in any way excuse them. David obviously forgot the faithful Abigail who had long cared for him and loved him when he was an outcast from the establishment. He forgot the lovely lady who had not only fed his stomach when he was very hungry but who had fed his mind and conscience with the promises of God and who had single heartedly turned him away from what would have been a major disaster in his life.

Why do men forget, so quickly, the woman who has stood by them so long? "It's wrong", wrote Florence Littauer, "For a man to reject a wife who has struggled through poor times and put up with the quirks of his mother just as he makes it to the top and can travel to Tahiti". Indeed, or just as he makes it to be king of all the land with time, at last, on his hands. A night with his wife Abigail would have served David ten million times better. So, tempted husband, go home early, tonight, to the wife of your youth.

J♦U♦L♦Y 4TH

"So David sent and enquired about the woman". 2 Samuel 11:2

Why didn't he turn away? Because he saw a beautiful woman was no sin but it was opening the door to disaster when he sent and enquired about her. He had adultery on his mind. He knew the clear teaching of the Word, "You shall not commit adultery", but he ignored the warning.

Let everyone of us carefully note the warning, when tempted. As James Olthius in his book "I pledge you my troth" has said, "The Scriptures warn man against adultery because it breaks troth (pledged word; fidelity), destroys mutual freedom and makes people unhappy. The Word is a cryptic warning protecting marriage. Since marriage does not break as fast as a crystal glass people flirt with the idea that fidelity is not really affected by an indiscretion here and there. However the Word reminds us to take care. The commandment is much like the 'No swimming' sign planted in front of a dangerous pond. The signs go up because someone cares enough about life to try to prevent drowning. So it is with the seventh commandment. When God forbids adultery He calls man to more than physical fidelity. Marriage is a total troth communication, which can be broken by any kind of infidelity, not just physical, as we have traditionally too often assumed".

Mr. Olthius is right. We are all prone to temptation. In fact, it would be safe to say that most men and women are guilty of mental adultery at one time or another. And this is where so many affairs begin - in our minds. Our thought life, our imagination is the spawning ground for our sinful actions. We must commit not just our behaviour to God but all our thoughts and feelings. Would that David had done just that on the night he first saw Bathsheba.

J•U•L•Y 5TH

"So David sent and enquired about the woman. And someone said 'Is this not Bathsheba, the daughter of Eliam, the wife of Uriah the Hittite?' Then David sent messengers, and took her; and she came to him ... and she returned to her house". 2 Samuel 11:3-4

Note clearly that God put an obstacle across David's path. An un-named person told him that Bathsheba was the wife of Uriah the Hittite. David was planning something evil but the Lord was gracious to him in trying to block his path. One of David's servants dared to remind his royal master that Bathsheba belonged to somebody else.

One of the great marks of those who love the Lord should be selflessness. To steal another person's money or possessions is bad enough but to steal his wife is the pits of selfishness. Most marriages fall apart because of selfishness on the part of one or both partners. Attraction became captivity for David. Despite God's shot across his bows he allowed himself to be captured. He should have heeded the teaching of Scripture, accepted his sexuality but removed himself from a romantic setting with Bathsheba. He should have continually fed, nurtured and maintained a need-fulfilling marriage, but he selfishly chose to ruin another.

The Bible teaches us in times of temptation to flee; we are to "Flee fornication" (1 Cor 6:18), to "Flee from idolatry" (1 Cor 10:14), to "Flee youthful lusts" (2 Tim 2:22) and to "Flee the lust of the world" (2 Tim 1:14). Flight may be the best answer to the problems you will face today. Remember; not all flight is cowardice, is it? If you doubt me, ask Joseph.

J◆U◆L◆Y 6TH

"Then David sent to Joab, saying, 'Send me Uriah the Hittite'. And Joab sent Uriah to David ... and David said to Uriah, 'Go down to your house and wash your feet'. So Uriah departed from the king's house, and a gift of food from the king followed him. But Uriah slept at the door of the king's house with all the servants of his lord, and did not go down to his house". 2 Samuel 11:6-9

David was put into his position as king by the Lord. All those put under his authority were there in a relationship of a sacred trust. Can you imagine how Bathsheba's husband felt when the great king of Israel called him back from the siege of Rabbah? He considered it a great honour to be re-called. Here he sat answering questions about how the war prospered, as to how David's commander in chief Joab was, as to how the people were doing. It was equivalent to a place at a cabinet meeting at Downing Street, to a de-briefing at the White House, to a morning at the Elysee Palace. It was heady stuff.

But behind it all lay a despicable motive. David was trying to induce Uriah to go home for the night to his wife so that his own sin could be covered. It is a few thousand years now since David held his meeting with Uriah, sugar-coated with his hypocritical concern and endowed with a fruit basket. Did he never stop to think that the Lord was watching his every move? Did it not even cross his mind that what you sow, you reap?

If something is given to you as a sacred trust and you betray it the consequences will be devastating. You will answer for it. Whether it be to parent little children in your home, to lead in your local church, to head up a business, to represent a people; these things are given to us in trust. To manipulate them for sinful and selfish ends is to soil the trust given to us. May our prayer be as we go about our work today; "Lord, help me to be sincere. Help me to be trustworthy, at all times. May I never use others to cover my wrongdoing".

J♦U♦L♦Y 7TH

"But Uriah slept at the door of the king's house ... and Uriah said to David, 'The ark and Israel and Judah are dwelling in tents, and my lord Joab and the servants of my lord are encamped in the open fields. Shall I then go to my house to eat and drink, and to lie with my wife? As you live, and as your soul lives, I will not do this thing"'. 2 Samuel 11:9-11

Here was a foot-soldier who never had or never would have David's literary or leadership gift, but who was, by far, the better behaved. Don't think that just because a person is gifted by God that they will necessarily use those gifts in a spiritual manner. Some of the least gifted of God's people are the best behaved.

Don't you find Uriah's reference to the ark in our text, haunting? What must David have felt when he heard Uriah plead that if even the ark was in a tent while the army of Israel were in the open fields, why should he go home to the comforts of his own bed? David had but recently pleaded with God to allow him to re-house the ark. God had refused his request because David was "A man of war". God was, in great kindness, using Uriah to remind him of his priorities and how he was now plunging into sin after sin because he had woefully neglected his priorities.

Is it not very moving to notice how that all through this disastrous episode of David's life that God kept graciously sending him warnings that he was out of line, all the time seeking to graciously draw him back into His will. If a godly christian stands in your way trying to warn you about wrong-doing in your life don't manipulate to remove him. Heed his warning and repent. The fact remains that even if you have sinned, the best kind of repentance is to do so no more.

The David who had danced with joy at the bringing of the ark to Jerusalem now hardens his heart at the very reference to the ark by Uriah the Hittite. After such fickleness, nothing should shock you. Turn your eyes today to your Lord; He is the same yesterday, today, and forever. What a relief!

" Then David said to Uriah, 'Wait here today also, and tomorrow I will let you depart'. So Uriah remained in Jerusalem that day and the next. Now when David called him, he ate and drank before him; and he made him drunk. And at evening he went out to lie on his bed with the servants of his lord, but he did not go down to his house". 2 Samuel 11:12-13

The pit into which David descends gets darker and darker. We feel almost like screaming at him his very own words at the death of Abner; "Should Abner die as a fool dies? Your hands were not bound nor your feet put into fetters; as a man falls before wicked men so you fell". Were David's own hands tied the night he walked on the roof in Jerusalem? Were his feet in the stocks? He was a free man. Now he gets himself run through with many sorrows that would burden him to the end of his life.

First he committed adultery, then he deceived Uriah and now he makes him drunk, hoping he would make him stumble home to his own bed, to be with his wife and thus to cover David's sin. The Scriptures have a very severe warning against anyone who makes a person drunk. "Woe to him", warns the prophet Habakkuk (2:15), "Who gives drink to his neighbour, pressing him to your bottle, even to make him drunk ... the cup of the Lord's right hand will be turned against you, and utter shame will be on your glory".

Did David have glory? Few lives have known as much. Did shame come on his glory? A storm of shame was to fall on his glory that was to make his name a target for the arrows of sarcasm. I was teaching a class of boys in a college once and began to teach them about David. Up went a lad's hand at the back of the class before I could even begin, and the lad threw David's behaviour up to me, immediately. Shame fell on David's glory, to this very day.

We comfort our hearts with the fact that no shame ever fell on the glory of our Lord Jesus Christ and never will. The Scriptures urge us to "Be strong in the Lord - be empowered through your union with him; draw your strength from him - that strength which his boundless might provides" (Eph 6:10 AMP). "But thanks be to God, who gives us the victory - making us conquerors through our Lord Jesus Christ" (1 Cor 15:57). It was the stumbling Peter who wrote "If you do these things you will never stumble; so an entrance will be supplied to you abundantly into the everlasting kingdom of our Lord and Saviour Jesus Christ". Let no shame fall on your glory today.

J♦U♦L♦Y 9TH

"Then in the morning it was so that David wrote a letter to Joab and sent it by the hand of Uriah. And he wrote in the letter, saying, 'Set Uriah in the forefront of the hottest battle, and retreat from him, that he may be struck down and die'". 2 Samuel 11:14-15

Playing with sin is playing with fire. If you don't drown the Hell spark of temptation it will become a fire that can quickly burn out of control. Faster than a man can run, what started as a lustful thought culminated in murder. Unwittingly Uriah carried his own death warrant in the form of David's letter to Joab. The letter outlined the message to put Uriah on the front battle lines and to abandon him there.

What was the motivation behind such heinous behaviour? Sheer pride; pride of reputation. People will resort to unbelievable ends in order to preserve their reputation. We have a saying in my part of the world which says "Get a reputation for rising early and you can lie in your bed until lunchtime". That's the way people are; they are often fooled by reputation. David couldn't bear to face the truth about himself and confess his sin so he cunningly tried to cover his sin by arranging Uriah's death. It was a dirty, miserable, conscienceless act done by a man who had forgotten his God and the moral obligations of one who had for so long served him well. Be careful of the cunning giant of reputation, he is much more cruel than any Goliath you will meet in life.

J♦U♦L♦Y 10TH

"So it happened, while Joab besieged the city, that he assigned Uriah to a place where he knew there were valiant men. Then the men of the city came out and fought with Joab. And some of the people of the servants of David fell; and Uriah the Hittite died also". 2 Samuel 11:16-17

David's plan worked and Uriah the Hittite died, but notice how the Scripture shows us the detail that Uriah was not the only one who died in David's devious plan. Joab had sent Uriah close to the wall of Rabbah with some of his bravest men, and, soon some of them too, lay dead.

Cause and effect is one of life's clearest principles. Be careful of your actions for they have repercussions away beyond your understanding. Sin has a way of blinding us to the result of our actions. "Let the Devil take tomorrow for tonight I need a friend", sang Kris Kristoffeson. Sadly, it became the psalmist David's song in reality and he took Bathsheba for a night and the Devil took his tomorrow for sure. In his devious plans to cover his sin some of his best men were killed. The pleasures of sin are only for a season and there were few as brief as David's. What a price he paid! The sad thing is the innocent had to suffer along the way.

Are you tempted to do wrong? Sit down for a few minutes and consider the long-term effect your action is going to have, not only on you but on others. There is no such a person as a person without influence. And, of course, if you are planning to do a good thing just remember that the smallest action for good can travel with blessings every bit as fast as an action for evil. Choose the good thing.

J◆U◆L◆Y 11TH

" Then Joab sent and told David all the things concerning the war, and charged the messenger saying, 'When you have finished telling the matters of the war to the king, if it happens that the kings wrath rises, and he says to you; 'Why did you approach so near to the city when you fought? Did you not know that they would shoot from the wall?' ... Then you shall say 'Your servant Uriah the Hittite is dead also'". 2 Samuel 11:18-21

David didn't like poor strategy, his chief of staff knew that only too well. An overall view of things, a tactical approach was always David's battle plan. A good strategist, a good tactician would never have exposed his best men to needless danger and Joab was now trying to break the news to David that some of his best men had been needlessly lost in battle. Notice how he did it. He did it by basically saying "If the king gets angry and asks why his best men were exposed so close to the wall tell him Uriah the Hittite is dead also".

Is it not amazing the things people will condemn in others and happily do themselves, if it suits them? As far as David was concerned, bad strategy was good strategy if it covered his sin. How wrong he was! His honour was besmirched that dastardly day, for as long as this world lasts. Despite David's sin there is such a thing as absolute values in this world; they do not change whether you live in the Seychelles or Saintfield. God's absolute values are not negotiable, even if you are David himself. Adultery is adultery, and murder is murder. No wonder the Soviet Academy of Science has recently had a special study of the effects of the ten commandments. Whether it be Marx, Angles, Lenin or David flouting them, the results will be the same.

J◆U◆L◆Y 12TH

" Then David said to the messenger, 'Thus you shall say to Joab; 'Do not let this thing displease you, for the sword devours one as well as another. Strengthen your attack against the city, and overthrow it'. So encourage him". 2 Samuel 12:25

Encourage him, indeed! Lying hypocrite! Smooth talking chancer! I would guess that few messengers in the history of the world would have been as surprised as Joab at the cool, calm and collected way in which king David took the terrible news of the deaths at the walls of Rabbah. Human beings can contrive the most cunning of phrases to cover what is really going on in their hearts. "Ah well", says David, "The sword devours one as well as another". Quite a few brave and great men, as well as Uriah the Hittite lay dead because of his secret, selfish connivance and he says what is tantamount to "All is fair in love and war!".

David, David, how could you forget the day your long lost friend Jonathan came down to the woods to encourage you, to strengthen your hand in God? How could you forget the God who strengthened you to kill a lion and a bear and who later drew you out of the burning remains of Zicklag to set you on the throne of Israel? What are you doing slaying the innocent and saying that it is really only chance that dictates things in the end?

What is the lesson out of all this sinning of David's? The lesson is that the flesh in the believer is no different from the flesh in the unbeliever. If the believer sows to the flesh that believer will reap the flesh just as surely as the unbeliever will. It goes against the flesh to truly serve God. There are paradoxes in it. In God's Kingdom if you want to be a great leader you must demonstrate true servanthood. If you want to be given broad responsibilities you must initially prove yourself faithful in little things. You will find that the most effective form of retaliation in the Kingdom of God is the absence of retaliation. The way to show yourself wise is not so much by speech but by silence. The way to stop a loud argument is by a soft spoken word. Those who give generously have much more than those who hoard. David had all of these qualities when he sowed to the Spirit. He had the opposite when he sowed to the flesh. So will we.

J♦U♦L♦Y 13TH

"When the wife of Uriah heard that Uriah her husband was dead, she mourned for her husband. And when her mourning was over David sent and brought her to his house, and she became his wife and bore him a son. But the thing that David had done displeased the Lord". 2 Samuel 11:26-27

David had pleased himself, that is for sure. He had completely deceived the nation , he had maintained his integrity in the eyes of the people and he was now sure he would enjoy Bathsheba as his wife. The burial of Uriah was past, the mourning seemed deeply sincere, no doubt the religious songs at the graveside were orthodox. After the official mourning was over, a decent, if short wait, and Bathsheba became David's wife. He was king. She was queen. After all, nobody apart from Joab knew a thing. That is, nobody except God.

"Do not let this thing displease you", David had said to Joab. There was no sign of any anxiety that the thing that he had done displeased the Lord. Ultimately, what does it matter who has been pleased or displeased on earth, if we haven't pleased the Lord we are wide off the mark? Everthing seemed outwardly fine in David's life but "The thing he had done had displeased the Lord". "David did what was right in the eyes of the Lord", says 1 Kings 15:5, "And have not turned aside from anything that he had commanded him all the days of his life, except in the matter of Uriah the Hittite". Now, the thing that David thought his people would never know about, the whole world knows about.

Just as it is possible to displease God, we must counterbalance this fact with the realisation that it is also possible to please him. Again and again Scripture highlights the things that bring God delight. Let me list a few. Obedience (1 Samuel 15:22). A just weight (Proverbs 11:1). The exaltation of Christ (Matthew 17:5). Our prayers (Proverbs 15:8). Giving the Kingdom to His people (Luke 12:32). Since we will judge angels (1 Corinthians 6:2-3) and reign on earth with Christ (2 Timothy 2:12 ; Revelation 2:26-28), let's do those things that please Him. There is a river of God's delight (Psalm 36:8). Let's plunge in!

J♦U♦L♦Y 14TH

" Then the Lord sent Nathan to David". 2 Samuel 12:1

At least a year had passed. The impact of David's sin on his relationship with God was devastating. David was to write about it, later, in Psalm 32 and describes how his very vitality was turned into the drought of summer. History teaches that nothing gained by sin is worth its price. "Can a man walk on hot coals and his feet not be scorched?

One day, whilst statesmen and soldiers were crowding the outer court of David's palace, a prophet, by right of old acquaintance made his way through them all and asked for a private audience with David. He was called Nathan and he was marked by a very powerful principle in his life; he cared enough to confront. David's long march back to repentance, forgiveness and restoration was to begin with this wonderful man.

Notice, though, the balance in Nathan's life. Though he cared enough to confront, he had previously been an encourager (See 2 Samuel 7:13). There are some people who seem to delight in pointing out the sins of others. They ooze with condemnation. A confronter who has not first been an encourager is ineffective. Encouragement is a normal christian activity; confrontation is exceptional. If you don't have the balance you will destroy people, not restore them.

Notice the timing. It was at least a year from the act of sin before the Lord sent Nathan to David. It wasn't cowardice on Nathan's part but the recognition that we need to be dependent on the Lord's guidance both as to whether or when we should

149

confront someone with their wrong doing. Follow these guidelines and you will bring about great blessing in broken lives.

J◆U◆L◆Y 15TH

"Then the Lord sent Nathan to David. And he came to him, and said to him;
'There were two men in one city, one rich and the other poor. The rich man
had exceedingly many flocks and herds. But the poor man had nothing,
except one little ewe lamb which he had bought and nourished; and it grew
up together with him and his children. It ate of his own food and drank from
his own cup and lay in his bosom; and it was like a daughter to him. Then a
traveller came to the rich man, who refused to take from his own flock and
from his own herd to prepare one for the wayfaring man who had come to
him; but he took the poor man's lamb and prepared it for the man who had
come to him". 2 Samuel 12:1-4

The tongue will sing babies to sleep all over the world tonight. It will communicate a nation's request through an ambassador. With words millions of pounds worth of money will move on the stock exchange today; words will express love and devotion, fear and anger, encouragement and hatred in college and palace, penthouse and hovel. If we had any idea of their power we would choose them more carefully.

Like Nathan. Notice Nathan's careful wording. He didn't rush in and blurt out condemnation. He didn't approach David in a way that would humiliate him before others. Nathan thought carefully about what he would say and how he would say it. David was a shepherd and taking his images from the world of shepherding he got passed all the labyrinths of David's cover-up, cleverness, connivances, and trappings of power and got to his heart.

Let all who communicate God's truth take a cue from Nathan's approach. Paul did. "To the Jew, I became as a Jew, to the Greek a Greek, that I might win some", he said. To the shepherd, Nathan became as a shepherd and even a royal palace environment couldn't prevent the truth of God which he was communicating finding its mark. Follow Nathan's approach, even when you communicate the Gospel and you will be amazed at the results.

"Then David's anger was greatly aroused against the man, and he said to Nathan, 'As the Lord lives, the man who has done this shall surely die! And he shall restore fourfold for the lamb, because he did this thing, and because he had no pity'". 2 Samuel 12:5-6

Nathan did not go on hearsay or second-hand information. He knew previously what had happened and he was able to deal with David on the basis of undeniable facts. He loved David enough to get the facts right and the facts were packed into the parable of the lamb he had just told David. Notice how Nathan's method presented the facts of the case before David without stirring up his opposition of self-love or resentment at being directly rebuked. David's sullen, uneasy conscience flamed out in his sentence on the rich man who had taken the poor man's lamb literally causing David to pass sentence against himself without being aware of it!

Levitical law only asked for a fourfold restoration in such a case (See Ex 22:1) but David pronounced the sentence of death on the man. There is no better illustration in the Bible of our Lord's story of a man struggling with the delicate operation of removing a speck of dirt from someone's eye while a plank in his own eye obscures his vision. We have a fatal tendency to exaggerate the faults of others while we minimise the seriousness of our own. David, though he was not aware of it, was experiencing the pleasure of self righteousness without the pain of penitence. Here is a particularly nasty form of hypocrisy. The man who takes a man's wife and murders her husband condemns a man who takes someone's lamb and passes a judgment of execution on him. If only David had enacted Christ's golden rule that we should act towards others as we would like them to act towards us. That is the answer to all hypocrisy.

Then Nathan said to David, 'You are the man!'". 2 Samuel 12:7

Nathan will go down in history as the perfect example of a man who graciously but firmly dealt with error and sin in another man's life. He did not take a cheap shot at David in public. He did not start a campaign of gossip behind the king's back. He had the integrity and godly courage to stand eye-to-eye before the king and spell out the truth. He challenged him with the absolute standards of Scripture. It was some moment when Nathan moved from storytelling to interpretation. Nathan revealed David to himself in the mirror of his own judgment and brought him to his knees.

"If your brother sins," said Christ, "Go and reprove him in private". Is there someone out there to whom the Lord wants you to be a Nathan? It will hurt to help and confront but think of the blessings of such a ministry. Millions of people in history have turned to the psalm's of David when they have fallen into sin and failure. Why? Because they identify particularly with the heartbreaking, confessional material in them. How did that come about? Through Nathan. What if Nathan hadn't bothered and simply said "See-if-I-care?" Let me illustrate what might have happened by a story.

The story concerns a case that came before the courts in the state of Massachusetts in 1928. A man had tripped over a rope and fallen into the water at a quayside. Near at hand a young man sat in a deckchair. "Help, I can't swim", shouted the man in the water. His friends who had been walking with him at a distance rushed to the quayside. But it was too late. The young man in the deckchair only turned his head to watch. The friends of the drowned man were so incensed at the callous indifference of the sunbather that they sued him in court. They lost the case. The court reluctantly ruled that the man in the deckchair had no legal responsibility whatsoever to try and save the other man's life. Thank God Nathan was not acting according to earthly rules, alone. Are you?

J◆U◆L◆Y 18TH

"Then Nathan said to David, 'You are the man! Thus says the Lord God of Israel; 'I anointed you king over Israel, and I delivered you from the hand of Saul. I gave you your master's house and your master's wives into your keeping, and gave you the house of Israel and Judah. And if that had been too little, I would also have given you much more!'" 2 Samuel 12:7-8

It is always a healthy spiritual experience to be reminded of the unstinting goodness of God. It must have been a haunting experience, though, for David on this occasion. As Nathan reminded David of all the way God had led him his heart must have sunk lower. He had forgotten the goodness of God and had coveted that which God had banned. Little did he think that God had more good in store for him than he could have ever gained by human devising.

Human covetousness is very blind to the goodness of God. Covetousness is a miserable beggar for it draws away from the God who satisfies, to false gods who pollute the fountainhead of blessing. Coveting a Babylonish garment led Achan to become a thief. Coveting money led Judas to treason. Coveting a piece of ground, a vineyard, led King Ahab to murder. Coveting the world rather than the service of Christ led Paul's friend Demas to spiritual disaster.

For all your life, and for the sake of your soul, be content with such things as you have. If that is too little, God, who knows what you need best, will give you more.

J◆U◆L◆Y 19TH

"Why have you despised the commandment of the Lord, to do evil in his sight? You have killed Uriah the Hittite with the sword; you have taken his wife to be your wife, and have killed him with the sword of the people of Ammon. Now therefore, the sword shall never depart from your house, because you have despised Me, and have taken the wife of Uriah the Hittite to be your wife". 2 Samuel 12:9-10

Sin affects the heart of God. David had despised not only God's word but God Himself. God will not allow us to continue to ignore Him if we are His children. He will bring us to confession and repentance. He will give us a horror of sin, like Chrysotom. Chrysotom?

The Emperor Arcadius and his wife had a very bitter feeling towards Chrysotom, Bishop of Constantinople. One day, in a fit of anger, the Emperor said to one of his courtiers, "I would I were avenged of this Bishop!" Several then proposed how this should be done. "Banish him and exile him to the desert", said one, "Put him in prison", said another. "Confiscate his property", said a third. "Let him die", said a fourth. Another courtier, whose vices Chrysotom had reproved, said maliciously, "You all make a great mistake. You will never punish him by such proposals. If banished from the kingdom, he will feel God as near to him in the desert as here. If you put him in prison and load him with chains, he will still pray for the poor and praise God in the prison. If you confiscate his property, you merely take away his goods from the poor, not from him. If you condemn him to death, you open Heaven to him. Prince, do you wish to be revenged on him? Force him to commit sin. I know him; this man fears nothing in the world but sin". Selah

J◆U◆L◆Y 20TH

"For you did it secretly but I will do this thing before all Israel, before the sun". 2 Samuel 12:12

The hand of God's judgement was going to fall on David in a very public way. God promised that as David had violated the sacredness of marriage in secretly stealing another man's wife, his own wives would be taken publicly by his adversary. That which was done in secret would, in effect, be shouted from the roof tops.

I know of a local church in the United Kingdom where the elders were having an out and out argument at a church leadership meeting. Accusations were being hurled at one another and the blood pressure of the church leaders was rising. Suddenly, one of the elders said, quietly, "Just a minute everyone; if a member of the public was standing outside this door tonight what on earth would he think of us all?" The men suddenly fell silent and godly order was restored. David never thought his secret sin would bring such public repercussions. "If you have to chasten me, Lord, please don't let it be before the people", prayed C. H. Spurgeon. There is no guarantee He won't. Let it be a deterrent to us all.

J◆U◆L◆Y 21ST

" Then David said to Nathan, 'I have sinned against the Lord'. And Nathan said to David, ' The Lord also has put away your sin; you shall not die. However, because by this deed you have given great occasion to the enemies of the Lord to blaspheme, the child also who is born to you shall surely die."' 2 Samuel 12:13-14

Confession and forgiveness go together. David at last recognised that what he had done was against the authority and glory of the Lord, apart from all the other repercussions to individuals down the line. It was the first step towards his restoration. No sooner were the words of repentance on his lips than they were met by a love which hates sin but loves the sinner. "The Lord", said Nathan, "Also has put away your sin; you shall not die". It is the story of the Bible. It is the very heart of God.

There are four kinds of love. There is affection. You can have affection for a favourite old coat or a childhood teddy bear. Affection is a form of love. There is friendship, where two people look out in life in the same direction, and who have the same tastes and interests. Friendship is also a form of love. There is, of course, Eros, which is infatuation and we see that all over the world. It is a form of love which makes the world go round. But then there is agape, which is God's love. It loves the unlovable. It stoops down to us before we ever think of reaching up to it. When David confessed his sin, God's love enveloped him faster than he could ever have imagined. God spared his life.

Don't you think we ought to praise God for what he has not done as well as for what he has done? The Lord has not dealt with us after our sins nor rewarded us according to our iniquities. If we confess our sins he is faithful and just to forgive us our sins and to cleanse us from all unrighteousness. But remember, God's love is not lazy good nature as a lot of people think it is and so despise it. It is rigidly righteous, and so Christ died. Love indeed.

J◆U◆L◆Y 22ND

"Then his servants said to him, 'What is this that you have done? You fasted and wept for the child while he was alive, but when the child died, you arose and ate food."' 2 Samuel 12:21

For seven days Bathsheba and David's baby lay on the edge of death. David's behaviour in those seven days showed very clearly how utterly repentant he was. He lay on the ground, beside himself with grief. He wouldn't eat, he pleaded with God for the child's life but it was not to be. I have been there myself with our firstborn lying sick and near to death and the grief is too deep for words. For us the answer was "Yes", for David, the answer was "No". After seven days the baby died. David accepted that answer and in acceptance lies peace. He got up, washed, changed and went to the temple and worshipped.

The people around David, though, couldn't understand his behaviour. Why would he now eat when the child was dead and he wouldn't eat while it was alive? But then there are few in the world who understand the motivation of a believer. David had hoped by fasting and praying that the little one would live but now God had said "No" he refused to blame God or become bitter. David picked up the pieces of his life and moved on. God had forgiven him and chastened him, now he accepted God's grace and got on with living. God was not through with blessing David any more than He is through with blessing you.

J♦U♦L♦Y 23RD

"But now he is dead; why should I fast? Can I bring him back again? I shall go to him, but he shall not return to me." 2 Samuel 12:23

Millions upon millions of bereaved parents have drawn immeasurable comfort from these deeply moving words of David. What do they teach us? They teach us that those that are dead are out of the reach of prayer. They teach us that grief and tears do not profit the dead. They teach us that babies who die go to be with the Lord. They teach us that the children we lose, though their loss break our hearts, they are better off with the Lord than they could ever be with us.

David's words also show, in my opinion, that we shall know one another in Heaven. He knew he would be going to Heaven not as an undefinable spirit but to an identifiable individual. "I" shall go to "Him" says David. He fully expected to be able to identify his child. There is immortality in a sentence. "He shall not return to me" shows that seances and mediums were taboo and ultimately dangerous. There the Spirit of God lets the matter rest and so must we.

J♦U♦L♦Y 24TH

"Then David comforted Bathsheba his wife ... so she bore a son, and he called his name Solomon. And the Lord loved him" . 2 Samuel 12:24

The chastisement of the Lord does not last forever. Soon after David's loss, David holds a new baby son in his arms. Born to be the wisest man who ever lived, he was called "Jedidiah" meaning "Beloved of the Lord". The balance of this amazing story is hope for us all. If you have known the chastening of the Lord in your life, if you have had to face the ugly reality of the wickedness of your own heart, of the repercussions of your own wrong actions, remember that the dark days you are now living through, will pass. Those who repent of wrongdoing will know the blessing of God again. They are not relegated to the scrapheap and accounted useless for the rest of their days.

With baby Solomon at home, David now sets out to do what he should have done in the first place; to take the city of Rabbah. He leads his army into battle and is successful. His thoughts as he draws near the walls of Rabbah must have been of Uriah the Hittite, the man he had sent to his death but recently. If only David had done his duty in the first place, Uriah would never have died. "If only" is the story of most of our lives but there is no need for us to sit down in the corner and quit because of it. There are new battles to be fought, new victories to be gained. Today is a fresh day. You must not spend the rest of your life worrying about the things you can now do nothing about; concentrate on the things you can do something about and get on with it.

J♦U♦L♦Y 25TH

"But when King David heard of all these things, he was very angry."
2 Samuel 13:21

David deeply loved his children. Time and again in his life the deep feelings he had for them surfaced. He knew, as every parent knows, that our children are the most valuable things we have. Yet, the surest way to make it hard for your children is to make it soft for them. When David's son Ammon sinned, David though very angry, did nothing. It was Eli's massive fault all over again for his sons "Made themselves vile and he restrained them not". To refuse to discipline your children is to refuse a clear command of God because a child who doesn't learn to obey his parents will find it much harder to learn to obey God.

Obedience to God leads to knowledge (1 John 2:3), to completeness (1 John 2:5), to character development (1 John 3:7), to discernment (1 John 3:10) and to victory (1 John 5:4-5). David lacked the application of discipline to his children's lives probably because he had despised the commandment of the Lord himself. He carried no moral weight with his children for the rules he fain would have applied to them, he had severely broken himself. The warning is clear. As the man said "If you want your boy to follow in your footsteps you've probably forgotten a few you took". Let's be careful that we keep the rules that we would have others keep.

J◆U◆L◆Y 26TH

"So Absalom fled and went to Geshur, and was there three years."
2 Samuel 13:38

Absalom would never have killed his brother Ammon if David had taken immediate action against Ammon in the first place. He was to reap a devastating harvest of sorrow for his indulgence of his son. Recently I read the story of a christian teacher who caught a thirteen year old boy reading a pornographic magazine in his class. The teacher immediately confiscated the magazine and since the class knew what was happening, he used the opportunity to talk about the dangers of such warped and dehumanising material. The teacher didn't let the matter end there. He wrote a letter to the parents, enclosing the magazine. He pointed out that he could control only what his pupils read in class and that he would continue to do so. He pointed out that it was the parent's job to oversee what the children read elsewhere.

A shepherd needs to protect his sheep from the wolves. The great David who had protected a number of sheep from those who would have wiped them out, declined to deal with the wolf at his own front door. Selah.

J♦U♦L♦Y 27TH

"So Joab the son of Zeruiah perceived that the king's heart was concerned about Absalom. And Joab sent to Tekoa and brought from there a wise woman, and said to her, 'Please pretend to be a mourner, and put on mourning apparel; do not anoint yourself with oil, but act like a woman who has been mourning a long time for the dead. Go to the king and speak to him in this manner.' So Joab put the words in her mouth".
2 Samuel 14:1-3

The woman from Tekoa was as wise as a serpent but she was not as harmless as a dove. She was set up by the Devil through the clever Joab to trick David into indulging his murderous son by allowing him back into court circles. She was told to pretend to be a woman in mourning and to put on mourning clothes. A subtle story was put into her mouth by Joab which would play on David's susceptible emotions. David fell right into her trap. He who had subtly played on Uriah's faithfulness for his own ends now found himself the victim of one who played on his parental emotions for the subtle ends of an astute Joab, backed by Satan.

If there is one lesson I have learned in life it is that things are never as they seem. The Devil has no difficulty in making sin look innocent. As William Gurnall said "No player has so many dresses to come in upon the stage with as the Devil has forms of temptation"! The Devil covers his tracks so carefully you would never dream of charging him with the sudden trouble that has emerged. Did David imagine for one moment that the mourning woman who fell on her face before him telling him a heartbreaking story was actually the Devil drawing him to draw Absalom into a place of favour from which he would almost take David's very throne? Just as God used Nathan's parable to be a blessing to David, Satan also used a parable to unseat David. Counterfeit is Satan's most natural method of resisting God's purposes. Be on your guard, today.

"So the King said, 'Whoever says anything to you, bring him to me, and he shall not touch you anymore.' Then he said, 'Please let the king remember the Lord your God, do not permit the avenger of blood to destroy anymore, lest they destroy my son.' And he said, 'As the Lord lives, not one hair of your son shall fall to the ground.'" 2 Samuel 14:10-11

The woman of Tekoa spun David a story and he believed it. David promised too rashly to protect her and far too rashly confirmed the same by an oath. Sentiment is a dangerous rationale. Pity can be dangerous. David rushed in too fast, he let a sweet-talking woman of Tekoa talk him out of his better judgment.

Are you ready to rush into supporting something today, throwing discipline aside for the sake of old times, or peace, or fear of what some might think? Are you ready to let your better judgments be clouded? You have not thought through the consequences and this can have serious repercussions.

I always remember what Neihmoller wrote of Germany during the Second World War. "In Germany they came first for the Communists and I didn't speak up because I wasn't a Communist. They came for the Jews and I didn't speak up because I wasn't a Jew. They came for the Trade Unions and I didn't speak up because I wasn't a Trade Unionist. Then they came for the Catholics and I didn't speak up because I was a Protestant. Then they came for me and by that time no one was left to speak up". There is a time to speak and a time to refrain from speaking. David didn't speak up and discipline his children and he didn't speak up and tell the woman of Tekoa that he had better check out her story before putting himself under oath to her. May God give us grace today whether to embrace a cause or to shun it.

"Your maidservant said, ' The word of my lord the king will now be comforting; for as the angel of God, so is my lord the king in discerning good and evil. And may the Lord your God be with you'". 2 Samuel 14:17

Will flattery really get you nowhere? One thing is certain; if you listen to flattery and believe it, it will get you into trouble. Gossip is what folks say behind your back that they would never say to your face and flattery is what they say to your face but they will never say behind your back.

The woman of Tekoa called David an angel of God but then she was set up to do it, wasn't she? The law condemned Absalom to death but David set it aside, through the persuasion of the woman of Tekoa who piled on the flattery to soften him up. It was sweet-talking Eve who pushed Adam into sin and it was the persuasive Sarah who pushed Abraham into believing in surrogate motherhood. It was sweet-talking Deliah who ditched Samson from her lap into the lap of the Philistines. It would not be very long until Israel was to be plagued with the problem of the wisest man in all the earth being flattered by heathen women into becoming an effeminate fool. Solomon is a colossal example of how easy it is to let flattery erode the things that matter until your life and witness is destroyed. Should a mourning, face-on-the-floor, pleading Tekoan woman herself tell you that you are an angel, don't let her flattery fool you.

J◆U◆L◆Y 30TH

"And when he cut the hair of his head - at the end of every year he cut it because it was heavy on him - when he cut it, he weighed the hair of his head at two hundred shekels according to the king's standard".
2 Samuel 14:26

Good looks. Few unattractive faces ever make the front cover of Vogue. When last did you see a disfigured body advertise a High Street shirt?

I looked at a magazine today and read an advertisement for a skin moisturiser. The message was clear; if any woman used it they would have, it said, "Fewer, less noticeable facial lines" and a "Renewed radiance and youthful glow". Lines and old age were obviously an enemy!

"In all Israel", says our text, "there was none to be so much praised as Absalom for his beauty; from the sole of his foot to the crown of his head there was no blemish in him". There are a lot of people who would give anything to be like him; everybody in Israel loved his good looks, and in our day the situation still applies. Good looks open doors, turn heads, influence people. But do you not think it speaks of a malaise in a nation if good looks are lauded above other more important things? Absalom was not valued for moral worth because he was a murderer, a schemer and totally lacking in justice and wisdom. The Bible teaches a good name is rather to be chosen than great riches and loving favour than silver or gold. What a woman is within is far more important than what she is without. What a man is in character is by far more meaningful than how he looks, as Israel was very soon to discover to their cost.

J◆U◆L◆Y 31ST

" Then the king kissed Absalom ... and so it was whenever anyone came near him to bow down to him that he would put out his hand and take him and kiss him" . 2 Samuel 14:33 ; 15:5

What's in a kiss? Love, affection and tenderness; but not always, is it? Judas kissed Christ to betray him in the garden of Gethsemane in order that he might get some money. What for? To buy some land for himself. There is nothing wrong with buying land as long as you recognise that you are not the ultimate owner. You will remember that God let out land to Israel but they wanted it without owning allegiance to him as the ultimate owner. They stoned his prophets and when He sent His Son they crucified Him and the man who betrayed His Son bought land for himself. Is it any wonder that Judas's field became a cemetery? All grabbing of things for myself, all ignoring of the ultimate owner will end in death. Nothing productive will come from it.

David kissed Absalom with a kiss of compromise and Absalom's kisses at the entrance to his father's palace had rebellion in their motivation. He wanted the land and the throne for himself and death on all his plans and ambitions soon swept over him. It is worth asking the question, once more; "Who owns me?" Recognise the ultimate owner in your life in all that you do and ultimate happiness is guaranteed.

A·U·G·U·S·T

A♦U♦G♦U♦S♦T

*M*illions of people have been touched by David's psalms but none more so than by his psalms of repentance. If ever anybody was sorry for his sins that person was David. The horror of what he had done almost overwhelmed his very sanity. But there is forgiveness with God and mercy. During August we shall look at some of David's confessional writings which have had such influence across history. They are truly restorative material.

A♦U♦G♦U♦S♦T 1st

"Have mercy upon me, O God, according to the multitude of your tender mercies. Blot out my transgressions". Psalm 51:1

What a change from the cynical tactician we have been studying, recently! Between that kind of David and the David of today's text stands Nathan the prophet. He brought God's word to David and that brought a transformation in David's attitude. God's word, of course, is powerful to the bringing down of the hearts most resilient strongholds. People you would never imagine could be touched by it, can be.

David knows very well that he, of himself, has no claim to the mercy for which he begs. Neither have we, for that matter, but it is a comfort to millions of us as David appeals to an attribute of God which we too can know. It is called God's loving-kindness. It is God's tender warmth. It is the kind experienced by Bartimaeus, despised, pushed aside, crying "You Son of David, have mercy on me!" He found it, as David did, and as you can.

God, though tender hearted, knows very well that David's sin, as yours and mine, still accuses. David pleads that God blots out or wipes away his sin. "Wash me thoroughly", he pleads, as a filthy garment needs to be washed and washed. Do you feel the accusing, frightening, power of guilt upon your life, today, christian? How can it be removed? Only one way; through the

Cross, of which all Old Testament sacrifices for sins spoke. Heartbroken one, meditate on Paul's words, whenever guilt accuses you; "And you ... he has made alive together with him, having forgiven you all trespasses, having wiped out the handwriting of requirements that was against us, which was contrary to us. And he has taken it out of the way, having nailed it to the cross. Having disarmed principalities and powers, he made a public spectacle of them, triumphing over them in it". Tell me, if this is true, where are your accusers, now?

A◆U◆G◆U◆S◆T 2ND

"For I acknowledge my transgressions, and my sin is ever before me. Against you, you only, have I sinned, and done this evil in your sight: that you may be found just when you speak, and blameless when you judge".
Psalm 51:3-4

"So this is the Bible's approach", sneers the cynic, "Were David's sins of adultery and murder, private sins? Surely they could not have had more public repercussions! So, now we go off into private confession to God and that's it?"

The Bible, though, goes right to the heart of the matter. Long before David's time, a young man was faced with every bit as tempting a situation as David had been. His name was Joseph and looking his temptress straight in the eye he said "How can I now do this great wickedness, and sin against God?" Yes, you can sin against your neighbour, your employer, even against a nation by treachery, but, ultimately, no matter what way you look at it, sin is against God.

When David acknowledges his sin was against God he quits trying to cover his tracks. He now realises how stupid such an action is before the all-seeing eye of God. Even forgiven, pardoned and restored, David was not to be what he might have been but, on confession to God, he is not what he once was. Thank God, as with the Prodigal Son, he never grew accustomed to the Far Country and he was homesick and restless until he turned his steps once more to the father's house. Prodigals come home somewhere in the world every day. How about you? Then, like David you can begin a new life in which you can spend yourself in gracious ministry for the reclamation and redemption of others.

A✦U✦G✦U✦S✦T 3RD

"Behold, I was brought forth in iniquity, and in sin my mother conceived me". Psalm 51:5

Do we sin because we are sinners, or are we sinners because we sin? The answer is that we sin because we are sinners. Sins come out of sin; our evil acts out of an evil nature. David, in our text, is not intending to blame his mother for his sinful state or action. He is not excusing himself. He is merely indicating that he, in common with all of us, are from the moment of birth sinners.

Today's text is often misunderstood and it is important to see that in its context David refers to his sin five times, as his own, as inexcusable and that sin is the very environment in which he lives. I heard Sir Peter Ustinov say recently in Belfast that we are not born bad, we are only made bad. Today's text stands against him.

A✦U✦G✦U✦S✦T 4TH

"Purge me with hyssop, and I shall be clean; wash me, and I shall be whiter than snow. Make me to hear joy and gladness, that the bones which you have broken may rejoice". Psalm 51:7-8

A leper was cleansed in Israel by being sprinkled seven times with the sacrificial blood into which a bunch of hyssop was dipped as a sprinkler. The leper was then pronounced, clean. David longs for the same pronouncement and puts it as only a poet of his standing could put it;

"Wash me and I shall be whiter than snow".

Is it possible? Is David merely fantasising? Could God remove the guilt of sin and make the sinner whiter than snow? "Come now", says God's word, "And let us reason together, says the Lord. Though your sins are like scarlet, they shall be as white as snow; though they are red like crimson, they shall be as wool". David is saying that if God cleanses, the result will be totally effective, there will be no half-measures. God has never put His hand to something yet and not finished it. As the thought of it grips David he knows that if such cleansing were available joy and gladness would result. He is anticipating an outcast's return. Hope begins to spring up in his broken, sinful heart.

So it was that David found what he longed for. "The Lord also has put away your sin", said Nathan. "Put away" is a even better than being whiter than snow. The scapegoat of the wilderness symbolically carried the sins of the people out of sight. It spoke of another who would bear away the sins of the world. Put your trust in Him and not only will He cleanse you from your sin, He will take it away. "I have formulated my creed", wrote the great Dostoyevsky as a prisoner in Siberia, "Wherein all is clear and holy to me. This creed is extremely simple, here it is. I believe that there is nothing lovelier, deeper, more sympathetic, more rational, more manly and more perfect than the Saviour; I say to myself with jealous love that not only is there no one else like him, but there could be no one".

A✦U✦G✦U✦S✦T 5TH

"Create in me a clean heart, O God, and renew a steadfast spirit within me. Do not cast me away from your presence, and do not take your Holy Spirit from me. Restore to me the joy of your salvation. And uphold me with your generous Spirit". Psalm 51:10-12

When you look into David's self-analysis in Psalm 51 you would think it would lead him to despair. He is face to face with himself and he does not like what he sees. But it leads him to prayer and to a quality of prayer he has not known in a very long time.

As long as a person prays, there is hope. It is when a person stops praying that darkness closes in. God speaks much better to an upturned face than to a pre-occupied back. You can see possibilities in prayer that you could never see outside of it. David prays for a clean heart, a steadfast spirit, and a restoration of the joy of salvation. It is the backsliders prayer and David was to receive all that he asked for; so can you. David who looked at himself now swiftly looks to God who will purge him (v.7), wash him (v.7), gladden him (v.8), heal him (v.8), renew him (v.10), deliver him (v.14), and restore him (v.12).

Have you been looking into your own heart recently? Are you filled with despair at what you see? Do you feel like Paul when he wrote "O wretched man that I am! Who will deliver me from this body of death? The answer was straight and effective; "I thank God - through Jesus Christ our Lord".

A◆U◆G◆U◆S◆T 6TH

" Then I will teach transgressors your ways, and sinners shall be converted to you". Psalm 51:13

Who do you think was, in New Testament times, an outstanding missionary? Paul? Certainly. Silas? Without a doubt. A host of people were great missionaries in New Testament days. But are we not forgetting one in particular. His name? The Prodigal Son.

"The people", one missionary has testified, "seldom grasp our meaning when we speak in abstract terms of sin and of God and of the divine forgiveness; but when we unfold the story of the Prodigal, our message becomes clear to them at once. For twenty centuries nobody has surpassed the Prodigal Son in evangelistic influence and appeal. On every continent and island he has been at work, night and day, summer and winter, for almost two thousand years pointing the prodigals of this world to the Father's house."

"I will teach transgressors your ways", says David, "And sinners shall be converted to you". Was his prayer answered? It was answered by the very psalm he was writing for since it was written it has shown generations of people the way back to repentance and back to the heart of God. This is the prodigal's psalm and it has become a great blessing in God's hands. Are you a prodigal? Repent and God will yet use you to teach transgressors His way. If you doubt me, ask President Nixon's hatchet-man, Charles Colson. He'll tell you.

A·U·G·U·S·T 7TH

"O Lord, open my lips, and my mouth shall show forth your praise. For you do not desire sacrifice, or else I would give it; you do not delight in burnt offering. The sacrifices of God are a broken spirit, a broken and a contrite heart - these, O God, you will not despise". Psalm 51:15-17.

It has been shown that the Old Testament has a way of saying "Not that, but this", where we would say, "This rather than that", or "Not that without this". Today's text is not saying that God was rejecting the offerings the Israelites were offering because the truth is it was God who appointed the offerings in the first place. What the text is saying is that no matter what we bring Him, it means nothing if there is not "A broken and contrite heart" behind what we offer.

Ellice Hopkins once put it this way; "Do you know the lovely fact about the opal? That, in the first place, it is made only of a desert dust, sand, silica, and owes its beauty and preciousness to a defect. It is a stone with a broken heart. It is full of minute fissures which admit air, and the air reflects the light. Hence its lovely hues, and that sweet lamp of fire that ever burns at its heart, for the breath of the Lord God is in it. You are only conscious of the cracks and desert dust, but so he makes his precious opal. We must be broken in ourselves before we can give back the lovely hues of His light, and the lamp in the temple can burn in us and never go out".

A·U·G·U·S·T 8TH

"Blessed is he whose transgression is forgiven, whose sin is covered. Blessed is the man to whom the Lord does not impute iniquity, and in whose spirit there is no guile". Psalm 32:1-2

After Prince Albert died Queen Victoria lived under a constant cloud of grief and nothing could comfort her. In the evenings she would weep as a lady-in-waiting read her passages from the Scriptures. One of the ladies dared to try to reason with the monarch.

"Your majesty, instead of feeling morbid, you should rejoice. One day in Heaven you will meet the great people from the Bible - Moses, Jacob, Abraham, Solomon, David". "No! No!" interjected Queen Victoria, "I will not meet David!" No matter what an English monarch might say God did forgive David on his repentance and in today's text is David's overflowing joy because of sins forgiven. He describes evil in four ways. It is "Transgression" which means rebellion against right authority. It is "Sin", which means missing the mark. It is "Iniquity" which means moral crookedness. It is "Guile" which means cunning, an attempt to cover up.

David uses three expressions for pardon and they are just beautiful. The first is that it is a "Taking away", a burden lifted off. Then it is "A covering", hiding from God's sight. Then it is "A debt not reckoned", a debt cancelled. Compare the two sides of the gulf; "'Transgression", "Sin", "Iniquity", "Guile" on one side and "Taken away", "Covered", "Cancelled" on the other. It was a mighty gulf that God spanned at Calvary. And remember, God is swifter to forgive than we are to confess.

A•U•G•U•S•T 9TH

"When I kept silent, my bones grew old through my groaning all the day long. For day and night your hand was heavy upon me; my vitality was turned into the drought of summer". Psalm 32:3-4

There are people all over the world who carry their secrets with them like festering thorns that infect their whole personality. It would be hard to calculate the amount of damage done by guilt. A mother or father embittered by guilt can start withdrawing from other members of their family and make their whole family into a disaster area. Too many teenagers filled with guilt these days have been turning to suicide. Guilt makes people harsh, unappreciative, suspicious and distrusting. They don't accept love from others, easily, in case that love will be withdrawn should people find out their secrets. Guilt takes a fearful toll of people's wellbeing.

Instead of facing the facts squarely and confessing his sins honestly to God, David had kept silent. Did it help? It only made matters worse. His silence did not bring him strength, it brought him weakness. Strength and freshness went out of his life and he was dried up and without enthusiasm. His vitality was sapped. Is that you? Please don't keep silent towards God any longer. It will only cripple your whole life. Confess to God what you have done wrong. Because sin is against Him, only He can forgive. There is no sin He isn't able to deal with, no sinner He can't restore. You are not an exception.

A٠U٠G٠U٠S٠T 10TH

"I acknowledge my sin to you, and my iniquity I have not hidden. I said 'I will confess my transgressions to the Lord', and you forgave the iniquity of my sin". Psalm 32:5

There is no subject which haunts me more than the subject of the Jewish Holocaust. When I think of Germany and its facing up to the truth of its recent history, there can be no doubt that there is relief for even a nation when it confesses that it did wrong. But David's confession is more than that kind of confession, his brought him far more than relief; it brought him God's forgiveness. The deadlock between himself and God was broken.

It has been suggested that our text throws incidental light on the situation that prevailed in Corinth. We read that the church at Corinth was behaving so badly that their sin was causing some to be weak and sick, and some to die. Could it be that they wouldn't confess and that their symptoms were indeed David's when he wouldn't confess? Confession on their part could have broken the deadlock for them just as it did for David. If we confess our sins, Scripture tells us that God is faithful and just to forgive us our sins and to cleanse us from all unrighteousness. Ours is not the religion of the merely pardoned it is that of the totally forgiven. Said Al Martin, "Is your life more fragrant than when the kiss of forgiveness is most fresh upon your cheek?" (For further study on the subject of forgiveness read Romans 4:5-7, 1 John 1:8-10 and Prov 28:13).

A•U•G•U•S•T 11TH

"For this cause everyone who is godly shall pray to you in a time when you may be found; surely in a flood of great waters they shall not come near him". Psalm 32:6

When you know God has forgiven you there is a security that comes into your life that nothing else can bring. David pictures himself as being like a person on a rock in the midst of floods that cannot reach him. Though not exempt from trouble, as we have clearly seen in David's life, he is not overwhelmed with it. It is interesting that today's text inspired Charles Wesley's hymn;

"While the nearer waters roll,
While the tempest still is high;
Hide me, O my Saviour, hide ..."

So prayer rises from David's heart amidst floods of trouble around him. Don't you think prayer has often turned into a guilt-ridden process rather than a tension restoring process? Prayer is more than a necessity or a moral duty, it should be a delight. Its reflex influence heals the human mind, releases the nervous system from pressures, restores a true sense of values in life. When you begin to really pray you will understand the meaning of the verse that promises God will keep in perfect peace the mind that is stayed on Him. Then you will know the meaning of the words "He who dwells in the secret place of the Most High shall abide under the shadow of the Almighty". Then you will know the "Peace of God which passes all understanding". You got peace with God when you trusted Christ which cannot be taken from you. You get the peace of God when you pray.

A•U•G•U•S•T 12TH

"You are my hiding place; you shall preserve me from trouble; you shall surround me with songs of deliverance". Psalm 32:7

When the Children of Israel came out of the Red Sea they sang, all two million of them! When Jericho was defeated, Deborah and Barak sang a duet, all two of them. When Israel faced a huge onslaught of enemies at the Wadi before the Wilderness of Jeruel a choir of singers was appointed "Who should praise the Lord ... as they went out before the army ... saying "Praise the Lord for His mercy endures forever"'. When they began to sing and to praise the Lord their enemies were defeated without any fighting whatsoever (See 2 Chron 20).

Job, bereaved, sick, criticised, lonely and baffled spoke of "God my maker who gives me songs in the night" and there is no question that with lacerated backs and feet fast in the stocks Paul and Silas sang those night songs. A believer's happiness does not depend on good happenings. If it did and their good happenings didn't happen to happen where would they be?! In the very worst of circumstances christians can still sing a song of deliverance. Who, studying what we have just studied of David's life would ever have imagined David would ever sing again? But he did and so will you.

A♦U♦G♦U♦S♦T 13TH

"I will instruct you and teach you in the way you should go; ...".
Psalm 32:8

Does God guide? In our text He not only says He does, He promises He will. Today I want to give you something to study regarding the subject of guidance. I have found these points very useful in my christian life and I pass them on to you.

God promises to instruct and teach us in the way we should go but let us learn how He does it. He may say yes to our petition but no to our desire. (See Numbers 11:1-33 ; Psalm 106:15). He may say no to our petitions but yes to our desires (Gen 18-19). He may say yes to both our petitions and our desires (Judges 16:26-30). He may say no to both our petitions and our desires because of the following: Unconfessed sin (Psalm 68:18). An unclear conscience (Matt 5:23). The wrong motivation of selfishness (James 4:3). Doubt (James 1:6-7). Unresolved husband/wife conflicts (1 Peter 3:7). Lack of faith (Heb 11:6). Lack of compassion (Prov 21:13). It is not His will (James 4:15). He wants to teach us divine lessons (2 Cor 12:9-10). He wants to use us as an object lesson to others (Hosea and Ezekiel). One of the best pieces of advice I ever read on guidance came from the pen of Haddon Robinson who said, "The question we should ask is no longer, 'What is God's will?' instead the question is, 'How do I make good decisions?' If we change the question, we change the direction of the answer ... God has given us the freedom to make good decisions and we're responsible for them".

A◆U◆G◆U◆S◆T 14TH

"I will guide you with my eye". Psalm 32:8

A surgeon doesn't always have to speak to his staff in the operating theatre to explain to them what he wants. Working with him daily they can often understand what he wants by his look. So it is that as we live in the spirit we begin to get to know what God wants by walking and talking with him daily.

What are God's methods of guidance? In the past they were by the pillar of cloud and fire, the blowing of trumpets, the use of urim and thummin and judge and prophet. Today he uses his written word (John 10:27), the inward urge of the Holy Spirit (John 16:13 ; Matt 10:19 ; Acts 10:19 ; 13:2 ; Romans 8:4 ; Gal 5:25 ; John 10:27) and outward circumstances (Rom 8:28). Test the inward urge of the Holy Spirit by Bible based wisdom (Acts 16:7 ; 2 Cor 2:13); guard against confusing it with mere human impression which can come from wishful thinking, fear, obsessional neuroses, depression, side effects of medication, and Satanic delusions. Any supposed guidance which disturbs your peace in Christ is to be stringently guarded against (Col 3:15 ; Phil 4:6). Don't forget, though, God will guide you with his eye. Remember the Lord turned and looked upon Peter.

A◆U◆G◆U◆S◆T 15TH

"Do not be like the horse or like the mule, which have no understanding....". Psalm 32:9

We were created differently to the animals. God did not talk to the animals - he talked to man. Only man has what David calls "Understanding". The Scripture is fascinating on the subject because it mocks and rebukes man when he fails to do by his mind and consent what animals do by instinct. The Scriptures speak of the swallow coming back but God's people refusing to repent and turn back to God. They speak of the stork knowing her appointed times but man ignoring them. It speaks of ants being industrious and prudent and man being lazy. When human beings fail to do by consent what animals do by instinct they are contradicting themselves. David knew only too well how contradictory to himself he had just been.

Three monkeys sat in a coconut tree
Discussing things as they're said to be
Said one to the other "Now listen, you
There's a certain rumour that can't be true
That man descended from our noble race
The very idea is a disgrace!"

And another thing you'll never see -
A monk build a fence around a coconut tree,
And let the coconuts go to waste
Forbidding all other monks a taste
Why, if I put a fence around the tree
Starvation would force you to steal from me.

No monkey ever deserted his wife,
Starved her babies and ruined their life,
And you've never known a mother monk
To leave her babies with others to bun
Or pass them on from one to another
Till they scarcely know who is their mother.

Here's another thing a monkey won't do
Go out at night and get on a stew,
Or use a gun, or club, or knife,
To take some other monkey's life.
Yes, man descended the ornery cuss
But, brother, he didn't descend from us!

(Anon)

A◆U◆G◆U◆S◆T 16TH

"... which must be harnessed with bit and bridle, else they will not come near you". Psalm 32:9

May God not have to use a bit and bridle upon us to draw us near to Him as you would have to draw some animals. David had just experienced the death of his child. Now the death of every child is not to be read as a judgment of God but David knew God was speaking to him through the death of his little one. Such experiences bring us closer to God. It is God's permitting and overruling of calamities which leads to our most exalting and refining discoveries. Let R. W. Service's lines prove that fact;

I sought him on the purple seas,
I sought him on the peaks of flame;
Amid the gloom of giant trees
And cannons lone I called his name.
The wasted ways of earth I trod;
In vain! In vain! I found not God.

I sought him in the lives of men,
In cities grand, in hamlets grey,
In temples old beyond our ken,
And tabernacles of today.
All vain I sought from cloud to clod.
In vain! In vain! I found not God.

Then, after roaming far and wide,
In streets, seas and deserts wild,
I came at last to stand beside
The death-bed of my little child.
Lo, as I bent beneath the rod,
I raised my eyes ... and there was God!

A◆U◆G◆U◆S◆T 17TH

"Be glad in the Lord and rejoice, you righteous; and shout for joy, all you upright in heart!". Psalm 32:11

From the broken spirit which we met earlier in the psalm which had "Turned into the drought of summer" to the gladness shouting for joy of today's text, is a very long way in David's experience. The world was still the same place but David was a different person; his attitude had changed. Don't you think life is ninety percent what happens to you and ten percent how you react to it? My house may burn, my money may be stolen, my health may break down, my work may dry up, but no matter what people may do to me or not do, no matter what circumstances surround me, no matter how dark the day or miserable my surroundings, people or things cannot take away my choice of attitude.

When I feel lonely I can give an hour of my time to someone who is lonelier. When I feel discouraged I can send a note of encouragement to someone who is in despair. When the world rushes passed me and shows me no care I can give a word of compassion to someone who is slow and easily overlooked. It all lies in attitude. The minister, much given to finding encouragement in everything once climbed into his pulpit on a very stormy morning. His congregation wondered what on earth he would have to praise the Lord for on such a day. His opening remarks were "Thank the Lord every day is not like today!". That's the attitude to have.

A✦U✦G✦U✦S✦T 18TH

"If you, Lord, should mark iniquities, O Lord, who could stand?".
Psalm 130:3

"What would you do if someone in one of your public meetings rose up and accused you of wrongdoing in the past, Mr. Whitfield?", asked an earnest enquirer of the great preacher. "I would let him finish", said George Whitfield, "And then I would tell the audience I could tell them much worse for I know my own heart". I went into a coffee shop in Ulster recently and the waitress, seeing me said, with a smile, "There wasn't a sinner in the place till you came!" Well now, I don't know that that is the most encouraging remark I've heard recently! Still, do you feel that you are, like Paul felt, the chief of sinners? There is only one answer to that statement and it is today's text.

There are no fewer than fourteen words in the Hebrew Old Testament for sin, and each one reveals sin in a different way. In this one David acknowledges that he is off the straight. If you are not standing, you fall. If the Lord was to observe and keep in remembrance all our iniquities, we would all be damned. Not one of us could stand. Remember that. But are we all damned? No, there is forgiveness with the Lord that he may be feared.

A✦U✦G✦U✦S✦T 19TH

"I wait for the Lord, my soul waits, and in his word I do hope".
Psalm 130:5

Waiting for God lies at the heart of the believers experience. There are people who are forever talking about God, criticising Him, saying what He should do or not do. You've heard them, haven't you? "Why does God allow suffering?" "Why does God allow death?" "Where was He when I lost my job?" "Why doesn't He do something?"

It was Dr. Martyn Lloyd-Jones who said "You do not begin to be a christian until you're mouth is shut, is stopped and you are speechless and have nothing to say". Sin and the law of God condemns us "That every mouth may be stopped and all the world may become guilty before God". Admitting our guilt and being in awed silence before God is the royal road to blessing.

To wait for God as a believer is to trust. It is to lose anxiety and fret. It is to stop becoming impatient. It is avoid the lure of self-management which is responsible more than anything else for tricking us into painful situations and inflicting hurtful sorrows upon us. It is to rest in the promises of God's Word, trusting that God will reveal His will.

Look what happened to Abraham and Sarah when they forced the pace regarding the birth of Isaac (Gen 16). The results of not waiting upon God were anger, selfishness, dissension, envy, enmity, jealousy, immorality, impurity and the single most volatile flashpoint in the world today, the Arab-Israeli conflict. No one has ever been disappointed who waited for God. Repeat; no one. Compare the fruits of the flesh and the fruits of the spirit in Galatians 5:19-20; with Galatians 5:22-23. Which fruit would you prefer?

A•U•G•U•S•T 20TH

"My soul waits for the Lord more than those who watch for the morning - I say, more than those who watch for the morning". Psalm 130:6

All kinds of people patiently wait for the morning; the patient nurse by a bedside, the insomniac burdened with worry that has long made sleep impossible, or, the lonely wife whose husband is far away. I am certain that many reading today's text may have longed for today to dawn. Maybe you have recently been bereaved. Maybe an alcoholic lives in your home, maybe your very own relatives don't speak to you any more; maybe you are like the person who wrote to me recently saying that "After sixty four years worshipping in a certain church I have been ostracised by many members". Day time is bearable for you but maybe the night is what you dread.

The reference in our text may be to the Levites on duty in the Temple eagerly watching for the dawn that they may offer the morning sacrifice; it may be a reference to sentinels on the city wall watching to end their watch, or, it may be to shepherds on a dark hillside. In the final analysis it refers to all watchers who wait for the Lord in a spirit of expectation.

Anna and Simeon watched and waited for the Lord and he came. So He will come a second time and the church that has for centuries been waiting and watching for His return, will not be disappointed. As Bill Freel said "As christians we should not be exitists, looking for our going but adventists looking for His coming".

A•U•G•U•S•T 21ST

"Hear my prayer, O Lord, give ear to my supplications! In your faithfulness answer me, and in your righteousness". Psalm 143:1

Psalm 143 is the last of the penitential psalms and begins with David pleading with the Lord to listen to his prayers. This is a feature of many Bible people in prayer. Jacob at Penuel would not let the Lord go until he blessed him. Moses pled with God for the erring Children of Israel to the extent of laying his own life on the line if that was the cost of God's sparing of them. Daniel asked God to open his eyes and see "Our despair and the city which is called by your name". "O Lord", he prayed, hear; O Lord forgive; O Lord heed and act". Daniel didn't let God's word drift over him or the world to drift by him. He was determined that the reality of the world around him must be made to conform with the reality of God's word. Earnest prayer was the key.

The list of Bible people taking God's promises and applying them in prayer to see them fulfilled in their lives is an inspiration. Hannah, Job, and Paul are more examples and our Lord himself in prayer is the holiest prayer ground of all. It was he who told the story of the man who had a visitor at midnight and who was not afraid to stir his next door neighbour from sleep to get his friend some food. Christ was teaching us that if we mean business we will not find our Heavenly Father reluctant to answer our prayers. Of course if we ask, seek and knock and don't care whether we are answered or not, we won't get what we are seeking, will we?

A◆U◆G◆U◆S◆T 22ND

"I pour out my complaint before him; I declare before him my trouble".
Psalm 143:2

David admits the guilt of all men and prays that judgment may not be visited upon him for his share in it. He knows, as you and I know that if desert and merit were to be the determining factors whether or not God will help us, our case would be hopeless. David is not content with the gloomy fact that no person can of themselves be righteous in God's sight. Implied in the statement is a request that God would grant him that righteousness which he alone can impart out of pure grace.

Strange, isn't it, how people in pride claim perfection? I heard recently of a man who claimed he hadn't sinned for months. Only problem was as he was putting this claim to a colleague of mine, my colleague noticed that he was breaking the speed limit!

No, David is asking in today's text for an audience at the mercy-seat and has no wish to appear before the judgment-seat. His statement is distinctly Pauline, long before Paul lifted his pen. As David found mercy at the temple's mercy-seat so you and I can find mercy at ours, which is Calvary's mighty work. Christians are totally unrighteous but see the one in whom they are hidden; Christ Himself? He is our righteousness and has obtained mercy with his Father for us. I know of no better pillow than that upon which to lay my head tonight, do you?

A◆U◆G◆U◆S◆T 23RD

"For the enemy has persecuted my soul; he has crushed my life to the ground; he has made me dwell in darkness, like those who have long been dead. Therefore my spirit is overwhelmed within me; my heart within me is distressed". Psalm 143:3-4

People have immense power to destroy any confidence you might have; even your confidence in the Lord. David describes in detail what he felt as his enemy rose against him. He felt his very soul was under persecution; spiritually he was under attack. He felt crushed to the ground and basically he was saying "I am already as good as dead". His spirit was overwhelmed; he couldn't even find himself amidst the severe assaults which were being made on his character. The problem was that since his sin with Bathsheba he was all too well aware that a lot of what his enemies were saying was true.

Is this your experience? Maybe an enemy has risen and used some sin of yours to seek to crush your soul and spirit. You know that what they are saying is true and yet you know that the Lord loves you still. What are you to do? You are to realise that the Lord is chastening you. Your enemy is totally unconscious of being God's instrument for your chastisement but this is a fact. As the Asyrians were a "Razor" in God's hands to shave Judah (See Is 7:20), as Nebuchadnezzar was God's instrument to chastise Israel by taking them away to captivity, as Ananias and Sapphira's judgment chastened the New Testament church, so what your enemy is doing is chastening you. Be patient, take it, you are pardoned by God but the present pressure is to bring you out as gold.

A♦U♦G♦U♦S♦T 24TH

"I remember the days of old; I meditate on all your works; I muse on the work of your hands". Psalm 143:5

It is easy when you are depressed, discouraged and down-hearted to think that your past days were the best days. Why, when the new temple at Jerusalem was built the young men rejoiced and the old men wept! The younger generation did not feel that the glory of the latter could ever be as great as the glory of the former. They were wrong then and such thinking is wrong now.

Is it wrong to remember good times in the past? Certainly not. We should be glad to remember victories of faith, occasions of joy and God's deliverance in the past but the whole direction of scriptural teaching is to spur us on to the future. The past is full of nostalgia but the future for the believer, no matter what way you look at it, is full of hope. Forgetting those things which are behind we press toward the mark of a high calling of God in Christ.

As David had taken on a few onery bears and lions in the past, it was now time to take on even greater tasks. As Moses had seen God open up the court's of Pharoah he had to now step out and see God open up the Red Sea. Paul had seen God work tremendously in the past in his life but he now set sail for Jerusalem, "Not knowing what will happen to me there". It certainly beat watching full sunsets at Miletus for the rest of his christian life . Go on, get out there and prove that God is the God of your future, not just the God of your past.

A♦U♦G♦U♦S♦T 25TH

"I remember the days of old; I meditate on all your works; I muse on the work of your hands". Psalm 143:5

There is no healthier exercise for our minds than to meditate on what God has created. I can tell what kind of person you are by the kind of books you read, the curtains you buy, the colours you chose in clothes, the state of your room, etc. So it is as we look on God's creation we can see the incredible variety of his mind. We can tell what a God our God is by the things he has created.

Take just one thing, for example; water. Someone with time on his hands has worked out that there are 320 million cubic miles of sea water alone and each cubic mile weighs 4,314,996 tons. If you look at a spoonful of sea water and put it under a microscope you would see 100,000 living things moving about! Above our heads are thousands of millions of tons more water in the form of vapour and cloud and so called dry land is wet for six miles down! If all the water in the ground was brought to the surface it would cover the earth to a depth of 1,000 feet and most of us would drown! Yet, Jesus said that not one single cup of water given in kindness, even in the name of a disciple, is without its reward!

We are only talking of water; what of the vast expanse of space? What of the intricacy of flowers and fauna? I watch the Chelsea Flower Show every year on television and I have yet to see the BBC give God a credit line for creating the exquisite beauty of the flowers filmed. Once in the Liverpool Planetarium I asked the lecturer if he thought there was a God behind it all. "We are not allowed to answer religious questions here", he answered with a frown! Poor man! If I had been him I would have resigned the job on the spot, wouldn't you?

A٠U٠G٠U٠S٠T 26TH

"I spread out my hands to you; my soul longs for you like a thirsty land".
Psalm 143:6

Again and again a little phrase has haunted me through recent months. Let me describe the background to the phrase. It concerns the christian writer called Philip Yancy and some of his friends who were invited to Moscow at the time of the recent fall of Communism. They met Gorbachov and Yelstin and visited various churches. Then came the day when they had to face the press. They were apprehensive. Reporters and journalists of all kinds gathered into the room and a beautiful, articulate, and famous T.V. presenter rose to ask her question. "How can we", she wondered, "Find God?" The visiting christians were flabbergasted; question after question followed from the rest of the journalists in the same vein.

Philip Yancy wondered what he would have had to face if he had been before the Press Club in America. He began to muse on the widespread spiritual decadence of the West and began to ask himself why it was that the spiritual surge in Eastern Europe was so incredible. He wrote that he had reached only one clear conclusion; "God", he said, "Always goes where He is wanted". That's the little phrase that's been haunting me. Sinful and all as David was, awful though his sins had been, he wanted God. He wanted him as a parched land wants rain. He longed to have him and he got him. Why? Because God always goes where He is wanted.

A◆U◆G◆U◆S◆T 27TH

"Answer me speedily, O Lord; my spirit fails! Do not hide your face from me, lest I be like those who go down into the pit". Psalm 143:7

We all long for a speedy answer from the Lord, but though our prayers will be answered, they may not be answered speedily. How well I remember the day that a friend of mine called at my home. He was seeking to encourage me in christian work and told me the story of how he and other of his friends had been involved in christian work in an Austrian castle. Ever since they had, as a christian organisation, bought the castle the Lord seemed to have touched their work with a spiritual harvest. They wondered at the secret until they discovered a Bible belonging to the original owner of the castle. In the fly leaf of the Bible he had written a prayer that God would use his castle to His glory. History has proved that the owner was greatly persecuted for his christian stand and died, heartbroken. Imagine the surprise of my friends when they discovered how old the Bible was. They discovered the castle owner's Bible, and therefore his prayer, was 700 years old!

A•U•G•U•S•T 28TH

"Cause me to hear your loving-kindness in the morning. For in you do I trust; cause me to know the way in which I should walk, for I lift up my soul to you". Psalm 143:8

The first waking moment of any day is very important. You know how it is, those delicious seconds before the first demand of the day blimps on the computer of the brain! You know you must rise in the next few minutes and face whatever has to be faced but it is a very healthy spiritual exercise to capture those precious seconds with a simple prayer. It can set the tone for the whole day. I find it is good to say in your heart "Lord Jesus, this day is yours. Let me do in it just whatever you want me to do. Cross my path with the people you want me to help or encourage". Following such a prayer of opening the mind to spiritual thinking, I find, is followed always by the Lord opening up thoughts of His loving-kindness to us. It speaks assurance, peace, joy, hope. Should your whole world be falling around you, should difficult decisions have to be taken, or even heart-breaking sorrows sweep through your day, the Lord's voice of loving-kindness comes to you this morning assuring you of the supply of your needs, strength for your tasks, safety in your danger and security for eternity.

Lifting Robert Murray McCheyne's Bible one day, handed to me by the caretaker of his church building in Dundee, I read the beautiful text from John's Gospel chapter 10 where Jesus said "I give to my sheep eternal life and they shall never perish". Mr. McCheyne had written over against these lovely words in the margin of his Bible this simple note; "Nothing can force them out". With such loving-kindness spoken to your heart this morning, christian, you can face the Devil himself, today, and win.

A•U•G•U•S•T 29TH

"Cause me to hear your loving-kindness in the morning, for in you do I trust; cause me to know the way in which I should walk, for I lift up my soul to you". Psalm 143:8

Why do we need God's guidance? Because life is made up of decisions. In fact in our generation in the western world we are faced with over-choice. A computer specialist sat down at a computer and recently put all the variations available in cars - body styles, colours, accessories -into his system. After the computer groaned and blinked for some time it revealed the startling find; American consumers could chose from 25 million different automobiles! Picking a car to buy is a relatively easy decision when compared to some of the big decisions of our generation, particularly in the area of careers, abortion, genetic engineering, etc.

If you decide to know God's guidance it is a healthy sign but you must get rid of a great widespread fear which millions of christians have. It is that God's plan for your life is like a itinerary drawn up by a travel agent. As long as you are in the right place, at the right time, to board each train, or bus, or boat, all is well but miss one of these pre-planned connections and the itinerary is ruined. A revised plan can only ever be second-best compared with the original programme. You will have God's second best and be God's second rate servant and on the scrapheap, forfeiting your usefulness, should you make a mistake in making a major decision. The fact is you will certainly face sad consequences from bad decisions but to think that God cannot put you back on track if you misconceive His will is downright unbelief. Moses, David, Peter, and many others made bad decisions but God restored them and used them again. Misconceiving God's will is less sinful than knowing it and not doing it. Selah.

A◆U◆G◆U◆S◆T 30TH

"Teach me to do your will, for you are my God; your Spirit is good. Lead me in the land of uprightness". Psalm 143:10

Can prayer effect guidance? David is obviously praying for guidance in today's text but he realises that a prayerless life can never be a God-guided life. Nothing could be simpler than prayer; an infant can pray and yet prayers relation to the provident government of the world is mysterious and profound.

Could your prayers effect guidance? Yes, certainly. Think about Gideon, for example. Gideon's prayers saved an army once. The fleece that he put out as a test to discover God's will for his life has caused a lot of discussion. Was it a sign of lack of faith on Gideons part? For seven long years the Midianites had simply come and taken from the Israelites what they wanted. But not this time; Gideon and an army of 32,000 men were waiting to be committed to battle. As Gideon waited for God he certainly needed to know if God was with him in the coming conflict. So the farmer decided to see if he could control the dew by his prayers. Why the dew? David tells us that dew represents unity amongst God's people (See Psalm 133). Gideon was no fool. He needed control of unity in his army and through prayer he got it.

Moses saved a nation by his prayers (See Exodus 32-33). Abraham saved his nephew through his prayers (Genesis 18-19). Hannah saved the spiritual leadership of the nation of Israel through her prayers (1 Samuel 2:1-3). Who and what will you save by yours? Only eternity will reveal it.

A♦U♦G♦U♦S♦T 31ST

"Revive me, O Lord, for your name's sake! For your righteousness sake bring my soul out of trouble. In your mercy cut off my enemies, and destroy all those who afflict my soul; for I am your servant". Psalm 143: 11-12

We have spent the month of August looking at some of the themes in the penitential psalms and it is appropriate that we should end on the note of David's restoration to a sense of his identity. An overwhelming sense of guilt and the devastation caused by sin in his life blinded David to his true identity. He had lost sight of the fact that he was still the Lord's and that the Lord was committed to him, despite his sin. When all was said and done David was still the Lord's servant. He takes no other boast. He does not glory in his gift of writing, his mastery of military or civil matters, his good looks, or his position as king; he glories in being a servant of the Lord. As such he knows that he may have got his own soul into trouble but only the Lord can bring him out of it.

Glory, christian, in the fact that you are a servant of the Lord. The Scriptures teach that angels are at your service in such a service. Christ himself was not ashamed to call himself a servant. He considered service to His Father his highest honour. So, christian, go today to your classroom, your business, your university, your farm, your kitchen, your palace, your factory, your office, or wherever God has placed you and serve the Lord. Service to the Lord, for example, as a long distance lorry driver is every bit as important as the service of some great evangelist. No work done for God's glory is insignificant. It is an old adage but worth repeating; wherever you go today remember "Whose you are and whom you serve". Such a knowledge and such an identity will lead to the most wholesome lifestyle possible.

SEPTEMBER

S◆E◆P◆T◆E◆M◆B◆E◆R

A storm in family life is the worst of all storms. It came, in David's case, from the pride of his son, Absalom. Pride always comes before a fall and the rise and fall of Absalom is a singular lesson in the stupidity of vanity. Poor David didn't have to go looking for trouble, it came looking for him; his son caused him more trouble, at this time, than his enemies. Trouble in any house is the same. Yet in the midst of it all God sent his alleviations and deliverances. Let's give September to a study of it all.

S◆E◆P◆T◆E◆M◆B◆E◆R 1ST

"After this it happened that Absalom provided himself with chariots and horses, and fifty men to run before him". 2 Samuel 15:1

An American Ambassador to the Court of St. James, Mr. Charles Price, arrived in Belfast one morning, quite recently. Addressing a dinner he told how ambassadors usually never have to buy plane tickets, wait in queues, drive cars or face the ordinary hassles of life while in office. He told us that he had recently gone back home to Texas for the wedding of his daughter and, forgetting where he was, had run down the stairs of his home and jumped into the back seat of the car at the door and nothing happened. He had forgotten he was at home and not on duty!

I liked the ambassador for his healthy balance of being able to laugh at the trappings of power rather than flaunting them. When George Thomas, the former Speaker of the House of Commons was elevated to the House of Lords and became Lord Tonypandy he was asked how he felt. He replied "I'll be the same size in the bath!" Woe to the person like Absalom who deliberately sets out to impress others with the trappings of power, for, there is even no room for God in the people who are full of themselves.

S✦E✦P✦T✦E✦M✦B✦E✦R 2ND

"Now Absalom would rise early and stand beside the way to the gate. So it was, whenever anyone who had a lawsuit came to the king for a decision that Absalom would call to him and say, 'What city are you from?' And he would say, 'Your servant is from such and such a tribe of Israel'. Then Absalom would say to him, 'Look, your case is good and right; but there is no deputy of the king to hear you"'. 2 Samuel 15:2-3

Imagine living in David's day and having a serious lawsuit to face. Imagine setting off for King David's palace to present your case. You have been waiting for some time and, though you have arrived early, you have discovered that there is no one to hear your case today. The King is busy and hasn't appointed anyone as a deputy to hear your case. You are disappointed, frustrated and feel you are only one of a number.

Suddenly, you are approached by the tall, striking figure of the king's son, Absalom. "What city are you from?", he asks. You tell him your city, your tribe and then into his apparently sympathetic ear you pour the details of you lawsuit. "You have a good case", he says, "but there is no one to see you. Pity, really. Bad administration around here. I'd do something about it myself but I can't. I'm not in power, you know". With a smile he is gone to pass on the same word to the next man in the queue. How would you react? I hope you would not forget that "Those are good, that are good in their own place, and do not pretend how good they would be in other people's places".

S✦E✦P✦T✦E✦M✦B✦E✦R 3RD

"Moreover Absalom would say, 'Oh, that I were made judge in the land, and everyone who has any suit or cause would come to me; then I would give him justice"'. 2 Samuel 15:4

C. S. Lewis has a brilliant analogy of the monkey who dressed up in the lion skin and started giving out the orders as king of the jungle. There are plenty of monkeys and lion skins, around yet. Absalom was certainly the grandfather of them. He wants to be judge in Israel, he who murdered his own brother and ought to have been judged himself for his crime. Those who have learned to obey make much better judges. We really must be careful, in life, that we are not taken in by the pushers and shovers who want what they are anything but qualified to have. Don't you think if Absalom had been a good son and a good subject, a man of wisdom, kindness and learning he would one day have made a fine judge? Don't you think that handsome is as handsome does?

The Scriptures teach a foundational truth about all promotion. "A man's gift makes room for him and brings him before great men". (Prov 18:16). Mark the proverb, well. Notice it does not say that his C.V. will open doors, or his knowledge of people in high places, or his cleverness in manipulating circumstances his way; it simply says his gift in and of itself will speak for itself without self-promotion. How do you know you have a gift? Check out the thing you find easy to do that everyone else finds difficult. There is your gift.

S◆E◆P◆T◆E◆M◆B◆E◆R 4TH

"In this manner Absalom acted towards all Israel who came to the king for judgment. So Abraham stole the hearts of the men of Israel". 2 Samuel 15:6

There is certainly a spiritual message here for all of us. Absalom set out to lower the sovereign in the eyes of the people. He was out to undermine a throne in order to have it for himself. Who else but Satan desired the very same thing? He tried to usurp God's throne and he is certainly out to steal our hearts. He who sought to tempt the sinless Saviour of the world will not hold back in seeking to seduce us.

Satan, corrupts everything he touches. He seeks to corrupt personal life, social life, and political life. He certainly tries to corrupt christian doctrine. He is a murderer (John 8:44); he is like a roaring lion stocking his prey (1 Peter 5:8) who roars after the kill, not before. He is a liar (John 8:44), the fountain of all falsehood, trickery and deceit. He is the god of this world (2 Corinthians 4:4). He sends out false prophets (Matthew 24:11), and insinuates false brethren into the church who "Step in to spy out our freedom ... that they may bring us into bondage" (Galatians 2:4). Don't let him steal your heart. Remember his power is limited, he is simply a usurper, Christ supremely bound him by the Cross. He cannot prevent the ultimate victory of God. He is cowardly and fears the name of his conqueror Jesus Christ. Its like a converted prisoner who wrote to me from his prison cell recently, "When Satan reminds me of my past", he wrote, "I remind him of his future".

S◆E◆P◆T◆E◆M◆B◆E◆R 5TH

"Fearfulness and trembling have come upon me, and horror has overwhelmed me. And I said 'Oh, that I had wings like a dove! For then I would fly away and be at rest. Indeed, I would wander far off, and remain in the wilderness"'. Psalm 55:5-7

Psalm 55 tells us how David felt during the conspiracy of Absalom. He felt like you might feel today. He felt betrayed and was living under an intolerable strain. He says he felt restless, distraught, depressed and oppressed; the walls of God's city whose walls should have been the reassurance of his people had become a parade-ground of rebels and terrorists. A hostile group under Absalom, were now on the ascendancy and David spoke of how they brought misery crashing down on him.

David was unquestionably one of the great spiritual giants of all time and is it not comforting to read the urge he felt when faced with seemingly impossible odds within his own family, never to speak of those that he faced within his own nation? He wanted to fly out of it all but it was a wish rather than a hope of escape. We all feel like getting out at times. Yet, I like what an old writer once wrote about our text. He wrote that "It would have been more honourable for him to have asked for the strength of an ox to bear his trials, than for the wings of a dove to flee from them". Which attitude would you rather have; an attitude of an Elijah sitting under a juniper tree wanting to quit or Paul who said "Hard pressed on every side, yet not crushed; we are perplexed but not in despair; persecuted but not forsaken; struck down but not destroyed - always carrying about in the body the dying of the Lord Jesus that the life of Jesus also may be manifested in our body"? The choice, christian, is yours. And remember, a fleeing dove may light on a thorn. You can never run away from trouble because there is no place that far!

S◆E◆P◆T◆E◆M◆B◆E◆R 6TH

" The words of his mouth were smoother than butter, but war was in his heart; his words were softer than oil, yet they were drawn swords" .
Psalm 55:21

David, ever the poet, incapsulates the treachery of Absalom in the words of our text. Let's learn from this period in David's life that people who use smooth talk to your face can have war towards you in their heart. As a bee can carry honey in her mouth and a sting in her tail, or the box-tree whose leaves are always green but her seeds are poison, we must not let a person's words alone sway us; treachery could be at the root of their smooth talk.

Of all the sins to scorn, treachery must be high on the list. It is a contemptible sin. Think of the list of biblical traitors: Baalam, Delilah, Saul, Joab, Rechab, Baanah, Absalom, Ahithophel, Jezebel, Samballat, Haman, Judas and Demas. Above all may we be true to our lovely Lord Jesus. Sitting in a restaurant recently I heard the piano player suddenly start to play the hymn "I'd rather have Jesus ...". I was challenged once again to loyalty to the One who died for me. "Than to be the king of a vast domain and be held in sin's dread sway, I'd rather have Jesus than anything this world affords today". Absalom's treachery ended in disaster but David's throne was established forever in the person of his greater Son, our Lord Jesus Christ. Be loyal to his throne wherever you go today.

S◆E◆P◆T◆E◆M◆B◆E◆R 7TH

"Cast your burden on the Lord, and he shall sustain you; he shall never permit the righteous to be moved" . Psalm 55:22

Was there ever a sentence written by David which has brought greater comfort than today's text? I know of the famous little poem called "Footprints" which tells us how there were no longer two sets of footprints on the sands of time but one and the little poem teaches the fact that God, at times, carries us in our trouble. That, in a very real sense, is true. Yet, that is not the truth presented in our text regarding casting our burdens on the Lord.

Here you are, like David, struggling with your appointed lot in life. David discovers that through prayer he can cast his burden upon the Lord. Good. What happens then? A promise comes into vogue. The promise is not that God will carry your burden, but that he will sustain you. Nehemiah has the best commentary on our text. Let these words inspire you. "Forty years you sustained them in the wilderness, so that they lacked nothing; their clothes did not wear out and their feet did not swell"(Nehemiah 9:21). Got it?

S◆E◆P◆T◆E◆M◆B◆E◆R 8TH

"Absalom said to the king, 'Please, let me go to Hebron and pay the vow which I vowed to the Lord. For your servant vowed a vow while I dwelt in Geshur in Syria saying, 'If the Lord indeed brings me back to Jerusalem, then I will serve the Lord"'. 2 Samuel 15:7-8

What believing parent would not have been delighted to hear their child say they wanted to serve the Lord? Could you blame the two hundred friends of David who innocently accepted Abraham's invitation to Hebron to the great religious ceremony he had there? Who could ever have guessed that behind the pious words and the outward show of praise and devotion to God lay a plot hatched in Hell?

Let's be informed. We must not be ignorant of Satan's devices. We must not be always saying "I never thought Satan would use so-in-so, or affect such a cover-up of his intentions". Let's be instructed. Satan's power is limited. He is not omnipotent and he is not omniscient. A wonderful and unique victory was won by the Lord Jesus at Calvary over all the powers of darkness. That victory can be experienced by every individual christian. Let's be imparting. Warn people dabbling in the occult or those disobeying God's Word. Show the way of deliverance. Let's be invading. Take the Bible to Satan's sphere of operation. The Gates of Hell are defensive, not offensive. They can be driven back.

S◆E◆P◆T◆E◆M◆B◆E◆R 9TH

"Then Absalom sent for Ahithophel the Gilonite, David's counsellor, from his city, namely from Giloh, while he offered sacrifices. And the conspiracy grew strong, for the people with Absalom continually increased in number". 2 Samuel 15:12

No action hurt David more in his entire life than the defection of Ahithophel. The Gilonite was David's close counsellor, a statesman who had long advised him in matters of state. When he was swept into Absalom's conspiracy it just about broke David's heart; "For", he wrote, "It is not an enemy who reproaches me; then could I bear it. Nor is it one who hates me who has magnified himself against me; then I could hide from him. But it was you, a man my equal, my companion and my acquaintance. We took sweet counsel together and walked to the House of God in the throng".

What was the motivation of Ahithophel's defection? There is a strong suggestion from a study of genealogical tables that Ahithophel was the grandfather of Bathsheba (See 2 Samuel 11:3 ; 23:34). One thing is certain, Ahithophel's son, Eliam, is listed with Uriah the Hittite as one of David's mighty men. They must have been close. How could David not have realised that the sin he had committed was going to affect his closest friends? It not only affected them; it sickened them and Ahithophel joined the enemy. Watch that your actions do not trigger a defection.

S◆E◆P◆T◆E◆M◆B◆E◆R 10TH

"So David said to all his servants who were with him at Jerusalem. 'Arise and let us flee; or else we shall not escape from Absalom. Make haste to depart, lest he overtake us suddenly and bring disaster upon us, and strike the city with the edge of the sword"'. 2 Samuel 15:14

"Flee". What a word! The seemingly secure domestic situation of the king of Israel is devastated and David becomes a fugitive once more. He who was once hunted like a partridge on the mountain is hunted again. David now faced yet another sudden reversal in his life.

We all face sudden reversals. The Scriptures teach that here we have "No continuing city but we seek one to come". Drastic changes can come very quickly and since things here are most impermanent the quicker we realise it, the better. It will save us a lot of heartache. Half our problem is that we have far too great expectations from things and that is why we are so often disappointed. Don't expect too much from your work, your date, your friends, your local church, your holiday, your ministry, even from your marriage. Unrealistic expectations always end in very real and devastating disappointment. The only one who will never disappoint your expectations is the Lord Jesus. All else is flawed. Get a grip of your expectations and you will uproot your disappointments at the same time.

S✦E✦P✦T✦E✦M✦B✦E✦R 11TH

"Therefore humble yourselves under the mighty hand of God, that he may exalt you in due time". 1 Peter 5:6

David knew very well that he was being chastened by God. Had the Lord not warned him through Natthan that evil would rise against him out of his own house? When Ahithophel defected to Absalom the results were soon nationwide. Ahithophel had huge influence and as a result "The people with Absalom continually increased in number". It must have been with sinking heart that David received the messenger who said, " The hearts of the men of Israel are with Absalom". What a humbling!

The great Victorian preacher Charles Hadden Spurgeon said during his ministry that if the Lord had to humble him, he prayed he would not do it in front of the people. The Lord now brought about the humbling of David, "Before all Israel" (2 Samuel 12:12). The lesson is clear. Don't ask the Lord to humble you for if he has to, it will be a mighty humbling. Rather "Humble yourselves under the mighty hand of God", writes the apostle Peter. So, christian, let's get to work. Let's humble ourselves before the Lord has to do it.

"And the king's servants said to the king, 'We are your servants, ready to do whatever my lord the king commands'". 2 Samuel 15:15

Not everybody defected to Absalom. Not everyone was fooled by the good looking, smooth talking, promise bearing Absalom. Not everyone was impressed by the fifty men who ran before Absalom's chariot every time he rode through town. When the messenger told David that the hearts of the men of Israel were with Absalom, it was generally true, but not altogether. There was mercy mixed with David's chastisement.

The Scriptures show that the servants in David's palace remained absolutely true to him. They were willing to do exactly as he directed. It has been pointed out that there is a principle in this; while we maintain close communion with Christ, who is the anti-typical David, the baits that Satan sets out for us will have no influence over us. In his second letter the apostle Peter expounds this principle clearly; we have to add to our faith virtue, knowledge, self-control, perseverance, godliness, and brotherly kindness. If we do we will not be "Barren nor unfruitful in the knowledge of our Lord Jesus Christ". What is more, adds Peter, if I may paraphrase it, "You will never stumble like me" (1 Peter 1:5-10). If Peter had kept close to Christ instead of running away, he would not have been baited so easily by Satan as he warmed his hands at the fire Christ's enemies had lit. Selah.

" Then all his servants passed before him; and all the Cherethites, all the Pelethites, and the Gittites, six hundred men who had followed him from Gath passed before the king". 2 Samuel 15:18

David did not compel anyone to go with him. They were all volunteers. Interesting, that while the people in Israel deserted him in droves some fascinating people remained loyal who were not Israelites at all! The Cherethites were a Philistine tribe in southern Palestine from whom David drew his bodyguard, commanded by Penaiah. The Gittites were natives of Gath, Goliath's town and six hundred of them were in David's bodyguard. Both these groups remained loyal to him. Sad, isn't it, that even today more Gentiles follow David's greater Son than do Israelites? But he compels none, any more than David did.

When Mrs. Raisa Gorbachov came to London, once, she was given the opportunity to visit whatever public place of interest she liked. She chose St. Paul's Cathedral and paused by Holman Hunt's picture "Christ the Light of the World". She read the text from Revelation 3 verse 20 underneath the painting and stepped back. We contacted the Dean of St. Paul's and he told us that he then stepped forward and explained to Mrs. Gorbachov that Holman Hunt's painting represented Christ knocking at the door of a person's life. He had deliberately omitted an outside door knob because he said the door of the human life must be opened from the inside to the knocking Christ. The Dean explained to Mrs. Gorbachov that the Lord Jesus never enters anyone's life by force. He enters by invitation. Thus it was that one of the most famous women in the world got the Gospel, pure and simple in the heart of London.

S✦E✦P✦T✦E✦M✦B✦E✦R 14TH

"In fact, you came only yesterday. Should I make you wander up and down with us today, since I go I know not where? Return, and take your brethren back. Mercy and truth be with you". 2 Samuel 15:20

Blood ties don't always guarantee friendship. David's own son was his worst enemy while Ittai, a total stranger and foreigner who seems to have been the leader of the six hundred Gittites in David's bodyguard, remains totally loyal to David. The king is so moved by Ittai's friendship that he gives him an opportunity to turn back. "Mercy and truth be with you", he says.

If you had opportunity today to turn back from following your king, the Lord Jesus, would you go? It makes us think of that wonderful verse in Hebrews 11 which speaks of Abraham and his call from God. Speaking of him as typical of all who leave many impermanent things for the permanent it notes "Truly if they had called to mind that country from which they had come out they would have had opportunity to return but now they desire a better, that is, a heavenly country. Therefore God is not ashamed to be called their God for he has prepared a city for them". Imagine if Abraham, having given up all the glories of his own country, arrived in Heaven and found it a disappointment; what would happen? God would be ashamed. Will it happen? No! Why? Because the verse says "Therefore God is not ashamed to be called their God for he has prepared a city for them". No one will be ultimately disappointed that they left anything for the Lord's sake; the very integrity of God would be at stake if it were otherwise.

S✦E✦P✦T✦E✦M✦B✦E✦R 15TH

"And Ittai answered the king and said, 'As the Lord lives, and as my lord the king lives, surely in whatever place my lord the king shall be, whether in death or life, even there also your servant will be"'. 2 Samuel 15:21

What had David to offer this man? Outwardly, very little. His cause now had minority backing. His throne was under fearsome attack. To be associated with him meant that you were taking your life in your hands. To be loyal to him meant that the establishment looked down on you. Promotion was out. Prospects were nil.

What drew such absolute loyalty? David's companionship. If it meant being associated with David's sufferings, so be it. Ittai had no doubt that David's companionship along the narrow path was much better than Absalom's companionship along a very broad one. Notice the emphasis in our text is squarely fixed on Ittai being with David; "Whatever place my Lord the king shall be whether in life or death, even there also your servant will be". As a lad, for about six months, I used to go to a Sunday School in a place called Ballywillwill. I can still feel the heat of the old pot-belly stove, hear the hiss of the gas lamps and hear the ticking of the old clock on the wall as I sat there as a little boy. I can still remember reading and re-reading the text above the inside door. It read "Where"; the Divine place. "Two or three";

the Divine testimony. "Are gathered"; Divine separation. "Together"; Divine fellowship. "In my name"; Divine authority. "There am I"; the Divine presence. "In the midst of them"; the Divine centre. It could almost be Ittai and his men's epitaph, couldn't it!?

S♦E♦P♦T♦E♦M♦B♦E♦R 16TH

"So David said to Ittai, 'Go, and cross over'. Then Ittai the Gittite and all his men and all the little ones who were with him crossed over. And all the country wept with a loud voice, and all the people crossed over. The king himself also crossed over the Brook Kidron, and all the people crossed over towards the way of the wilderness". 2 Samuel 15:22-23

Isn't there something fascinating about the name of rivers and brooks? They weave in and out of our lives and it is not for nothing that signs are put up by highway bridges to tell you the name of the river you are crossing. No christian eye could fail to notice the connection between the brook in today's text and the life of Christ. The brook, called the Kidron, over which the persecuted David and his few followers passed was the very same brook over which the persecuted Saviour passed on his way to the cross.

For me rivers speak of time, of place, of history. You never cross the same river twice. Next time it is a different river and you are a different person. Have you ever stared at a river bubbling by and thought "Where is my life going? What is it all about?" Millions of people have had that experience. David's sorrows have long since passed. Today, perhaps, it is your turn to know deep sorrow or anxiety. Think of the one who crossed the Kidron to Gethsemane on that infamous night. He looked into the cup of sorrow that he was soon to drink at Calvary and willingly he went on and drained it, completely. Take your griefs and your sorrows to him. Life certainly flows on but as He stood still at the cry of a Bartimaeus, He will do the very same at your cry. The Kidron crosser is the grief bearer. He is Jesus Christ the same, yesterday and today and for ever.

S✦E✦P✦T✦E✦M✦B✦E✦R 17TH

" Then the king said to Zadok, 'Carry the ark of God back into the city. If I find favour in the eyes of the Lord, he will bring me back and show me both it and his habitation. But if he says thus: 'I have no delight in you,' here I am, let him do to me as seems good to him" '. 2 Samuel 15:25-26

David knew very well that he was being chastened by the Lord for his sin. He refused to allow the ark of God to be exposed to all the dangers of his present circumstances and ordered it back to Jerusalem. He knew also that if the people saw the ark of God in his camp they would reckon that he had God on his side and David refused to pretend that all was well with him spiritually. He decided rather to throw himself upon the "Favour", or, grace of God; if God wanted him back in Jerusalem he would bring him back, despite Absalom.

No person who ever threw themselves on the grace of God was yet disappointed. If you put God between yourself and your failures in repentance and fear and trust in his grace to order your ways, you will be forgiven and guided. It stops arrogance, rebellion and scheming in your life. Throw yourself on God's grace and grace itself will come shining through in every detail of your life. It will oil your marriage, it will help eradicate jealousy in your heart, it will transform you. Look at how kind and considerate David is at this time in his life. It is his best side. Why? Because he is submissive to the grace of God. May you be the same.

S✦E✦P✦T✦E✦M✦B✦E✦R 18TH

"So David went up by the ascent of the Mount of Olives, and wept as he went up; and he had his head covered and went barefoot. And all the people who were with him covered their heads and went up, weeping as they went up". 2 Samuel 15:30

The way of the transgressor is hard. The sight of a weeping, barefooted, head covered David going up the Mount of Olives and the people following him, weeping, must have been a very moving sight. If you are tempted by sin's lure, today, remember what it did to the mighty David. See the conquering hero of the valley of Elah, the giant killer, the sweet singer of the world, the founder of a dynasty of kings, a prophet, inspired and taught by the Holy Spirit, laid so very low.

Is this weeping, heartbroken, barefooted man the same David who danced with joy in that city over there when God gave his people a great victory? It is the very same David, his sin ever before him (Psalm 1:3). But see, years down the line David's greater Son enter Gethsemane by this very same city and with "Strong crying and tears", not for his own sins but ours, ready himself for Calvary's cross. Are you like David, crying today, if not outwardly, inwardly? Crying, perhaps, for sins you have done? Aren't you glad you have the answer? Rejoice in it. If our greatest need had been for information, God would have sent us an educator. If our greatest need had been technology, God would have sent us a scientist. If our greatest need had been money, God would have sent us a economist. If our greatest need had been pleasure, God would have sent us an entertainer. But our greatest need was forgiveness, so God sent us a Saviour.

S✦E✦P✦T✦E✦M✦B✦E✦R 19TH

"Then someone told David, saying, 'Ahithophel is among the conspirators with Absalom'. And David said, 'O Lord, I pray, turn the counsel of Ahithophel into foolishness!"'. 2 Samuel 15:31

As if things were not bad enough! As David climbs the Mount of Olives weeping sorely over his troubles the news of his best friend's treachery is given to him. The man he had taken "Sweet counsel" with; the man with whom he had "Walked to the House of God"; "My own familiar friend", wrote David later, "In whom I trusted, who ate my bread, has lifted up his heel against me". It was an awful twisting of the knife of David's sorrows.

Do your friends despise and forsake you? Take it to the Lord in prayer. David did. He knew that one good head was worth a thousand hands and if Ahithophel could be baffled then Absalom could be defeated. He asked the Lord to turn Ahithophel's advice into foolishness. He didn't plot to kill him or rage against him, he just took him to the Lord in prayer. Do you see the wise and lovely side of David's character coming out again when he is contrite and humble? Do you see him being exercised by the chastening of the Lord?

The Scripture says "Now no chastening seems to be joyful for the present, but grievous; nevertheless, afterward it yields the peaceable fruit of righteousness to those who have been trained (disciplined) by it. Therefore strengthen the hands which hang down, and the feeble knees and make straight paths for your feet, so that what is lame may not be dislocated, but rather healed". Little did the barefooted David realise as the "Arrow" of Ahithophel's defection hit him on the slopes of Olivet that by handing him over to the Lord and accepting him as God's chastening rod that he was forging a straight path for himself back to healing, restoration and the throne. Selah.

S◆E◆P◆T◆E◆M◆B◆E◆R 20TH

"Lord, how they have increased who trouble me! Many are they who rise up against me". Psalm 3:1

Could it be that David sang the third psalm at the top of the Mount of Olives? There is a strong hint of it. The third psalm is the first psalm to bear a title and it says "A Psalm of David when he fled from Absalom", and we are told that the weary David worshipped God when he finally ascended the Mount of Olives.

David opens the third psalm with a question which had arisen at this time. It was a rumour that God had withdrawn from him. "Many are they who say of me, 'There is no help for him in God'." Now we are talking about the greatest spiritual poet in history; we are talking about a man, the bent of whose whole life was after God's own heart. Yet, many, had set a rumour going that such a man, once he fell into sin, could expect no help from God. And rumour spreads. And it hurts. Shakespeare got it right when he wrote;

"Rumour is a pipe, blown by surmises, jealousies, conjectures, and of so easy and so plain a stop, that the blunt monster with uncounted heads, the still-discordant wavering multitude, can play upon it."

Have you played on the pipe of rumour, today? You may add great sorrow to an already sorrowful heart when your tune is heard. Save your breath to encourage someone, for encouragement is the oxygen of the soul.

S✦E✦P✦T✦E✦M✦B✦E✦R 21ST

"But you, O Lord, are a shield for me, my glory and the one who lifts up my head". Psalm 3:3

Fewer heads in history have gone lower than David's. Look at the pressures on him. "How they are increased that trouble me", he writes. He writes of "Tens of thousands of people who have set themselves against me all around". His family has fallen apart, his throne has been challenged, his very nation is rent with disorder and rebellion, his own sin haunts him, his moral authority is gone, he is, in the eyes of many, finished. His head is down, his life seemingly wrecked.

But, no. Look at David's expectation. It is this in him that makes him so appealing to millions of us whose lives have known the onslaught of Satan and failure and distress. He does not turn now to his former scheming and living on his wits; the Lord, he says, is his shield. And yours? Of course. "My glory and the lifter up of my head". All earthly glory fades. Where now the Pharaoh's, the Roman Emperor's, the Ottoman's, the Napoleon's, the Stalin's, the Hitler's, the Lenin's? Gone. Let him who glories, glory in the Lord. David did just that and that's why his life is a blessing to this very day. Whether your life is a blessing or not depends on one thing; it lies in whom you glory.

S✦E✦P✦T✦E✦M✦B✦E✦R 22ND

"I lay down and slept; I awoke, for the Lord sustained me". Psalm 3:5

One of the most popular places for tourists in London are the War Cabinet Rooms where one can go underground and see where the British War Cabinet met during the dark days of World War II. There you can see the bed Sir Winston Churchill slept in as bombs exploded all around him. It certainly is not the world's most luxurious bed and sleep could never have been easy.

Are you suffering from insomnia? It is interesting that David writes of sleep during this dark hour of his life, not of what he ate, or drank, or whatever. Why, sleep? Staying in New Jersey once I came to breakfast and asked my hostess how she had slept. "I don't know", she said, "I was asleep!" I laughed. David knew, though, where the secret of his peaceful sleep came from. "The Lord", he said, "Sustained me". It was the sense of forgiveness, of pardon, of the love of God in his soul, that kept him going. I can testify that over twenty years of travelling, writing and preaching in the service of Christ, the thing that keeps me going is the joy of the Lord. Even if illness itself is keeping you awake, the joy of the Lord will be your strength. Such was David's certainty that God had heard and would answer his prayer he knew he could face the worst. So can you. Let the certainty of the peace of God be your pillow, tonight.

S✦E✦P✦T✦E✦M✦B✦E✦R 23RD

"Now it happened when David had come to the top of the mountain, where he worshipped God, that there was Hushai the Archite, coming to meet him with his robe torn and dust on his head. David said to him, 'If you go on with me, then you will become a burden to me. But if you return to the city, and say to Absalom, 'I will be your servant, O king; just as I have been your father's servant previously, so I will now also be your servant' then you may defeat the counsel of Ahithophel for me". 2 Samuel 15:32-34

I honestly wish that I didn't have to write about today's text. I wish I could by-pass what happened next. David had been behaving so well, trusting so wisely, walking so carefully and suddenly, there before him stood Hushai, an old friend. That Hushai's robe was torn and dust was on his head showed publicly how he felt about Absalom's rebellion. His dress was akin to a Victorian black armband. He mourned the departure of David from his throne.

It has been suggested that Hushai was sent by God at that precise moment in David's life as a test. The more I think about it, the more I am convinced that suggestion is true. All of us are tested by God in what we say and David had said his trust was in God alone. Why then did he send Hushai back to Jerusalem to be a spy, under the pretence that he was a true servant of Absalom? The thing was a lie. God overruled, yes, just like he overruled the lie of Rahab the harlot, but his overruling didn't make David's lie any less a lie. Don't make David's mistake for your scheming will leave a blot on your testimony for generations to come, just like the blot it left on David's.

S✦E✦P✦T✦E✦M✦B✦E✦R 24TH

"When David was a little past the top of the mountain there was Ziba the servant of Mephibosheth, who met him with a couple of saddled donkeys, and on them two hundred loaves of bread, one hundred clusters of raisins, one hundred summer fruits, and a skin of wine". 2 Samuel 16:1-2

David was hungry and tired, abandoned by friends, and was heading for seeming oblivion. Suddenly he is approached by a man profering kindness. He has donkeys for David's servants to ride on, food for his young men to eat, wine for those who are near exhaustion in the wilderness. It was no mirage; David, the deposed king is being offered support. Who would have realised that the whole operation was a trap? David, particularly susceptible to kindness, walked right into the trap. Ziba was snaking his way passed David's defences to further his own end.

Here was Satan in the guise of an angel. Here was a wolf in sheep's clothing. Here was poison covered by sugar coating. Here is a warning to all of us not to be fooled by outward appearances. There are plenty of examples in modern life of the Ziba approach.

Just the other day I read of gifts being showered on the International Olympic Committee members, for example, by city fathers wanting the Olympic Games in their city. Bribery stalks the corridors of power in politics, big business often reeks with back-handers. Few are the men and women of this world who cannot be bought or influenced by material gain, especially when they are going through a time of financial trouble or material scarcity. Watch the Ziba approach. Better that you walk than ride his donkeys, better that you go thirsty than drink his wine, better that you go hungry than feast on his luscious summer fruits.

S•E•P•T•E•M•B•E•R 25TH

" Then the king said, 'And where is your master's son?' And Ziba said to the king, 'Indeed he is staying in Jerusalem, for he said, 'Today the house of Israel will restore the kingdom of my father to me'. So the king said to Ziba, 'Here, all that belongs to Mephibosheth is yours'. And Ziba said, 'I humbly bow before you, that I may find favour in your sight my lord, O king!"' 2 Samuel 16:3-4

Don't you think that some people are very good at spending other people's money? All that Ziba was now offering David belonged to Mephibosheth. It was obvious that David was going to ask about Mephibosheth and Ziba had long planned the moment. He answered with a downright lie. He told David that Mephibosheth had stayed behind in Jerusalem in order to see Israel restored to the house of Saul. The thing was a slander because, as we shall soon see, Mephibosheth couldn't have been more loyal to David.

Few of us have not succumbed to believing slander. The Scriptures teach that we must not receive an accusation against anyone except at the mouths of two or three reliable witnesses. David misjudged Mephibosheth because he had a prejudice in his heart. He was so angry at Absalom's treachery, so angry at Ahithophel's defection, so frustrated at his own seemingly helpless position that the couldn't see the wood for the trees. Prejudice is the greatest enemy of truth. Be very careful that you are not so consumed by your present problems that you judge everything and everybody by them. Don't get paranoiac and abandon friends who are loyal to you. It was a cruel action when David gave Mephibosheth's lands to the flattering Ziba. Notice that Ziba didn't accompany David into the wilderness. He stayed on the safe side to see how things would turn out.

I tell you, there are people you might abandon friends for today who wouldn't take time off to go to your funeral tomorrow.

"Now when King David came to Bahurim, there was a man from the family of the house of Saul, whose name was Shimei the son of Gera, coming from there. He came out, cursing continuously as he came. And he threw stones at David and at all the servants of King David. And all the people and all the mighty men were on his right hand and on his left". 2 Samuel 16:5-6

We have been to Bahurim before in this story. It was to Bahurim that the weeping Paltiel came when David wrested Michal back (See 2 Samuel 3:14-16). It was a very different David who walks through Bahurim now. Then he got what he wanted, now he is aware he would be better taking what God wants. Running among the rocks of the glen above David is a man called Shimei. For years Shimei had hated David and now his fury erupts. He curses David, ruthlessly. He calls him a rogue and a bloodthirsty man.

Although this incident was allowed by God to humble David it in no way excuses what Shimei did. It is very wrong to take advantage of someone's trouble and to hurt them when they are down. Yes, David deserved to be cursed. Yes, David was certainly guilty of shedding innocent blood but to abuse and curse him when he was down was wrong. Never rejoice when your enemy falls or use the occasion to turn the screw on him. Be silent. Shimei was later to bitterly regret what he had done (See 2 Samuel 19:19-20). If you lift hand or foot to hurt a man when he is down you too will bitterly regret it.

S✦E✦P✦T✦E✦M✦B✦E✦R 27TH

And David said to Abishai and all his servants, 'See how my son who came from my own body seeks my life. How much more now may this Benjamite? Let him alone, and let him curse; for so the Lord has ordered him. 'It may be that the Lord will look on my affliction, and that the Lord will repay me with good for his cursing this day'. And as David and his men went along the road, Shimei went along the hillside opposite him and cursed as he went, threw stones at him and kicked up dust". 2 Samuel 16 - 13

"So, let him curse", is a good watchword as you go on with your life today. So, someone has found flaws in your life? Why should that stop you serving God? Who hasn't got flaws? Because they are pointing them out to all and sundry doesn't mean you should give up. Wasn't Moses a murderer? Wasn't Jacob a con-man? Wasn't Paul a ruthless bigot?

Wasn't John Newton a slave trader? Didn't D. L. Moody throw a man down the stairs in a temper and break his leg? Didn't George Muller say "Lord I want to be a missionary. If you want me to be one then let the horse I back in this race win and then I'll know you want me to be a missionary!". All of us sin and make silly mistakes and any Kitty Kelley could easily find them and catalogue them in an unofficial biography of our lives but that does not disqualify us from God's forgiveness and willingness to use us again. So, "Let him curse" was one of the wisest things David ever said.

S✦E✦P✦T✦E✦M✦B✦E✦R 28TH

"Now the king and all the people who were with him became weary; so they refreshed themselves there" . 2 Samuel 16:14

It was a surprise. I discovered the American who had opened the service at which I was speaking was called Mr. Bert Elliot, brother of the famed christian martyr to Ecuador, Mr. Jim Elliot. Later, at tea, we struck up conversation and got to talking about preaching and the various different approaches that are taken to it. Then Mr. Elliot let slip a little statement that has lived with me ever since. He pointed out that Isaiah had been given a word from God to "Them that are weary". "If you have a word for "Them that are weary"', said Mr. Elliot, "Other preachers mightn't like it but the weary sure will!"

All my life I have tried to remember that there is a broken heart in every congregation. A word to the broken-hearted is never wasted. Wherever you go today, you will not go far before you come across people who are weary with life and its circumstances. Even a king like David, as our text shows, becomes weary. Wouldn't it be good if you could say something or do something to refresh the weary today? If that weary one may be;

"Stronger for the strength I bring, Sweeter for the songs I sing, Happier for the path I thread, Lighter for the light I shed, Richer for the gifts I give, Purer for the life I live, Nobler for the death I die, Not in vain have I been I."

"And so it was, when Hushai the Archite, David's friend, came to Absalom, that Hushai said to Absalom, 'Long live the king! Long live the king!' So Absalom said to Hushai, 'Is this your loyalty to your friend? Why did you not go with your friend?' And Hushai said to Absalom, 'No, but whom the Lord and this people and all the men of Israel choose, his I will be, and with him I will remain"'. 2 Samuel 16:16-18

Absalom was not long in setting himself up as king in Jerusalem. Hushai, David's great friend had been sent in to Absalom's camp as a spy and it was not long before Absalom challenged him as to his loyalty. "Is this your loyalty to your friend?", he asks. There never was anything in the Bible to commend Absalom; he was a heartless, ungrateful, spoilt, miserable character who wouldn't stop at killing his own father for his own end. God had left him to himself and there is no telling what human nature will stoop to when that happens. Yet, he put a very haunting question to Israel's great politician, Hushai. There is even honour among thieves and Absalom was very surprised to see Hushai in his camp; "Is this your loyalty to your friend? Why did you not go with your friend?", he asks. Even Absalom couldn't understand Hushai's not being with David.

Could it be that some debauched, ungodly person has found you in some place this week and wondered why you were there? Could it be that the language I used or the jokes I told at that dinner or function this week made an ungodly mind question as to whether or not I was truly a christian? Hushai's answer was ambiguous but if he had done what he truly should have done, and identified with David in his situation outside Absalom's camp, his answer would never have been ambiguous.

"Is this your loyalty to your friend?
You, warming your hands by that crackling fire?
Why do you curse and to what end?
Explain these oaths mixed with your ire.

Is this your loyalty to your friend?
You, who kiss the Son of God,
Would you the Christ to Calvary send,
To buy a piece of this earth's sod?

Is this your loyalty to your friend?
You who love this present world,
How could you leave an imprisoned Paul,
And keep your flag unfurled?

Much may happen today, my Lord,
But when it comes to an end,
May all I have done strike up this chord,
He was loyal to his heavenly friend."
                                        D.B.

S✦E✦P✦T✦E✦M✦B✦E✦R 30TH

*"I will come upon him while he is weary and weak, and make him afraid.
And all the people who are with him will flee, and I will strike only the
king". 2 Samuel 17:2*

Ahithophel was no fool. He knew David as no man knew
him. For years the counsel of Ahithophel had been to David as
if he had been enquiring at the oracle of God. Now evil had got
hold of Ahithophel and instead of being an oracle of God he was
the very oracle of Satan. Notice Satan's strategy about
Ahithophel's advise in capturing David; it was to strike him
when he was weary and weak.

Even armies use this strategy. The Russians let Napoleon
attack Moscow, leaving the city to him, and then when the
winter came they let it starve him homewards. As his weary,
freezing army staggered in retreat the Russian army picked
them off. Beware when you are tired. Watch what you say,
where you go. Satan is watching. Call in Heaven's reinforce-
ments, for when you are weak, then you are strong. But you are
only strong in the Lord. If I can pass on my experience to you I
would say this; in twenty years of "Full time" christian service
I have often failed most and made my biggest mistakes when I
was weary. "No major decisions should be taken after 10.00 p.m.
at night", warns my experienced friend Dr. Harold Love. I wish
I had known that earlier in life. Now you know it, remember it.

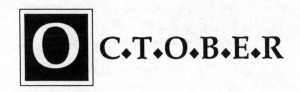

OCTOBER

O✦C✦T✦O✦B✦E✦R

*I*t happens in all our lives; it is called the law of cause and effect. Your harvest is directly proportional to your sowing. David sowed to the flesh and he reaped the flesh. If he had, in middle age, sowed to the Spirit he would have reaped the Spirit. The rebellion of Absalom and its consequences came as a chastisement from God upon David and there are deep spiritual lessons to learn from it. "No chastening seems to be joyful for the present", says the Book of Hebrews, "But grievous; nevertheless, afterwards it yields the peaceable fruit of righteousness to those who have been trained by it". Thankfully some lovely peaceable fruits of righteousness flowed from David's experience and, during October we shall seek to gather some of them for a spiritual harvest.

O✦C✦T✦O✦B✦E✦R 1ST

"So Absalom and all the men of Israel said, ' The counsel of Hushai the Archite is better than the counsel of Ahithophel'. For the Lord had proposed to defeat the good counsel of Ahithophel, to the intent that the Lord might bring disaster on Absalom." 2 Samuel 17:14

Where does the centre of power lie in our world today? The United Nations? The European Community? Washington? Paris? Moscow? Peking? Every christian knows that the centre of power lies in the Lord's hands for "The Most High rules in the kingdom of men and gives it to whoever he will" (Dan 4:17,25,32). The Lord works a purpose out through all the deliberations of political leaders in international affairs, and through much lesser lights as well. In the story of David's deliverance from Absalom, if you study it carefully you will see that the Lord used a prominent politician, two priests, a maidservant and a farmer and his wife to get David out of Absalom's net.

I often think of Lord Radstock (a relation of William Waldergrave the prominent British politician). Radstock was guided by God to visit St. Petersburg in the late 1800's. Quietly he presented the Gospel in the drawing rooms of the aristocrats. One by one people started to be converted and the word of the Gospel spread. I have it on good authority that as a direct influence of Radstock's preaching two million people across Russia and Poland were converted over the next 100 years and that the policy of "Perestroika" was heavily influenced by the christian corner of the former Soviet Union, which brought about, in particular, the fall of Communism. Don't despise the day of small things. The Gospel you speak today might touch a whole generation to follow you.

O✦C✦T✦O✦B✦E✦R 2ND

"Therefore I counsel that all Israel be fully gathered to you, from Dan to Beersheba, like the sand that is by the sea for multitude, and that you go to battle in person". 2 Samuel 17:11

Ahithophel had counselled an immediate attack on David. "Now let me chose 12,000 men and I will arise and pursue David tonight", he had said. Hushai David's spy, is asked for his advice and he stalls for time to allow David to escape. He tries to show that taking David is no easy task and all Israel needs to be mobilised. Ahithophel had wanted to lead his 12,000 men against David but Hushai counsels that Absalom had better lead Israel himself.

Immediately Absalom responds to Hushai's advice. "The counsel of Hushai the Archite is better than the counsel of Absalom," he concludes. We can see very clearly the underlying vanity. Absalom wanted to be the big man, Absalom wanted to be "No. 1". Everything had to be related to him and if it wasn't he was going to make sure that it was. Pride, though, always goes before destruction and a haughty spirit before a fall. Absalom's vanity led him straight to his death. If he had listened to Ahithophel he would have stayed back in Jerusalem but by leading Israel he ended up hanging in death in the bough's of an oak.

Has some crafty individual arisen in your district and is he or she causing mayhem to the peace of your home, your church, or your community? Do you feel there will never be an end to the heartache being caused? Let me turn your attention to a little text in the book of Job. It says God "Catches the wise in their own craftiness and the counsel of the cunning comes quickly upon them. They meet with darkness in the daytime and grope at noontime as in the night". Selah

O◆C◆T◆O◆B◆E◆R 3RD

"Now when Ahithophel saw that his counsel was not followed, he saddled his donkey, and arose and went home to his house, to his city. Then he put his household in order, and hanged himself, and died; and he was buried in his father's tomb". 2 Samuel 17:23

Suicide. No more chilling word exists in human experience. Yet, the Bible draws a strange curtain of silence around it. Let us not be too quick to condemn those who have committed this awful act. Who knows what intolerable pressure has come to bear down upon the mind of the suicide? Yes, Ahithophel certainly felt thwarted when his advice was refused by Absalom. Yes, Ahithophel had been the most outstanding political adviser in Israel and it must have been galling to play second fiddle to Hushai. Yes, his pride was hurt. But as we read this solemn, heartbreaking account of the great Ahithophel setting his house in order and then hanging himself can we not see a deeper motivation? It was disillusionment with David's behaviour that sparked his rebellion in the first place and led him to suicide.

We live in a "Devil-may-care" society. The philosophy of the Western world is "Do your own thing". In our technological society we often tend to think that people are like machines, too! But they aren't. Folk's hearts are the same today as they were 2,000 years before Christ, in David's day. If someone puts their trust in you and you betray that sacred trust, you could lead them to suicide. If you think I am exaggerating pay a visit to the house of Ahithophel.

O♦C♦T♦O♦B♦E♦R 4TH

" Then David went to Mahanaim. And Absalom crossed over the Jordan, he and all the men of Israel with him". 2 Samuel 17:24

Mahanaim means "Double camp". It was named by Jacob on his way to meet Esau because some angels of God met him there. He was saying "This isn't just my camp, this is God's camp". He was saying "If God be for me, who can be against me?" Let us pause at Mahanaim ourselves, for a moment's meditation.

What does this truth mean that "If God be for us who can be against us?" It is a truth, if you get a hold of it, that will correct emotional thinking with evangelical thinking. It means no opposition can finally crush us. It means no good thing will finally be withheld from us. We will get all the good that God can think of, not that we can think of. It means no accusation can ever disinherit us. With such assurances you can get out there and face the day or night.

O♦C♦T♦O♦B♦E♦R 5TH

"O God, you are my God; early will I seek you; my soul thirsts for you; my flesh longs for you in a dry and thirsty land where there is no water. So I have looked for you in the sanctuary, to see your power and your glory".
Psalm 63:3-4

David was knocked down but he was not knocked out. Psalm 63 is set at this time in David's life and, as with other Psalms, it gives us a very clear indication of how he felt. The thing he missed most of all was not his throne, nor his family, nor the opportunity to wield power; the thing he really missed was God's house. Passing through some of the wildest and most discouraging country in all Israel, (I've been across it myself and wilderness it certainly is), David felt thirst but it was nothing to his longing for God. Even when fleeing his throne in the heart of a wilderness David was after God's own heart.

As John Philips has said "Pleasure is God's invention. Satan has never been able to manufacture a single genuine lasting pleasure. We are drawn back to God for the true enjoyment of life and David knew that better than most. The word David uses for "Longing" can be translated "Fainting". The word occurs nowhere else. David's craving after God was not just mental, emotional or volitional, but an actual physical craving. It left him physically weak. This desire, above all other qualities in David's life marks him out far above his contemporaries'. Does it mark you?

O◆C◆T◆O◆B◆E◆R 6TH

"Because your loving-kindness is better than life my lips shall praise you"
Psalm 63:3

Life. What is it? A vapour that soon vanishes away. There is that young fellow jogging along the road, fit, resolute, sleek, all of life in front of him. Yet the Scriptures tell us that "Even the youths shall faint and be weary and the young men shall utterly fall". Time, eventually touches everything. The loveliest home soon needs new window sashes, or a fresh paint. The most brilliant Prime Minister and his or her cabinet has their day. The most expensive car, corrodes. The greatest singer's voice goes. The greatest artist's eyes grow faint. The glory of life in whatever form is transient.

Time, though, is foiled in God. His loving kindness is better than life. No ravage of time can corrode or taint, mar or sweep away the grace of God. In the midst of a miserable wilderness and a spate of desperately sad circumstances David refuses to let anything dissuade him from the assurance of the loving kindness of God. Life is a desert without it. He lifts up his hands in praise and in service as loving kindness is shown to him.

How easy it is to forget a kindness. Is there any sin in all the world worse than the sin of ingratitude? That the Lord Jesus should die for me and then for me, in ingratitude to take my own life and try to run it my own way, is ingratitude of the worst kind. Let's live our lives out in gratitude to the one who died for us.

O◆C◆T◆O◆B◆E◆R 7TH

"My soul shall be satisfied as with marrow and fatness, and my mouth shall praise you with joyful lips". Psalm 63:5

One thing is for sure, the Bible teaches that you don't need comfortable, secure, compatible circumstances in order to be content and happy. Here is David stripped of everything that people would believe to be conducive to the "Good Life". And he is saying "I have a God who keeps me satisfied and a God who keeps me singing".

It reminds us of Paul who had exactly the same experience, though in somewhat different circumstances. Paul was brought up from the cells before King Agrippa, in chains. There the great king sits in pomp and circumstance and Paul stands before him dishevelled and bound. "You are permitted to speak for yourself", says the king. Now, what did Paul say? Did he complain about his chains and say he would make Rome ungovernable, that he would mobilise the christians to march on Agrippa's palace? His first words are priceless; "I think myself happy, King Agrippa". What? Happy? He then proceeds to tell the king his conversion story and his heart overflows as he speaks of Christ. "Therefore", he says, "Having obtained help from God, to this day I stand, witnessing both to small and great saying no other things than those which the prophets and Moses said would come - that Christ would suffer, that he would be the first to rise from the dead and would proclaim light to the Jewish people and to the Gentiles". "You almost persuade me to become a christian", said Agrippa. No wonder!

David and Paul would teach us, today, not to feel sorry for ourselves. You, christian, have the Lord and He is enough. Let others see that He is in the depths of your circumstances, even this very day.

O•C•T•O•B•E•R 8TH

"When I remember you on my bed, I meditate on you in the night watches".
Psalm 63:6

David's bed was certainly not in the Wilderness Hilton, was it? He had an army chasing him, ready to "Fall on him as the dew falls on the ground". Their purpose was that "Of him and all the men who were with him there shall not be left so much as one". Insomnia would invade David as he lay under the stars but instead of worrying and fretting, he thought about God. All minds will be kept in perfect peace who stop at God.

"Because you have been my help", says David, "Therefore in the shadow of your wings I will rejoice". Obviously David let his mind run back through the times when God had helped him in the past. It is a good cure for insomnia. It is a most healthy spiritual exercise which, unfortunately, we do not often practise. F. B. Meyer put it this way; "Do you think", he asked, "That the God who brought you across the Atlantic is going to drown you in a ditch?" Recall all the help of God to you in the past and it will fire you for the future. The God who found you, saved you, kept you, loved you, guided you, blessed you is not going to desert you now.

O•C•T•O•B•E•R 9TH

"Because you have been my help, therefore in the shadow of your wings I will rejoice". Psalm 63:7

I was always told that eagles pushed eaglets out of nests and as the eaglets plummeted through space they just had to use their wings. Then the eagles would swoop and catch the eaglets on their wings and bring them to safety. That, I was told, was the interpretation of the Bible verse which speaks of God bearing Israel on eagle's wings.

The only problem was I could find no ornithologist to back up what I had been told. "By the time the eaglets are ready to fly", I was told by an expert, "It would be aerodynamically impossible for their parents to catch them on their wings". So, what did the verse mean? Then, one day, I discovered the answer when reading about the American bald eagle. It seems that the eaglets fly themselves and then the parent comes behind and the flapping of his or her wings creates air currents to give the eaglet, lift. The Hebrew word for "Bear" is "Lift". Can you imagine the comfort of having the shadow of those mighty wings around you, if you were an eaglet, flying? Far greater the comfort, christian, that you abide under the shadow of God's wings. They will give you "Lift" as nothing else will.

O◆C◆T◆O◆B◆E◆R 10TH

"My soul follows close behind you; your right hand upholds me".
Psalm 63:8

Do you not find it incredible that suddenly you arrive in a situation in your christian life and God has been there ahead of you? This, of course, is the work of the Eastern shepherd. He goes before his sheep. No good shepherd would take sheep into territory that he had not first of all checked out for himself. He would take weedkiller, or bags of salt or whatever, to clear the way for the flock he is about to lead onto that ground. So David knows that the Lord, his shepherd, goes before him, even though most of Israel is coming after him to try to kill him!

David crept closer behind God the closer Absalom got to him. God's mighty hand came down and encircled him. So, whatever way you look at your problem today, christian, the Lord is ahead of you dealing with it. Follow him and he will make your mountain a way.

O◆C◆T◆O◆B◆E◆R 11TH

"But those who seek my life, to destroy it, shall go into the lower parts of the earth. They shall fall by the sword; they shall be a portion for jackals".
Psalm 63:9-10

Bismark said "Might is Right". Voltaire said "God is on the side of the big battalions". "Even Jesus Christ himself couldn't sink this ship", someone wrote on the side of the Titanic when she sat in the slips in Belfast. Bismark and his armies have gone. Voltaire died screaming " The Nazarene! The Nazarene! The Nazarene!". An iceberg sliced the mighty Cunard's liner and she sank to the bottom.

At the stage David wrote today's text the battle with Absalom hadn't been enjoined. David had but a few people around him. Yet, he knew the Lord would not fail him. What actually happened when the fateful day came? The battle was enjoined in the woods of Ephraim and, we are told, "The woods devoured more people that day than the sword devoured". God used the terrain to affect what David could never affect. God knows not only the timing in our lives but the place where we are. Don't despise "The place", even if it be a wood. Has God placed you in an obscure place? No place is obscure to God. The woods of Ephraim became one of the most famous places of victory in the history of God's people.

O✦C✦T✦O✦B✦E✦R 12TH

"Now it happened, when David came to Mahanaim, Shobi the son of Nahash from Rabbah of the people of Ammon ... brought beds and basins, earthen vessels and wheat, barley and flour, parched grain and beans, lentils and parched seeds, honey and curds, sheep and cheese of the herd, for David and the people who were with him to eat" . 2 Samuel 17:27-29

When you come into tough, heartbreaking circumstances it is always a good thing to make a note of the things God sends to comfort you. Keep a diary (or a mental note). When you get depressed it makes good reading to go over the means God has used to lift your spirits in the past. If you have a note of it then you can pass it on to someone in a similar circumstance; always pass comfort on.

But comfort isn't always accepted, is it? You may try to pass on comfort and be rebuffed. We are told that when the king of the people of Ammon died David tried to comfort his son, Hanun by showing him kindness, as his father had shown kindness to David in the past. But Hanun suspected David of ulterior motives, treated the men he sent disgracefully, and raised an army to fight Israel! Some reaction to comfort, wasn't it?

See, though, how God rewards David for his attempt to comfort. Years later, when hounded by Absalom, Shobi the very brother of Hanun the king of the people of Ammon arrives from Rabbah loaded with provisions for David and the people who were with him. David's attempt to comfort was despised but not by the Lord; he who tried to comfort was himself comforted. It was the law of divine compensation. It still operates.

O✦C✦T✦O✦B✦E✦R 13TH

"Machir the son of Ammiel from Lo Debar ... brought beds and basins, earthen vessels and wheat, barley and flour, parched grains and beans, lentils and parched seeds, honey and curds, sheep and cheese of the herd, for David and the people who were with him to eat for they said, 'The people are hungry and weary and thirsty in the wilderness'".
2 Samuel 17:27

Life takes amazing turns. When Saul and Jonathan died the immediate family were so frightened of the consequences that Mephibosheth, Jonathan's son was hidden away in the house of Machir the son of Ammiel in Lo Debar. It was to Machir's house that David sent his servants to bring the lame Mephibosheth to eat at his table, continually. Now David's table is empty; in fact he hadn't got a table at all! "Hungry, weary and thirsty", our text tells us, David had touched rock bottom.

Who is this then coming across the wilderness with wheat, barley, flour, parched grain, beans, lentils and parched seeds, honey and curds, sheep and the cheese of the herd? Machir! Who is all this for? David! Why, David had shared his rich table with Mephibosheth and now Machir, who loved David for what he had done for Mephibosheth, spreads a table in the wilderness fit for a king. Years later John Wesley said "I give God spoonfuls and he gives me back shovelfuls!" Selah

"And Barzillai the Gileadite from Rogelim, brought beds and basins, earthen vessels and wheat, barley and flour, parched grains and beans, lentils and parched seeds, honey and curds, sheep and cheese of the herd, for David and the people who were with him to eat". 2 Samuel 17:27-29

Is this a young man who comes with all this food? Is this a middle aged man who now helps David and his few followers as "All Israel" musters to kill him? Who now lays down these bags of wheat and these jars of honey? As the boiling sun pours down on the wilderness, scorching all before it, we see an eighty year old man lift the God sent provender for David who was on the edge of despair. No one is too old or too young to show a kindness. How well I remember a dying man, Mr. David Bond Walker, my old Sunday school teacher, send me down a £5 note from his deathbed as we gathered to comfort his loved ones. I was a very young full-time preacher at the time but no £5 note ever touched me more. My friend remembered me even in his dying moments.

As I think of Barzillai, the eighty year old, I think of Simeon. Into the temple comes David's greater Son with Mary and Joseph, so poor that all they could afford for a sacrifice was "A pair of turtle doves or two young pigeons" (See Lev 12:2-8). But there was old Simeon, nearing death, waiting to minister to them. "He came by the Spirit into the temple ... and he took him up in his arms and blessed God", referring to the little baby, despised by Israel and hounded by Herod, as "The glory of your people Israel". And there too was Anna, and "She was of a great age ... a widow of about eighty-four and coming in that instant she gave thanks to the Lord and spoke of him to all those who looked for redemption in Jerusalem". Two old people did more to glorify Christ than all Israel did on that particular day.

"And David numbered the people who were with him, and set captains of thousands and captains of hundreds over them. Then David sent out one-third of the people under the hand of Joab, one-third under the hand of

Abishai the son of Zeruiah, Joab's brother and one-third under the hand of Ittai the Gittite. And the king said to the people, 'I also will surely go out with you myself'' . 2 Samuel 18:1-2

"I prepare as if there were no Holy Spirit and then I preach as though I had never prepared", said G. Campbell Morgan. Fortune favours the prepared. Indeed, it is my experience that faith breeds organisation. In christian work, as any other work, people soon know if you haven't done your homework. "But God says that if I open my mouth he will fill it", says someone who doesn't believe in preparation. True, but ask such a person to expound the book of Ezekiel without having first studied it! The priests in the temple had to put fresh wood on the fire each day when they were presenting their sacrifices. The old ashes were not allowed to be stoked up in the morning and laziness was not to mark the presentation of each days sacrifice.

Are you and I, christian, not presenting the sacrifice of the Lord Jesus to the world around us? That is, we are preaching the message of the sacrifice of Christ on the cross and we too need a fresh approach to presenting that sacrifice, daily. As David trusted God for the coming battle he wasn't lazy in his attitude to it. He picked his best generals, his best captains and organised things with all diligence. In the christian battle we must be the same. Give christian work your very best, today.

O✦C✦T✦O✦B✦E✦R 16TH

"Then David sent out one-third of the people under the hand of Joab, one-third under the hand of Abishai the son of Zeruiah, Joab's brother and one-third under the hand of Ittai the Gittite. And the king said to the people, 'I also will surely go out with you myself'. But the people answered, 'You shall not go out. For if we flee away, they will not care about us; nor if half of us die, will they care about us. But you are worth ten thousand of us now. For you are now more help to us in the city'" . 2 Samuel 18:2-3

David's supporters had now rallied. His army had risen to thousands in number and David desperately wanted to lead his army into battle. His supporters wouldn't hear of it. They loved him and said he was worth ten thousand of them. The affection

David at this point is extremely tender. There was a quality about him that inspired affection, even in his darkest hour.

The shadow of the Cross of Calvary falls over this section of Scripture. We think of David and the disciples doing their best to dissuade Christ from going to Calvary as David's supporters had tried to dissuade David from enjoining battle with Absalom. The contrast couldn't have been greater, though, could it? It was David's sin that had brought all this trouble on his country. He didn't want to stay inside a city wall while people were suffering for his sake. It was, by contrast, our sin, not Christ's, that took him to Calvary. There was no staying behind a city wall for him in the battle to be enjoined with one who sought to usurp God's throne. It was on a hill "Without a city wall, where the dear Lord was crucified who died to save us all".

I have no doubt that David would have tried to save Absalom's life on the field of battle, if he had been there. God the Father, mystery of all mysteries, did not interpose at Calvary on his Son's behalf. "Yet, it pleased the Lord to bruise Him", wrote Isaiah, "He has put him to grief". Why? For our sakes that our sin might be forgiven. No wonder Isaiah adds that God says "I will divide him a portion with the great, and he shall divide the spoil with the strong because he poured out his soul on to death, and he was numbered with the transgressors and he bore the sin of many and made intercession for the transgressors".

O♦C♦T♦O♦B♦E♦R 17TH

"Now the king had commanded Joab, Abishai, and Ittai, saying 'Deal gently for my sake with the young man Absalom'. And all the people heard when the king gave all the captains orders concerning Absalom".
2 Samuel 18:5

Everyone in King David's army heard his command that his son Absalom be handled gently. We think again of Calvary. No such command came from Heaven's throne when the gentle Saviour hauled his awful cross up Calvary's mountain. No such command to be gentle came when they nailed the hands that created every gentle baby ever born, to the cross. There was the clearing of throats and the filthy spittle on that sacred face. There was the crown of thorns pushed into that sacred head. There was the dislocation of all his bones. There was his fierce thirst, his dried up strength as they crucified him, the Prince of Glory. Gentle with him? They laughed him to scorn. No eye pitied and no arm saved. He was no rebel. He never sinned, yet "His visage was so marred more than any man's and his form more than the son's of men".

So it is that his cross is our glory. He went into the dark and we have light. He was torn that we might be made whole. That you might be gentle, he was beaten beyond recognition. Fathomless thoughts. Unspeakable love. The centre of history. The joy of eternity. Calvary.

O٠C٠T٠O٠B٠E٠R 18TH

"For the battle there was scattered over the face of the whole countryside, and the woods devoured more people that day than the sword devoured".
2 Samuel 18:8

The wonderful providence of God is seen in the defeat of Absalom and his army. "God helps those who help themselves", we are told by people who think lightly of God's providence. They think God's providence is relegated to being dependent on our activity. What, in fact, does providence mean? The basic meaning of providence is "Foresight" and the activity that results from foresight. If providence is foresight then only God can have it, perfectly. None of us can tell what a day will bring. You couldn't even spell out for me what will happen before you put your head on your pillow this evening, never to speak of how your career will go or how your old age will be.

God alone foresees the end from the beginning. He alone is able to act upon the basis of foreknowledge. Absalom's rebellion was going to be exposed for what it was and little did he know that the location of the battle near a wood was to be his undoing. God uses uneventful beginnings to bring about unbelievable endings. Events that are secular and carnal cannot hinder God's plans. Just remember that the Lord has laid a plan and prepared means for the deliverance of His people even before their enemies have prepared the plot for their destruction.

O✦C✦T✦O✦B✦E✦R 19TH

"Then Absalom met the servants of David. Absalom rode on a mule. The mule went under the thick boughs of a great oak tree, and his head caught in the oak; so he was left hanging between heaven and earth. And the mule which was under him went on". 2 Samuel 18:9

Wit may win people friends. Good looks may find them favour. Flattery may gain them a following. Manipulation may put them high in society. Clever strategy may help some of their aspirations to be realised. The fact remains, though, if God is kept out of their reckoning and they rebel against his word and will, then their folly will be exposed.

Could there ever be a more ridiculous scene than Absalom hanging in a tree, caught by his head and hair, utterly unable to do a thing about his situation? Where now his great army? Where now the favour he had won in the hearts of the men of Israel? His half-brother Solomon described him perfectly in one of his famous proverbs. "The eye that mocks at his father and despises to obey his mother, the ravens of the valley shall pick it out and the young eagle shall eat it". even the mule he was riding on left Absalom to it.

Let us not be afraid of Satan and all that he throws against us in these days. As God made an open show of Absalom's folly, so through Christ's cross Satan has been shown up for what he is. Paul writes that Christ "Having disarmed principalities and powers, he made a public spectacle of them, triumphing over them in it". Since Christ has made such an open show of what Satan is and what he stands for, let us not be tempted by all his subtleties as we go about our work today.

O✦C✦T✦O✦B✦E✦R 20TH

"But the man said to Joab. 'Though I were to receive a thousand shekels of silver in my hand, I would not raise my hand against the king's son. For in our hearing the king commanded you and Abishai and Ittai, saying 'Beware lest anyone touch the young man Absalom!' Otherwise I would have dealt falsely against my own life. For there is nothing hidden from the king, and you yourself would have set yourself against me"'. 2 Samuel 18:12-13

He is an unnamed servant of David's. He is simply called "A certain man". He happened to see Absalom's plight and described what he had seen to the commander in chief of David's army, Joab. "You just saw him!", said Joab, "And why did you not strike him to the ground? I would have given you ten shekels of silver and a belt". His answer was the epitome of loyalty, money didn't come into it, David had asked that Absalom be spared and he would obey David.

Unfortunately, for some people, money comes between them and the most important things in life. There is a very moving interview in the New Testament between a young man who was very rich and the Lord Jesus. He was full of eagerness, humility, discernment, and had a tremendous respect for morality. But the tragedy was that the young man who came so eagerly to Christ went away with leaden footsteps. Why? Because he refused to do what Christ asked him to do. He had been concerned to keep the commandments but he was even more concerned to keep his money. He had bent the knee but was unprepared to bend his will. He had bowed his head but not his heart. He knew what he needed but he would not forego what he wanted. Christ called him to sacrifice for the future but he sacrificed for the present. He gave up the one thing that is vital for the many things that are vain. He turned away unconverted and he and his wretched money have never been heard of since. Whatever happens don't let his fate be yours. Take Christ as your Saviour and you will learn that his blessings make rich and add no sorrow. And, remember, money has never made anyone rich.

O٠C٠T٠O٠B٠E٠R 21ST

"Then Joab said, 'I cannot linger with you'. And he took three spears in his hand and thrust them through Absalom's heart, while he was still alive in the midst of the terebinth tree". 2 Samuel 18:14

What is it about the character of Joab that never inspires warmth? He fights loyally for David, to a point. He certainly wants David on the throne and David's government to be stable. Joab was prepared to support David long before David ever reached the throne but there is a cold, calculating, materialistic streak in him. We never read of him offering a prayer, truly exalting the Lord, or inspiring anyone to know or follow God. He follows David because it suits him. He is motivated by selfishness. It suited him to use the widow of Tekoa to persuade David to allow Absalom back into David's court, now it suits him to kill Absalom. David's desire or command in the matter is not paramount.

The sad thing is that it is possible to have an outward service for Christ because it suits; what the Lord's commands are on issues need not be paramount. Again and again ecclesiastics debate on the media and never, no never, do they seem to quote the Scriptures on the issues they discuss. On all the great burning issues of our day the Scriptures are not even referred to. Beware of the unspiritual in leadership. David sold himself into Joab's hands in the matter of Uriah the Hittite and he became, in his later years, a weak and nominal king. For anything, don't hand yourself into the hands of the unspiritual.

O✦C✦T✦O✦B✦E✦R 22ND

"Now Absalom in his lifetime had taken and set up a pillar for himself, which is in the King's Valley. For he said, 'I have no son to keep my name in remembrance'. He called the pillar after his own name. And to this day it is called Absalom's Monument". 2 Samuel 18:18

For all David's faults what do we particularly remember him for? We remember him for those occasions when he took a great stand for God and threw his own selfish ambition to the side. We remember him for his sins, yes, but particularly for those psalms which pour out his repentance and sorrow for his sin. Those psalms have been such an inspiration to millions struggling with guilt. We remember David because he loved the Lord.

Absalom stands in complete contrast. Here was someone who set himself up as a leader. At every turn he exalted himself. He wanted to be remembered so he set up a monument to his own glory in his own lifetime. It reminds me of an old man in America who spent one quarter of a million dollars on a monument to himself and his late wife and died in a poor house. The monument now stands sinking in the Kansas soil. When people kept suggesting that he perhaps might donate a swimming pool to the area, or whatever, he always replied "This town aint done nothin for me". All Absaloms are not dead yet, are they? The word of God has the final say on the matter; "Whoever exalts himself shall be abased". Always remember that you and I are not big enough to be the sole goal of our own existence.

O✦C✦T✦O✦B✦E✦R 23RD

"Then Ahimaaz the son of Zadok said, 'Let me run now and take the news to the king, how the Lord has avenged him of his enemies" '.
2 Samuel 18:19

All around David are a kaleidoscope of characters who are loyal to him. They surface at different points in his life and they are an inspiration for all who would serve Christ, David's greater Son. There is, for example, Hushai, the great politician. There was Jonathan the king's son. There was Mephibosheth, Jonathan's grandson and Ittai the Gittite. There was of course, the lovely Abigail and his friend Zadok and Abiathar. To meet David's needs God sent him not just one friend but a group of faithful supporters. Though their names are obscure, the nature of their friendship shines clearly to enlighten us all.

I like to think of Ahimaaz as "The Gentle One". He pleads with Joab to be allowed to tell David the news of how the battle had gone. Perhaps remembering David's behaviour when he slew the man who told him of Saul's death, Joab first refused to allow Ahimaaz to tell David what had happened. He sent a Cushite to do it. But Ahimaaz pleaded and got there, first. No one ever sought to bring bad news more tactfully. The Lord has his servants for all kinds of tasks. Perhaps you will be called on to be the bearer of terrible news, one of these days. It comes to us all. May you be like Ahimaaz, gentle and tactful. There are few with such an approach around. When you have to pass on bad news try to follow these four principles. Be real. Be quiet, Your presence, not your words, will be most appreciated. Be supportive. Be available.

O✦C✦T✦O✦B✦E✦R 24TH

"Just then the Cushite came, and the Cushite said, 'There is good news, my lord the king! For the Lord has avenged you this day of all those who rose against you'. And the king said to the Cushite, 'Is the young man Absalom safe?' And the Cushite answered, 'May the enemies of my lord the king, and all who rise against you to do you harm, be as that young man is!'"
2 Samuel 18: 31-32

The Cushite was a wise man. When he arrived with the news of events he was asked about Absalom and answered with tact. He did not tell David that Absalom had been speared by Joab through the heart three times, that the ten young men who bore Joab's armour had surrounded Absalom and finished him off, that his body had been thrown into a large pit in the woods and that a huge heap of stones had been placed over him. The Cushite simply wished all David's enemies to be as Absalom was; dead.

We are into explicitness in our generation in matters of life and death, of love and family, and few areas are left to be private or sacred. More's the pity. Even little children have to carry immense burdens in our generation in their minds far too early in life because of explicitness. David's grief was enough without having to bear graphic details. Having witnessed, particularly in Eastern Europe, macabre scenes at funerals I find the Cushites approach to tragedy a wise one. The voyeurism of television has desensitized our generation. May God make us sensitive shielders of people's lives and give us wisdom as to what is worth telling and what is worth withholding.

O✦C✦T✦O✦B✦E✦R 25TH

"Then the king was deeply moved, and went up to the chamber over the gate, and wept. And as he went, he said thus; 'O my son Absalom - my son, my son Absalom - if only I had died in your place! O Absalom my son, my son"'. 2 Samuel 18:33

There have been few cries of grief ever spoken like David's cry at the death of his son Absalom. Next to the 23rd Psalm his words about Absalom's death are probably the best known words from the life of David. But, they were, although understandable, definitely ill advised. David shows more grief for a heartless, cruel son than he does for the nation Absalom had ripped apart and the twenty thousand deaths he had caused in his rebellion against God and his own father. He had allowed affection for Absalom to cloud his duty to God and the nation that God had set him over.

In times of great stress it is very easy to burst out and say things that cast slight on God. David was saying to God that he wished he had died instead of Absalom. What father, when he sees his son die does not feel the same? But Absalom had died under the judgment of God. The Lord had placed David on the throne, not Absalom. It is foolish to question God's wisdom of putting us where we are and letting us live when others die. Be glad you are where you are in the will of God, no matter how trying. Set a guard on your lips. Be like my friend Mrs. Margaret Hawkins of Newtownards. Standing watching her dear young son's funeral cortege leave her home she turned to me and said, "The Lord gave and the Lord has taken away. Blessed be the name of the Lord". Brave, wise, good words.

O◆C◆T◆O◆B◆E◆R 26TH

"You love your enemies and hate your friends. For you have declared today that you regard neither princes nor servants; for today I perceive that if Absalom had lived and all of us had died today, then it would have pleased you well". 2 Samuel 19:6

When Joab discovered David overwhelmed with grief over Absalom's death and neglecting his duty to his friends and his nation he gave him the edge of his tongue. Joab berated him for not thanking his army for saving his life and the life of his nation. It was a rough speech, spoken heartlessly, in the circumstances, but there was much truth in it. He summed David's stance up in a very terse phrase; "You love your enemies and hate your friends".

Don't we often do just that? We often forget the long faithfulness of friends in crises and exalt those who never were our friends in the first place. Joab's statement is still heard in the modern day phrase "You always hurt the one you love" or "Home, the place where we grumble the most and are treated the best". Loyalty to friends is not easy, sticking to duty amid overwhelming emotional circumstances calls for great courage and Joab, for all his lack of respect, was right to remind David of their importance. Let him remind us, today, too. Those who have been kind to us, who have stood by us, must not be forgotten. As Neil Strait has said "He who forgets the language of gratitude can never be on speaking terms with happiness".

O◆C◆T◆O◆B◆E◆R 27TH

"Then the king arose and sat in the gate. And they told all the people, saying, 'There is the king, sitting in the gate'. So all the people came before the king. For everyone of Israel had fled to his tent". 2 Samuel 19:8

It is always wise to heed good advice. It came to David from a proud and intemperate Joab and came roughly, but he listened to it. Grief is lazy, it is hard to shake yourself into action when someone you love is taken from you. You want the world to stop and take notice but it carries right on. You feel aggrieved and hurt but it is good to be shaken out of lethargy and get back to duty. David listened to Joab's advice and went out to face the public.

Perhaps someone has given you some advice. Perhaps that person is not a very pleasant individual, perhaps they have even given you advice in a bad temper. Never despise advice if it is the truth, no matter how it comes. David's own comment on this incident is worth remembering; "Let the righteous strike me", he wrote, "It shall be kindness and let him reprove me; it shall be as excellent oil; let my head not refuse it". As we have learned, often, even the dumb animals give us good advice in their lifestyle. It doesn't matter how a person is dressed or what kind of house they live in; if they are giving good advice, heed it.

O✦C✦T✦O✦B✦E✦R 28TH

"Now all the people were in a dispute throughout all the tribes of Israel, saying 'The king saved us from the hand of our enemies, he delivered us from the hand of the Philistines, and now he has fled from the land because of Absalom. But Absalom, whom we anointed over us, has died in battle. Now therefore, why do you say nothing about bringing back the king?"'
2 Samuel 19:9-10

The people wanted David to become king in Jerusalem again. He was the rightful heir because he had just won a major victory. Yet, although he had huge support, nobody did anything but talk! The need to have a sovereign back on the throne was paramount for the administration and safeguarding of the country but nobody would make the move to do the necessary thing. Nobody would act.

It is amazing in life how many people are often agreed that something vital should be done in a certain situation but nobody makes a move to do it. The most obvious thing, the thing staring them in the face is the thing that they refuse to act on. Isn't it a great thing that Mr. Dunlop, down in May Street in Belfast, acted on the question that arose in his mind when he saw his son playing with a rubber tyre; "Now, what would happen if I put air into that tyre?" The pneumatic tyre was born. Isn't it interesting that Mr. Eddison who invented the mouthpiece, the transmitter part of the telephone, the electric lamp bulb and the gramophone, who helped to make the first successful typewriter and in turn, deeply influenced the invention of the radio valve was, in fact, taken away from school because the teacher thought his continual questions were a sign of stupidity! I'm glad Mr. Eddison acted on what seemed obvious to him. I'm glad Mr. Franklin invented eyeglasses or I couldn't focus on what I have just written! A good thing, which may seem obvious to you, might never be acted on because you didn't act on it. The world will be a poorer place as a result. Got the message?

"You are my brethren, you are my bone and my flesh. Why then are you the last to bring back the king?" 2 Samuel 19:12

Help in your life doesn't necessarily come from where you expect it. Does it? I have always found the following poem challenging;

"My neighbour was passing my garden one day,
She stopped,
And I knew right away,
It was gossip not flowers,
She had on her mind,
And this is what I heard her say.

"That girl down the street,
Should be run from our midst,
She drinks and she talks quite a lot,
She knows not to speak
To my child, nor to me",
My neighbour smiled, and I thought.

A tongue can accuse and carry bad news,
The seeds of distrust it can sow,
But unless you've made no mistakes in your life,
Be careful of stones that you throw,

Then a car speeded by and the screaming of brakes,
A sign that made my heart grow still,
For my neighbour's one child had been pulled from the path,
And saved, by a girl lying still.

The child was unhurt,
And my neighbour cried out, 'Oh who is that brave girl so sweet?'
I covered the crushed, broken body,
And said, 'The bad girl who lives down the street'"

Anon

O◆C◆T◆O◆B◆E◆R 30TH

"Then a ferry boat went across to carry over the king's household, and to do what he thought good. Now Shimei the son of Gera fell down before the king when he had crossed the Jordan. Then he said to the king, 'Do not let my lord impute iniquity to me or remember what wrong your servant did on the day that my lord the king left Jerusalem, that the king should take it to heart. For I, your servant, know that I have sinned. Therefore here I am, the first to come today of all the house of Joseph to go down to meet my lord the king"'. 2 Samuel 19:18-20

People can change. One day Shimei is cursing David and stoning him and calling him a rogue, now he is the first to greet David as he crosses the Jordan, returning to Jerusalem as the restored king of Israel. Shimei pleads for forgiveness and casts himself on David's mercy.

So it is that people are lemons today and oranges tomorrow. They cannot speak to you civilly this morning but why, this afternoon they are all over you. A name that people once recalled with deep emotion they now hardly even react to. Circumstances change people. Opportunism is often their Master. They like you, if it suits them.

It is lovely to know that nothing will change the attitude of our Lord Jesus to the one who trusts Him as Saviour. Neither time, circumstances, nor temperament can change his commitment to you. Nothing will move him away from his love for you. So, why fawn on the fickle temperaments of people around you? Why be moved from your path of duty and devotion to Christ because of them?

"Some will hate you, some will love you,
Some will flatter, some will slight,
Cease from man and look above you,
Trust in God and do the right".

O◆C◆T◆O◆B◆E◆R 31ST

"But Abishai the son of Zeruiah answered and said, 'Shall not Shimei be put to death for this, because he cursed the Lord's anointed?' And David said, 'What have I to do with you, you sons of Zeruiah, that you should be

adversaries to me today? Shall any man be put to death today in Israel?
For do I not know that today I am king over Israel?"' 2 Samuel 19:21-22

After all the darkness, the sorrow, the penitence, the heart-ache of David's sin and its aftermath in Absalom's rebellion, a wonderful flash of the old David returns. The David who had forgiven Saul, spared Nabal, shown great hospitality to Mephibosheth, comforted the king of the Ammonites, now stays the hand of Abishai from slaying Shimei. Mercy marks the restored David as he returns to Jerusalem, chastened of God. The old kindness surfaces again.

Has the Lord been pruning the tree of your life? Has this present month been a time when God took away all your props to cast you on himself? You are humbler and wiser at the end of this month than at the beginning. Do not be angry at God's pruning process. To be honest I have experienced that process during the time of writing this book myself and it has been a sobering experience. It is to make us kinder, gentler, more Christlike. It is training us for reigning. Let us remember the wise words of Robert Murray McCheyne; "If we saw the whole, we would see that the Father is doing little else in the world but training his vines". May you and I bear much fruit, like David, from recent pruning.

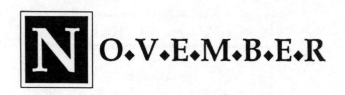

N O·V·E·M·B·E·R

N•O•V•E•M•B•E•R

*I*t was not the end of his life but it was the beginning of the end. David moves back towards Jerusalem, the rebellion of Absalom now well and truly over. It is a fascinating interlude in his life, full of spiritual teaching for us all. It reveals the value of God's chastening, it reveals an older and wiser David. We shall meet David's old friends and old enemies coming into view once more as he settles into the last years of his reign. Biblical principles were once more given their rightful place. The prodigal had come home.

N•O•V•E•M•B•E•R 1ST

"Now Mephibosheth the son of Saul came down to meet the king".
2 Samuel 19:24

The story of David now returns to the much maligned Mephibosheth. In the day of David's great need Mephibosheth had remained faithful to David but his servant Ziba had slandered his name to David. All through the time of Absalom's rebellion David had believed Mephibosheth to be disloyal. He was about to find out how very loyal he had actually been.

We judge things too fast. We don't check out the stories we hear. We are not certain of our facts. We are not as wise as serpents and harmless as doves. We forget that talk is cheap and that "Man shall give an account of every idle word that he speaks". Take my friend Pastor Val English. Sitting in a hospital one day talking to a stranger, the stranger started to speak of Pastor Val English. "Do you know him?", said Val, with his tongue in his cheek. "O yes, Val and I are like that", replied the stranger, crossing his second finger over his index finger. "Pure talk", said Val to me as he recounted the story, laughing. Watch them, the talkers.

"And he had not cared for his feet, nor trimmed his moustache, nor washed his clothes, from the day the king departed until the day he came back in peace", 2 Samuel 19:24

Mephibosheth really did love David. He grieved that his king was away. He longed for the day of his return. He cared little for himself, everything hung on the reinstatement of the one who had shown him kindness. He would, surely, sit at the king's table once more.

This verse is related to Paul rebuking the Corinthian church. While Paul and his colleagues went across continents "As men condemned to death ... a spectacle to the world ... fools for Christ's sake ... dishonoured ... poorly clothed ... beaten ... homeless ... reviled ... persecuted ... defamed ... made as the filth of the world ... the offscouring of all things ...". The Corinthian leaders were "Full ... rich ... strong ... distinguished" and "Reigned as kings", wrote Paul, "Without us" (See 1 Cor 4). The coming king has his people but, it seems to me, some are not desperate for his return and some don't seem to mind how long he tarries. In which category are you?

"So it was, when he had come to Jerusalem to meet the king, that the king said to him, 'Why did you not go with me, Mephibosheth?'"
2 Samuel 19:25

It was a fair question, and it showed David's return to the balanced life of walking in God's will. Gone was the ferocious cruelty when he took Rabah, when he poured out on others the hardness he ought to have dealt out to himself. Gone was the quick execution order he meted out on the young man who came from Saul's camp "With his clothes torn and dust on his head" (See 2 Samuel 2:2). Now Mephibosheth who had not "Cared for his feet, nor trimmed his moustache, nor washed his clothes from the day the king departed until the day he came back in peace", got a fair hearing. Mephibosheth got a chance to explain himself.

In life we must be fair. We truly must listen to both sides of a question. I have discovered particularly when counselling in the area of a marriage breakdown, one tends to believe the story of the first partner who comes. It is a fatal mistake. Let's hear both sides of the problem before we judge.

N✦O✦V✦E✦M✦B✦E✦R 4TH

"And he answered, 'My lord, O king, my servant deceived me. For your servant said, 'I will saddle a donkey for myself, that I may ride on it and go to the king', because your servant is lame. And he has slandered your servant to my lord the king, but my lord the king is like the angel of God. Therefore do what is good in your eyes. For all of my father's house were but dead men before my lord the king. Yet you set your servant among those who eat at your own table. Therefore what right have I still to cry out any more to the king?"' 2 Samuel 19:26-28

If someone has listened to a false story about you and been prejudiced against you because of it, don't be too hard on them. When you get a chance to put the record straight don't berate them for believing the lie. Don't wipe the floor with them. Concentrate on the good things they have done to you in the past, mention those kind actions, and appeal to the better side of their character. Be a statesman.

Notice Mephibosheth before David. He points out that he has been personally slandered but that David had saved his life and provided for him. He did not forget that David had given him a place at his table even though he hadn't deserved it. Mephibosheth's vindication speech is a gem for all who have been slandered. He tells the truth about himself but he does not blunt the truth with intemperate language. "Slander", said Saurin, "Is a vice that strikes a double blow, wounding both him that commits and him against whom it is committed". Slander, therefore, commits enough wounds without you and I wounding anyone as we try to counteract it.

"Therefore what right have I still to cry out any more to the king?"
2 Samuel 19:28

Mephibosheth knew his place. He had been given lands and servants and a place at the king's table. He, by the standards of the day, should have been executed but instead he had been shown mercy and kindness and love. Yes, he had been slandered by a wicked man but he could afford to be magnanimous. Why? Because he had been shown magnanimity! Why complain?

Are you full of complaint, today? Are you grousing and moaning around the house? Are you a pain to live with? Is everybody wrong but you? Just stop a moment and think of the hospital wards in this nation. Think of the heartache and the hellholes of poverty in Calcutta or Madras. In a world where 150 million children under five are malnourished, 7 million are refugees from war or famine, 100 million never step into a classroom, 30 million live on the streets, 10 million in Africa, alone, will have lost at least one parent to AIDS by the year 2000, what are our little complaints in the affluent Western world in comparison? Yes, go count your blessings and you'll be easier to live with, today.

"So the king said to him, 'Why do you speak any more of your matters? have said 'You and Ziba divide the land'. Then Mephibosheth said to the king, 'Rather, let him take it all, inasmuch as my lord the king has come back in peace to his own house"'. 2 Samuel 19:29-30

Today's two verses have produced much discussion. Was David unfair? Was David unconvinced by Mephibosheth's defence? Was David trying to sit on the fence? Was Mephibosheth, after all, suspected of disloyalty? Was David in a hurry in saying "Oh, sort it out yourselves. Ziba might be right and so might you, just divide the land between you?"

Don't you think that David was testing Mephibosheth? A materialistic Mephibosheth would have said "Fine. I'm delighted to get back half my lands so falsely taken from me", for remember when David was deceived about Mephibosheth he had given Ziba all that belonged to Mephibosheth! No. Mephibosheth was not David's devoted servant for what he could get out of it. Now that David had been restored, his presence in Jerusalem meant far more to him than lands. He was like the lady who stole the baby in Solomon's day. When two women claimed to be the mother, Solomon suggested that the child be cut in two. The false mother thought "Fine" but the true mother thought "Never" and cried out against Solomon's advice, willing to let the false mother have the baby in order that the baby live. So it was that Solomon discovered who the true mother was. By the same method David discovered the true loyalty of Mephibosheth. David's servant had passed his test with flying colours. In practical terms it is as the man said; "Who cares who gets the praise as long as the Lord gets the glory?"

N◆O◆V◆E◆M◆B◆E◆R 7TH

"I am today eighty years old. Can I discern between the good and bad? Can your servant taste what I eat or what I drink? Can I hear any longer the voice of singing men and singing women? Why then should your servant be a further burden to my lord the king? Your servant will go a little way across the Jordan with the king. And why should the king repay me with such a reward? Please let your servant turn back again, that I may die in my own city, and be buried by the grave of my father and mother".
2 Samuel 19:35-37

Barzillai was an old man and the normal pleasures of life were no longer attractive to him. He would accompany David across the Jordan for part of the way but he would not take up his offer of a special place at David's special victory celebrations at Jerusalem. He was feeling the weight of his years.

I like the anonymous prayer I came across once, let me share it with you. "Lord, Thou knowest better than I know myself that I am growing older. Keep me from getting too talkative, and thinking I must say something on every subject and on every occasion. Release me from craving to straighten out everybody's affairs. Teach me the glorious lesson that occasionally it is possible that I may be mistaken. Make me thoughtful, but not moody, helpful but not bossy; for Thou knowest, Lord, that I want a few friends at the end".

N◆O◆V◆E◆M◆B◆E◆R 8TH

"But here is your servant Chimham; let him cross over with my lord the king, and do for him what seems good to you". 2 Samuel 19:37

"Old age", said the wit, "Is when you get out of the shower and you're glad the mirror is all fogged up!" "The seven years of man", said R. J. Needham, "Is spills, drills, thrills, bills, ills, pills, and wills!"

Barzillai had probably made his will by the time that David crossed the Jordan. Note, though, that he didn't have the attitude to young people that some older people have. He wasn't arrogant, crabby, austere and critical towards them. The fact is that after you lose membership in it, the younger generation seems pretty bad. Barzillai didn't let such a prejudice rule him. As Matthew Henry said "They that are old must not begrudge young people those delights which they themselves are passed the enjoyment of nor oblige them to retire as they do". Barzillai let Chimham go with David to enjoy his big day without a word of complaint. He set an excellent example.

N◆O◆V◆E◆M◆B◆E◆R 9TH

"And the king answered, 'Chimham shall cross over with me, and I will do for him what seems good to you. Now whatever you request of me, I will do for you "'. 2 Samuel 19:38

Barzillai had come in the past to help David in the day of his trouble. Now, in the day of David's great victory, David is happy to return the kind act. Note that this kind action was not finished with for when David was an old man he gave strict instructions to Solomon; "Show", he said, "Kindness to the son's of Barzillai the Gileadite and let him be among those who eat at your table for so they came to me when I fled from Absalom your brother" (2 Samuel 2:7).

There is not a person on the face of the earth who does not understand the language of a kind act. A boy was once standing on a platform of a railway station, weeping. He had lost his ticket. A gentleman, spotting him, bought him a ticket and on handing it over said "Whenever you find someone in a position like yourself, one day, do the same for him. Pass it on!" As the railway carriage pulled out of the station the boy shouted out of the window, "I'll pass it on, sir. I'll pass it on". For all we know that act of kindness is still reverberating around the world.

N◆O◆V◆E◆M◆B◆E◆R 10TH

"Just then all the men of Israel came to the king, and said to the king, 'Why have our brethren, the men of Judah, stolen you away and brought the king, his household, and all David's men with him across the Jordan?' So all the men of Judah answered the men of Israel, 'Because the king is a close relative of ours. Why then are you angry over this matter? Have we ever eaten at the king's expense? Or has he given us any gift?' And the men of Israel answered the men of Judah, and said, 'We have ten shares in the king; therefore we also have more right to David than you. Why then do you despise us - were we not the first to advise bringing back our king?"'.
2 Samuel 19:41-43

Incredible, isn't it? A battle had just been fought. A rebellion had just been quashed. A dynasty had just been saved. God's king was just on his way to being reinstated on his throne in Jerusalem and an argument breaks out amongst his people as to who should be leading him back! The men of Judah said they had the right to do it because David came from their tribe. The men of Israel retorted that they had more right to David than the men of Judah for they had "Ten shares in the king"!

Things haven't changed, have they? Human nature is a fickle business. What did it matter who led David back to Jerusalem as long as he was led back? Why fight over it? It is C. R. Swindoll who tells the story of the missionary family who liked peanut butter. Not being able to get peanut butter in the country in which they were serving, they decided to have some shipped in. But other missionaries who sat at their table thought it was a true sacrifice to the cause of Christ not to have such a luxury. Believe it or not they made it so difficult for the peanut butter loving family they forced them to leave the mission field.

N✦O✦V✦E✦M✦B✦E✦R 11TH

"Yet the words of the men of Judah were fiercer than the words of the men of Israel". 2 Samuel 19:43

Interesting little verse, isn't it? The emphasis is that the men of Israel stated their case in a more reasonable manner than the men of Judah. It is not always what you say but the way you say it. The fierceness of the way the men of Judah said that they had the right to lead David back to Jerusalem is marked down against them.

Proper communication can make all the difference. Did you hear about the man who said to his wife "Look, you've been cooking all week, tonight I am going to take you out for a really decent meal". His wife cried! She thought he was making a comment about her cooking! Wiser was the man who said to his wife "You always look good, dear, but tonight you look terrific!" Remember, good communication is hard work. It means careful choice of words. Inability to communicate represents a very real problem in our day and age. Though we have more communication facilities than man previously has ever had, most of us are isolated from our neighbours and friends. Some spend many hours listening to radio and television and yet can't establish or maintain satisfying relationships with members of their own household. It is worth remembering that more tears are shed in our theatres over fancied tragedies than in our churches over real ones. We must learn to care for real problems and to communicate kindness. Let the law of kindness, not fierceness rule your tongue today.

"And there happened to be there a rebel, whose name was Sheba the son of Bichri, a Benjamite. And he blew a trumpet, and said: 'We have no part in David, nor do we have inheritance in the son of Jesse; every man to his tents, O Israel!' So every man of Israel deserted David, and followed Sheba the son of Bichri". 2 Samuel 20:1-2

Poor David. The way of the transgressor is hard. He took another man's wife and killed her husband and God promised him that the sword would never depart from his house, "Because you have despised Me". No sooner had Absalom's rebellion been quelled and Israel and Judah had vied to bring David back in glory than another rebel rose seeking to bring David's throne down. Sheba, the Benjamite called for war against David and every man of Israel deserts the man whose victory parade they had just strenuously argued they should lead!

Are you disappointed over the way people change? Let it teach you that you should never put your absolute faith and trust in people in the first place. It is a fact that one minute people applaud a Moses, and, the next they want to stone him. One minute they thank God for a Paul, next they say his "Speech is contemptible" and his bodily presence "Weak". One minute they strew Christ's way with palm leaves and the next they bay for his blood. "See", they said to a great French playwright, "The crowds queuing to get in to see your play". "The same crowd would come to see me hung", he replied. Indeed, they would. "You are worried about what they think of you?", said Billy Strachan. "Don't worry about them for the truth is they don't think about you at all". Though spoken as a generalisation, all too many of us know the particular truth of what Billy said. It is painful truth, but worth remembering.

"But the men of Judah, from the Jordan as far as Jerusalem, remained loyal to their king". 2 Samuel 20:2

The rebellion of Sheba against David exposed the false but it also revealed the true. Life with all its swings and moods brings its tests and the lovely thing is there will always be people in this world, no matter what temptations are thrown at them, who will remain loyal to the Lord Jesus just as the men of Judah had remained loyal to David.

The next few years in the United Kingdom will see a real challenge to the lordship of Christ. We are now in a generation which believes that all roads lead to God. The Gospel and its Lord are no longer regarded as unique. But the Bible will not allow such a view. One day, I was approached by Leith Samuel after I had spoken at a service about the uniqueness of our Lord. He gave me a little book of his called "Time to wake up" and it helpfully highlights five things that are unique to Christianity. They are worth remembering.

First, Christianity is the only faith in the world which offers the individual a direct relationship with the holy, sinless founder of the faith. Secondly, Christianity is the only faith in this world which offers the forgiveness of sins at the expense of the founder of the faith. Thirdly, Christianity is the only faith in the world which offers eternal life as a free gift, now, through the grace of the founder of the faith. Fourthly, Christianity is the only faith in the world which allows you to bring nothing, nothing but your sins. Salvation is entirely undeserved. Fifthly, Christianity alone shows the futility of standing on tiptoe trying to reach up to God. Christianity's message is God in sheer love and mercy reaching down to us. To remain faithful to these truths will not be easy. May God keep us faithful to David's greater Son and his Gospel as the men of Judah were to David.

N✦O✦V✦E✦M✦B✦E✦R 14TH

"Now David came to his house at Jerusalem. And the king took the ten women, his concubines whom he had left to keep the house, and put them in seclusion and supported them, but did not go in to them. So they were shut up to the day of their death, living in widowhood". 2 Samuel 20:3

I shall never forget my good friend Philip Hacking speak one evening on the subject of sin. He said something that has always stayed with me. Coming to the area of repentance from sin he said "Repentance is not just saying sorry, it is stopping".

Today's text shows us that the best kind of repentance is to do so, no more. For years David had broken God's law about multiplying wives and concubines. Now, chastened by the Lord through the rebellion of Absalom, he cares for his wives and concubines, but is no longer sexually indulgent. Pity it was that such severe chastening had to come. Pity it was that it took the rocking of his very throne to wean him away from this great weakness in his life. But he had learned his lesson. It is the last we read of David and concubines. Even when a very old man and no doubt severely tempted by a situation brought about by his servants with a beautiful young woman (See 1 Kings chapter 1) he did not fall again. It is a note of great hope in David's final tortuous days. Let us learn, before God has to teach us, that repentance is stopping.

N♦O♦V♦E♦M♦B♦E♦R 15TH

"Then the king said to Amasa, 'Assemble the men of Judah for me within three days, and be present here yourself'". 2 Samuel 20:4

A hand had arisen against David and all the men of Israel had supported it. That is a lot of men. From Dan in the north to Bethel in the south, from Tyre to Joppa, David was in trouble. Today's verse tells us that though the men of Judah were on David's side, they had all gone home after they had brought him back to Jerusalem. They were all behind him, true, but they were so far behind him he couldn't see them!

Few there are who are quick and ready to respond when danger arrives. We all hope the danger will pass without us having to do anything about it. We hope somebody else will do something about it all, but for the moment we want to "Sit tight". Think through your circumstances at the moment. Is there a life in danger of being swallowed up by sin and evil in your circle of friends and acquaintances? If nobody does anything about it that life will be spiritually lost. Is there a marriage in danger and straightforward advice could save it? Why not give that advice? Is there someone who is ready to give up and a simple word of encouragement could save the day? Why not give that word of encouragement? Better that the men of Judah assemble themselves to David's defence rather than David having to bid them do it.

"So Amasa went to assemble the men of Judah. But he delayed longer than the set time which David had appointed him". 2 Samuel 20:5

Amasa had been a high ranking captain under Absalom. David wanted him to replace Joab as commander of his army and hearing of it Amasa did not go out with the rebelling army against David. Now, after Absalom's death, David moves to put Amasa in charge of his army during a time of crisis. Was it any wonder that there was a delay amongst the men of Judah in carrying out David's plans? It would be very difficult for the men of Judah to unite under a man who had once been loyal to the arch rebel Absalom.

Leadership has been defined as "The activity of influencing people to co-operate towards some goal which they come to find desirable". David's choice of Amasa was unwise. Amasa was not the man for the job. He divided David's people, made them uneasy. Are you choosing someone for a position? Mark well the words of President Dwight Eisenhower; "In order to be a leader a man must have followers. And to have followers, a man must have their confidence. Hence the supreme quality for a leader is unquestionably integrity. Without it, no real success is possible, no matter whether it is on a section gang, a football field, in an army, or in an office. If a man's associates find him guilty of phoniness, if they find that he lacks forthright integrity, he will fail. His teachings and actions must square with each other. The first great need, therefore, is integrity and high purpose".

"And David said to Abishai, 'Now Sheba the son of Bichri will do us more harm than Absalom. Take your lord's servants and pursue him, lest he find for himself fortified cities, and escape us'. So Joab's men, with the Cherethites, the Pelethites, and all the mighty men, went out after him. And they went out of Jerusalem to pursue Sheba the son of Bichri. When they were at the large stone which is in Gibeon, Amasa came before them. Now Joab was dressed in battle armour; on it was a belt with a sword fastened in its sheath at his hips; and as he was going forward, it fell out".
2 Samuel 20:6-8

It was certainly confusing. David's deft tough in strategy was gone. Here, because of Amasa's delay David had put Abishai, Joab's brother, in charge of his trained men and sent him after the rebel, Sheba. Joab, meanwhile, impetuous, unscrupulous, and ruthless had decided to go after Sheba with his men. Amasa and his men eventually meet up with both armies at the "Large stone which is in Gibeon". Not the most united of strategies in the history of warfare, was it?

Joab, of course, was the fly in the ointment. Because of his knowledge of David's sin in murdering Uriah, Joab could do as he liked. He didn't care who he rode over, if anyone got in the way of his plans he removed them, as we shall soon see. He knew David wouldn't defy him. So it is that the warning rises again; sin is extremely costly. David let Satan get a foot in his door and he took almost his very life. The repercussions of his sin came down to the uneasy, disunited army that stood by the stone of Gibeon. Sin is a spiritual malignancy and if we do not deal with it then it deals with us.

N✦O✦V✦E✦M✦B✦E✦R 18TH

" Then Joab said to Amasa, 'Are you in health, my brother?' And Joab took Amasa by the beard with his right hand to kiss him. But Amasa did not notice the sword that was in Joab's hand". 2 Samuel 20:9-10

History has shown that many an outwardly kind word has hidden a murderous heart. Who, in the great company of men who stood by the stone of Gibeon would have imagined that the Joab who now asked after the health of Amasa and reached out to give him a welcoming kiss, was about to murder him? Don't be fooled by everyone who asks after you.

Joab was jealous of Amasa because he knew David wanted to give him his job. His jealousy led him to murder Amasa. All of us need to experience deliverance from the hellish giant of jealousy. Jealousy ruins friendship, wrecks romances, undermines marriages. Jealousy decimates team spirit, separates preachers, poisons executives, fosters competition, deplores others successes. It is a finger-pointing, squinty-eyed giant. Listen to the words of C. R. Swindoll; "I lived many of my earlier years in the dismal, gaseous, subterranean pipelines of jealousy, breathing its fumes and obeying its commands. It was gross agony. But finally, by the grace of Jesus Christ, I realised I didn't have to live in darkness. I slew the giant and crawled out ... and the releasing sunlight of freedom captured my heart. The air was so fresh and clean. Oh the difference it has made! It is utter delight". Care to join him?

N✦O✦V✦E✦M✦B✦E✦R 19TH

"Then a wise woman cried out from the city, 'Hear, Hear! Please say to Joab, 'Come nearby, that I may speak with you'. When he had come near to her, the woman said, 'Are you Joab?' He answered, 'I am'. Then she said to him, 'Hear the words of your maidservant'. And he answered, 'I am listening'. Then she spoke, saying, ' They shall surely ask counsel at Abel', and so they would end disputes. 'I am among the peaceable and faithful in Israel.....why would you swallow up the inheritance of the Lord?'
2 Samuel 20:16-19

The Bible is not a book that simply chronicles sweeping crusades or mass movements. It is the story of individuals. People like us. Average people who decided to do something, to make a contribution, to stand up and be counted. Like the wise woman of the city of Abel. She pled with Joab that there was no point in slaying the people of Abel if all Joab wanted was the traitor Sheba who was hiding in the city. After all, Abel was full, she argued, of people who were "The Lord's inheritance". "Deliver him only and I will depart from the city", said Joab. And so they delivered him and so Joab left.

The wise woman of Abel carries a message to us all across the centuries. It is the message that one person can make a difference. So, be like her and speak up. Speak up in the university where idologies rage. Speak up on the shop floor of the factory where unbelieving employees check out how christians are in every day life. Speak up at home where life makes up its mind. Speak up in your business life for the moral principles that are right. Speak up in your local church for the maintenance of spiritual health and life. Speak up in hospital where reality never sleeps. Speak up like the wise woman of Abel and a whole city can be saved.

"Now there was a famine in the days of David for three years, year after year; and David inquired of the Lord". 2 Samuel 21:1

Famine is a frequent subject of Scripture. Whenever it occurs the underlying lesson seems to be that it must not cause the believer to panic and run from the will of God. Abraham, for example, was led by the will of God to Canaan but when he found a famine there he seems to have felt he had misread the will of God and fled in panic to Egypt. He even endangered the promised seed of the Messiah by his behaviour. If it had not been for the intervention of God, a real disaster would have come upon his life.

Joseph's life in famine times was an inspiration. Accepting the direction of God he was used to save virtually the whole of North Africa in crises times. The chastened David faced three famines at this time in his life but being close to God he enquired of the Lord about it. He knew that God had a purpose in it all. Rather than panic, he sought God's help to make good decisions.

Mark well the words of Habakkuk; "Though the fig tree may not blossom, nor fruit be on the vine; though the labour of the olive may fail, and the fields yield no food; though the flock be cut off from the fold, and there be no herd in the stalls - yet I will rejoice in the Lord, I will joy in the God of my salvation. The Lord is my strength; he will make my feet like deer's feet, and he will make me walk on my high hills" (Habakkuk 3:17-19).

"And the Lord answered, 'It is because of Saul and his bloodthirsty house, because he killed the Gibeonites"'. 2 Samuel 21:1

Science deals with what we see but the Bible deals with the moral reason behind why we see what we see. That is a very important principle. If someone says "Anyone for tennis?", the rules of tennis will then come into action. Yet, if anyone says "why do human beings play tennis?", the rules of tennis cannot deal with such a question.

Here in David's life is a very clear example of the Bible's dealing with the moral reason behind circumstances, even the physical phenomenon of the famine in David's day. Years before Israel had made a solemn league with the Gibeonites, in Joshua's day, "To let them live", but king Saul later broke the treaty and sought to exterminate them. God had not forgotten and the three years of famine David and his nation now faced was directly related to God's anger at king Saul's broken promise years before. The lessons? Time does not wear out the guilt of sin. We must not build hope of impunity upon the delay of judgements. To break a promise is a very serious thing. It can bring a famine.

N♦O♦V♦E♦M♦B♦E♦R 22ND

"Therefore David said to the Gibeonites, 'What shall I do for you? And with what shall I make atonement, that you may bless the inheritance of the Lord?" 2 Samuel 21:3

A great theme is raised by David's question in today's text. It is the question of atonement. The displeasure of the Lord has been raised and David wants to do something to turn it away; atonement is made for the express purpose of turning away the displeasure of the Lord. It means to appease, to pacify and the root idea is to "to cover". It occurs one hundred and ten times in the Old Testament.

The Gibeonites had been wronged, therefore it was but fair that they should decide what form the reparation should take. They chose that seven men of Saul's descendants should die as punishment for the slaughter of their people. David accepted this.

And what of our sin against God? Whose death will God accept as that which will pacify His wrath against our sin? The amazing answer is that the substitute for the law-breaker is none other than the law-maker. John Stott has put it this way; "The Cross ... was not a punishment of a meek Christ by a harsh and punitive Father, nor a procurement of salvation by a loving Christ from a mean and reluctant Father; nor an action of the

Father which bypassed Christ as mediator. Instead, the righteous, loving Father humbled himself to become in and through his only Son flesh, sin and a curse for us, in order to redeem us without compromising his own character ... the biblical gospel of atonement is of God satisfying himself by substituting himself for us". Such love.

N♦O♦V♦E♦M♦B♦E♦R 23RD

"But the king spared Mephibosheth the son of Jonathan, the son of Saul, because of the Lord's oath that was between them, between David and Jonathan the son of Saul". 2 Samuel 21:7

This is the last occurrence of Mephibosheth's name in the Bible. Moving, is it not, to see the deep lasting impression Jonathan had left on David? It would have been very easy to have given Jonathan's son Mephibosheth to the Gibeonites as an atonement for Saul's wickedness. But David could never forget the promise he had made to Jonathan. Had not Jonathan pleaded "You shall not cut your kindness from my house forever, no, not when the Lord has cut off everyone of the enemies of David from the face of the earth"? David had vowed "For", says Scripture, "He loved him as his own soul".

Have you made a promise? Maybe long ago you promised a friend that you would care for someone. Have you fulfilled that promise? David was now secure on his throne, though troubled. Famine raged around him and Mephibosheth looked expendable. To David's eternal credit, he kept his vow. Mephibosheth was spared. May we too be people of our word.

N♦O♦V♦E♦M♦B♦E♦R 24TH

"When the Philistines were at war again with Israel, David and his servants with him went down and fought against the Philistines; and David grew faint. Then Ishbi-Benob, who was one of the sons of the giant, the weight of whose bronze spear was three hundred shekels, who was bearing a new sword, thought he would kill David. But Abishai the son of Zeruiah came to his aid, and struck the Philistine and killed him."
2 Samuel 21:15-17

Those Philistines, again! And, what's more, they once again sent a giant to kill David! The problem of his youth was the problem of his last days. The victory over Goliath was great but there were more giants, right up to the end. At this time we read of four giants stalking the land, one of which had six fingers on each hand and six toes on each foot! As with David, so with us; there is no holiday in the fight of faith.

The new giant David faced was called Ishbi-Benob. And he had a new sword. There was no questioning what was on his mind; he thought he could kill David. Notice that David, despite his years, was no "Stand-off" leader. The Scripture tells us that "David and his servants with him went down and fought against the Philistine; and David grew faint". Abishai came to his aid and slew the giant Ishbi-Benob.

You may think me strange in saying this but if you think about it, you'll find it to be true; the greatest test of your faith does not come in your youth. It comes in old age. Satan does not attack the older person in the way he attacks the younger. Satan lures youth with the glitter of the world but the older person has seen it all and knows only too well how empty it is. No, in old age, when the giants of loneliness, pain and regret come lumbering across the landscape, Satan then cries "Where is your God, now?" Your God will be there just as powerfully as in your youth. Older person, it is you who really carry the torch in a special way and the younger generation is looking to you for the victory of faith. David had it and so can you.

N♦O♦V♦E♦M♦B♦E♦R 25TH

"Then the men of David swore to him, saying, 'You shall go out no more with us to battle lest you quench the lamp of Israel"'. 2 Samuel 21:17

There is no lovelier title given to David than the description of him as "The lamp of Israel". Despite the fact that Satan constantly tried to blow his light out, David remained a witness to the God who had preserved him from his youth. And, to this very day, his psalms continue to shine as a lamp to the four corners of the earth.

It reminds us of Gideon standing with his three hundred men on a hillside with a multitude of Midianites in the valley below. They had torches hidden in pitchers. When the pitchers were broken all the Midianites could see were three hundred torches blazing on the hillside. They couldn't see the weakness or fears of the men behind the torches and they fled!

Imagine yourself going down a road at night and along comes a car. You see the lights but you cannot immediately identify if the car is a Porche or a Mini Minor! The light is the thing. So you may feel depressed today about the seeming insignificance of your witness for Christ. You may be filled with self-doubt yet if only one person this year, this month, this day catches sight of something different about you, namely the presence of Christ the light of the world, in your life, and that person is led to come to know that light in their darkness, does it matter if they cannot see you and your weaknesses for the light that is shining through you? The light is the thing, discouraged one, the light is the thing.

N◆O◆V◆E◆M◆B◆E◆R 26TH

"Again the anger of the Lord was aroused against Israel, and he moved David against them to say, 'Go, number Israel and Judah"'. 2 Samuel 24:1

Once more, as David grew grey at his ruddy temples, Satan tried to blow out the lamp of his witness. This timely attack was one of the subtlest of all. It came from what seemed like a very innocent action; David commanded Joab to take a census. Our text tells us that God moved David to take the census and 1 Chronicles 21:1 tells us that "Satan stood up against Israel and provoked David to number Israel". Is this a contradiction? No. God permitted Satan to tempt David and David being left to himself yielded to the temptation and sinned.

David's decision to take the census reveals, it seems, that David was starting to lean on the strength of numbers. All his enemies had been subdued and we are told " That the fame of David went out into all lands". It is not easy to hold a full cup of fame and success and there is a great temptation to say "Look how strong I am". Gideon, who we thought of yesterday had to learn, just like David, that big is not necessarily great. His army had to be whittled down from 32,000 to 300, "Lest", God said, "Israel claim glory for itself against Me saying, 'My own hand has saved me'". David's motivation was wrong and let the weight of his wrong motivation challenge us today to make sure that our's is pure.

N✦O✦V✦E✦M✦B✦E✦R 27TH

"And Joab said to the king, 'Now may the Lord your God add to the people a hundredfold more than there are, and may the eyes of my lord the king see it. But why does my lord the king desire this thing?' Nevertheless the king's word prevailed against Joab and against the captains of the army. So Joab and the captains of the army went out from the presence of the king to count the people of Israel". 2 Samuel 24:3-4

Not much good has been recorded in Scripture about the ruthless, coldhearted Joab but here, at least, is a word in his favour. Joab questioned David's motivation in taking a census; "Why does my lord the king desire this thing?"

David did not give any reason as to why he wanted a census. It would seem that having reached the very summit of his life he was unaccountable to anyone around him. He answered to nobody. We don't read of him praying about this thing, we don't read of him seeking God's counsel or of him turning to God's Word to look for guidance in his decision. He simply decided to do it and allowed no questions to be asked.

Be careful if you are in a position where your authority is unquestioned. It is a very dangerous place. All of us should be accountable for the things we do. Let others put integrity on an unassailable pedestal - not you.

"And David's heart condemned him after he had numbered the people. So David said to the Lord, 'I have sinned greatly in what I have done; but now, I pray, O Lord, take away the iniquity of your servant, for I have done very foolishly. 2 Samuel 24:10

In Exodus 30:12 we read "When you take the census of the Children of Israel for their number, then every man shall give a ransom for himself to the Lord, when you number them, that there may be no plague among them when you number them". David, it seems, forgot or deliberately refused to take the ransom money for the Lord as his census was taken. His heart and conscience now strikes him. Ransom money reminded Israel that they were no ordinary people, that they had been redeemed at great price from Egypt, that they still depended upon the Lord for their position and protection. Numbering the redeemed was no mere statistical exercise; they were the Lord's people, every one of them. The warning of a plague amongst the Children of Israel if the Lord's command was not kept was very clear.

There is a very clear parallel to christians today. "Conduct yourselves throughout the time of your sojourning here in fear", writes Peter, "Knowing that you were not redeemed with corruptible things like silver or gold". If David forgot how precious each redeemed life was by bypassing the importance of the ransom money; how much more should a christian remember that he or she was redeemed at an infinitely greater price? We forget it at our peril (See 1 Corinthians 11:29-34).

"So Gad came to David and told him; and he said to him, 'Shall seven years of famine come to you in your land? Or shall you flee three months before your enemies, while they pursue you? Or shall there be three days' plague in your land? Now consider and see what answer I should take back to him who sent me'. And David said to Gad, 'I am in great distress. Please let us fall into the hand of the Lord, for his mercies are great; but do not let me fall into the hand of man"'. 2 Samuel 24:13-14

Did David ever have to make a more difficult decision? Notice, though, that the verse we dealt with on November 26th says that in this whole affair, "The anger of the Lord was kindled against Israel". In chastening David, God was punishing Israel. There had been a national defection from the Lord. Not everyone loved the Lord like David did nor even cared what the Lord thought. It was David who clearly pointed out this problem of worldliness amongst God's people in his prayer in Psalm 12. "Help, Lord", he prayed, "For the godly man ceases! For the faithful disappear from among the son's of men". There was no repentance on their part as there had been on David's. David was a man after God's own heart but not after man's own heart. David had many enemies, as much in his own camp as any other because of his love for the Lord.

David, though, chose to "Fall into the hands of the Lord" rather than "Fall into the hands of man" in this matter. David knew God's heart and he knew that God's mercies were incalculable. I'd rather have God's frown than man's smile any day. Wouldn't you? Though he slay me, yet will I trust him.

N♦O♦V♦E♦M♦B♦E♦R 30TH

"Then the king said to Araunah, 'No, but I will surely buy it from you for a price; nor will I offer burnt offerings to the Lord my God with that which costs me nothing'. So David bought the threshing-floor and the oxen for fifty shekels of silver". 2 Samuel 24:24

David had been commanded by the Lord to erect an altar to the Lord on the threshing floor of Araunah the Jebusite during the time of the three day plague that fell upon the Children of Israel. Araunah immediately offered David oxen for sacrifice and wood for the fire, free of charge. David refused. He bought the threshing floor and the oxen for fifty shekels of silver. 1 Chronicles 21 tells us that he actually eventually bought all of Araunah's place, which probably included all of his land for six hundred shekels of gold. The threshing floor of Araunah became the eventual site for the great temple at Jerusalem.

So many treat spiritual things as if they came from some kind of free supermarket. David never looked on things from that angle. He refused to offer anything to the Lord that was cheap. To be quite honest it appals me when I often see local christian churches run "On the cheap" while their members live like kings. Let's get, like David, our priorities right. And he did because in our journey through 1st and 2nd Samuel the narrative ends with David's offering being accepted by God and we are shown David in full fellowship with the Lord. The prodigal had come home.

D E·C·E·M·B·E·R

D♦E♦C♦E♦M♦B♦E♦R

L ast words are always fascinating. Obituaries can also make interesting reading. An actor was rumoured dead whereas he was, in fact, merely ill. The actor was amazed to read his obituary in the newspaper which said that although he could never be deemed a great actor he was "Invaluable in small parts!" We could never write that of David for he was truly great and in this advent month his greatness and all he learned of God point us to his Greater Son, laid in a lowly manger at Bethlehem. Come, let us adore Him.

D♦E♦C♦E♦M♦B♦E♦R 1ST

"Now Adonijah the son Haggith exalted himself, saying, 'I will be king', and he prepared for himself chariots and horsemen, and fifty men to run before him" . 1 Kings 1:5

So, David ends his life in peace and tranquillity? That might be what the fairy story books would want to say but it certainly is not what the Bible says. Almost seventy, David now faces yet another rebellion against his throne from within his own household. Adonijah, Absalom's brother rises up and follows his brother's evil example, preparing chariots and horsemen and fifty men to run before him. Almost to the letter he does what Absalom did, making a feast, getting the people about him and inciting them to proclaim him as king. Older brothers should be very careful of the example they set to their younger brothers.

It is a sad fact that often a person's worst enemies can be those from within their own household or even their own circle of colleagues at work. If you are discovering that fact in your life don't be surprised. A young MP took his seat on his first day in the House of Commons. Turning to an older colleague and looking at the Opposition benches before him he said "Isn't it good to get a close look at the enemy?" "You will soon find", said his older and wiser colleague, "That the enemy is not over there but around you, here". Selah

D•E•C•E•M•B•E•R 2ND

"And his father had not rebuked him at any time by saying 'Why have you done so?' He was also a very good-looking man. His mother had borne him after Absalom". 1 Kings 1:6

David always had a weakness when it came to disciplining his children. His unruly son, Adonijah, was determined to exalt himself, even though he knew that Solomon had been appointed by God to succeed his father. David said nothing against him. He refused to cross his good-looking son and discipline him. By such parental neglect David was but preparing a rod for his own back.

"Chasten your son while there is hope", wrote Solomon, years later, "He who loves him disciplines him promptly". Disciplining in family life is vital, but let's keep the balance. We are often either inconsistent with not enough discipline or too much. Abundant love does not make discipline unnecessary and discipline without abundant love is a crime. May God give us the right consistency.

D•E•C•E•M•B•E•R 3RD

"Then he conferred with Joab the son of Zeruiah and with Abiathar the priest, and they followed and helped Adonijah". 1 Kings 1:7

Isn't it great to have a friend who loves you just for what you are and not for who you are? Isn't it grand to have someone loyal to you no matter what your circumstances, no matter who says what against you? There are not many things in life greater than true friendship and there are not many things more uncommon.

Joab proves in David's last days that he was, at heart, a self-centred, mercenary member of his administration. He was no real friend to David. Time always has a way of flushing out the true principles by which a person lives. The only real principle Joab seemed to have lived by was the principle of self-interest. He knew David wanted to replace him as army chief (See 2 Samuel 19:13) and so, to make his own position secure he supported Adonijah's rebellion against his master. He who had speared Absalom to death because Absalom was of no use to him now supports Adonijah against David because it is more advantageous to his position. Tell me, do you admire Joab for his subtle manipulation and cleverness? No? Then cut out any temptation to be manipulative or clever in your own friendships. "A friend that aint in need", said Ken Hubbard, "Is a friend indeed". (Think about it!)

D✦E✦C✦E✦M✦B✦E✦R 4TH

"But Zadok the priest, Benaiah the son of Jehoiada, Nathan the prophet, Shimei, Rei, and the mighty men who belonged to David were not with Adonijah". 1 Kings 1:8

Today's text is a very honourable roll-call, indeed. Disloyalty to David was seething again but this list gives honourable mention to the loyalists. Nathan stayed true despite all he knew of David's dark side for he knew his king's heart was after God. The ever loyal Benaiah who "Killed the lion in the midst of a pit on a snowy day" did not desert his master. Neither did the rest of David's mighty men; men like Eleazar who once fought so loyally for David that his hand stuck to his sword. Shammah, Asahel, Helez and all the others, thirty-six in all remained faithful. And Solomon, God's heir, gave his brother's rebellion no backing.

Our text tells us that none of these men went to Adonijah's special feast. Wasn't it, in effect, a great honour not to be invited? Could it be that you weren't invited to a particular social event, recently? You maybe didn't get invited to join the "In crowd" you used to go around with. It hurts, but perhaps you very well know that it has to do with your loyalty to Christ and the christian lifestyle. Stay true, christian. Your lack of an invitation has shown where your loyalties lie.

D✦E✦C✦E✦M✦B✦E✦R 5TH

"And just then, while she was still talking with the king, Nathan the prophet also came in". 1 Kings 1:22

The Lord overruled in Adonijah's rebellion. The key to it all lay in the way Nathan behaved. He called in Bathsheba to remind David of his promise to place Solomon on his throne. Then, at the precise moment when he was needed Nathan returned to David's palace and confirmed the point Bathsheba had made.

Nathan's behaviour underlines a very important principle found in the Bible. We read in Deuteronomy 19:15 that "One witness shall not rise against a man concerning any iniquity or any sin that he commits; by the mouth of two or three witnesses shall the matter be established". A. W. Pink comments "Much needless trouble had been avoided in the church (Matthew 18:11), many a false accusation had been exposed (John 8:13,17), many a breach had been healed (2 Corinthians 13:1) and many an innocent servant of God had been cleared (1 Timothy 5:19), if only this principle had been duly heeded". The lovely thing is that as a result of Nathan's application of the biblical principle great bloodshed was avoided and great heartache assuaged. May God give us grace to apply the same principle in our lives when someone rises to accuse anyone of sin.

D✦E✦C✦E✦M✦B✦E✦R 6TH

"And Benaiah the son of Jehoiada answered the king and said, 'Amen! May the Lord God of my lord the king say so too. As the Lord has been with my lord the king, even so may he be with Solomon, and make his throne greater than the throne of my lord king David"'. 1 Kings 1:36-37

There is a heartiness, a joy, a blessing in the "Amen" Benaiah uses to affirm his agreement to David's proposal to put Solomon on the throne. The use of the word "Amen" in our conversation is a thoroughly biblical practice. The root meaning of "Amen" is to "Confirm" or to "Support". It is to say, as Benaiah meant it, "So let it be". In the Old Testament it is used with doxologies, assent by congregations to laws, oaths and appointments. In the New Testament it is used as assent of a congregation to utterances of a leader.

Unfortunately the use of the term is slipping in many Western church congregations. Listen to Paul argue for its use: "I will pray in the Spirit", he says, "And I will also pray with the understanding ... otherwise if you bless with the Spirit how will he who occupies the place of the uninformed say 'Amen' at your giving of thanks since he does not understand what you say". Paul expected his congregation to say an audible "Amen", and so should we. (I tell you, when you hear an Eastern European congregation say "Amen" to a spiritual point you have made it does your heart much greater good than the Wembley roar!). Let's have more "Amens" in both our conversations and congregations.

D✦E✦C✦E✦M✦B✦E✦R 7TH

"And all the people went up after him; and the people played the flutes and rejoiced with great joy, so that the earth seemed to split with their sound".
1 Kings 1:40

Israel and Judah were by no means perfect but when it came to celebrating they certainly knew how to celebrate! We, in the West, are not so good at celebrations. If I say my leg is sore someone will tell me somebody they know of who recently had their leg amputated! If you say your spin drier has a wheeze somebody will tell you they had a friend whose spin drier caught fire and burned their house down!

We tend to remember the people who have hurt us rather than the people who have helped us, the insensitive rather than the inspirational. Life tends to be a drudgery to be endured rather than something to be enjoyed. Don't tell me you don't have something to celebrate; all of us should be grateful for even being alive. Stop letting your reminiscences run along the lines of the flat tyre you had on the motorway yesterday or the week you had in hospital last year. Rather, concentrate on the good Christmas's or holidays you have known: the happy weddings and the joyous births amongst your family and friends. Get out the confetti, or tinkle the old ivory keyboards, go out for dinner tonight or ease back with a coffee at your favourite coffee shop. Go on, celebrate the joy of living. If you want a biblical example just read today's text.

D•E•C•E•M•B•E•R 8TH

*"Now David assembled at Jerusalem all the leaders of Israel ... and said ...
But God said to me, 'You shall not build a house for my name, because you
have been a man of war and have shed blood. However the Lord God of
Israel chose me above all the house of my father to be king over Israel
forever, for he has chosen Judah to be the ruler; and of the house of Judah,
the house of my father, and among the sons of my father, he was pleased
with me to make me king over all Israel '". 1 Chronicles 28:1-4*

David had turned his last corner. He was about to come to the
end of his long and eventful life. As Dr. Luke said in his Book of
Acts, "He had served his own generation by the will of God". His
end was a very dignified one because David did not waste his
last hours. He used his fast-failing energies to set his house in
order and there is no question that the glory of the Lord was the
motivation for all he did and said. No one had more famous last
words than David and we shall look at them for inspiration as
the final month of our year together slips away.

David, in his final speech, concentrates first on an unfulfilled
desire. All of us have unfulfilled desires and dreams and David's
had been to build a magnificent home for the sacred ark of the
covenant. But God said "No". Notice there is not even a trace of
bitterness and resentment in David at God's decision. Instead of
wasting energy on thinking of what God didn't let him do, he
rejoices in what God did let him do. He was content with just
that. Can't you be, too?

D•E•C•E•M•B•E•R 9TH

*"And of all my sons (for the Lord has given me many sons) he has chosen
my son Solomon to sit on the throne of the kingdom of the Lord over Israel.
Now he said to me, 'It is your son Solomon, who shall build my house and
my courts; for I have chosen him to be my son, and I will be his Father'".
Chronicles 28:5-6*

Is there a career person reading today's text? Have you been
overlooked in promotion? Is there someone who is suffering a
broken relationship that you had placed great store by? Is there

perhaps a great unfulfilled ambition in your life and you know, at this time, that God has shown it will never be fulfilled in your life time? Meditate, then, on those very moving words of David as he faces up to knowing he will never see his great dream of building the temple, fulfilled.

Yesterday we saw how David rejoiced in what God did let him do in his life rather than what God didn't let him do. Now we see him concentrate not on what was unfulfilled because of God's will but on what will be fulfilled in God's will. David knew that what he now did in the coming few days and hours left to him would deeply affect the future. He knows the biblical principle that "He being dead yet speaks". So, he concentrates on Solomon, God's choice for the work, and encourages him. The lesson is clear; if God won't let you do something, encourage those He will!

D♦E♦C♦E♦M♦B♦E♦R 10TH

"As for you, my son Solomon, know the God of your father".
1 Chronicles 28:9

What better advice could any believer give his child? David advises Solomon not just to know about God but to know God. He is a God who can be actually known. All eternity will not reveal all that He is, never to speak of all of life. Getting to know Him is a great unending adventure. A lot of people in life can be known very quickly and how very boring they often are. But not God.

Infinite, invisible, immutable, inexhaustible, imperial, incorruptible, impartial, immortal, indispensable; He is God. No variableness ever lessens the resources of this great Quencher of thirst. No expenditure He makes ever lowers the reserves of His riches in glory. Here is, as C. R. Rolls put it; "Truth to sanctify, love to edify, peace to purify, gifts to gratify, grace to beautify, power to fortify, and Himself to satisfy". No wonder David told his son to get to know God. You can know Him too; just as well, and, in just as satisfying a way.

D✦E✦C✦E✦M✦B✦E✦R 11TH

"... And serve him with a loyal heart and with a willing mind; for the Lord searches all hearts and understands all the intent of the thoughts. If you seek him, he will be found by you; but if you forsake him, he will cast you off forever". 1 Chronicles 28:9

God is the great heart searcher. He knows if you mean business. No matter how many faces we may put on to other people, no matter how much flannel we use to cover our ultimate intentions, even our thoughts are heard in Heaven.

True loyalty to the Master and willingness to serve Him surely must flow from the fact that we have love for Him. You can have all the seminars you like about the subject but people need to love the Lord before they will ever serve Him.

"Though cities bow to art,
and I am its true lover,
It is not art, but heart,
which wins the wide world over".

We take it for granted that we serve Christ because we love Christ; but, is the assumption always safe? The Lord would search our hearts today and ask, as He did of Peter, "Do you love me?" Service for the Lord should never be a half-hearted thing. Put your whole heart in it. When you do it is infectious.

D✦E✦C✦E✦M✦B✦E✦R 12TH

"If you seek him, he will be found by you". 1 Chronicles 28:9

David is stating a truism, if ever there was one. Spiritual light crosses everybody's path whether you were born in Manhatten or in the jungles of Vietnam. We are all left without excuse and we shall be judged according to the light God has given us. Did not the aged Anna seek the Lord with all her heart? And Simeon too and all those who looked for redemption in Israel? They followed the light God gave them and when they saw David's greater Son, our Lord Jesus, they immediately realised he was the same light they had been following for, as John the Baptist put it, "This is the light which lightens every man that enters into the world". They trusted Him as Saviour.

In the Chad there was a tribe who constantly worshipped the one true god. My friend, Mr. Neville Taylor, a veteran christian missionary, told me when the Gospel was first preached to them virtually the entire tribe were converted to Christ. They could see that this was the light which had already crossed their path. So, preach the Gospel and you will find amongst those who have never heard it before an immediate recognition of it as the truth.

D♦E♦C♦E♦M♦B♦E♦R 13TH

"And David said to his son Solomon, 'Be strong and of good courage, and do it; do not fear nor be dismayed, for the Lord God - my God- will be with you. He will not leave you nor forsake you, until you have finished all the work for the service of the house of the Lord"'. 1 Chronicles 28:20

I rose recently to preach at the great Keswick Convention, the oldest Christian Convention in Britain. Was I nervous? Very. Was I frightened? Yes. What was my problem? Well, it had to do with the long line of faithful men of God who had preached there before me. The list was daunting. In 1883 it was J. Hudson Taylor. In 1885 it was H. C. G. Moule. In 1887 it was F. B. Meyer. In 1892 it was D. L. Moody. In 1937 it was Harry Ironside and the list goes on until it frightened the life out of me!

Are you frightened and daunted? Don't you think Solomon was daunted? "My son Solomon, whom God alone has chosen, is young and inexperienced and the work is great", said David (1 Chronicles 29:1). Are you daunted by some task of great responsibility in christian work which has come your way? Don't be overcome by it. The God of our fathers is our God and His power is the same today as ever it was. He won't leave you and He won't forsake you until the work is finished. Isn't that enough?

An older Keswick Convention Council member gave me a word of advice which I have never forgotten. He said "The problem we have here is that some preachers come to this

Convention and while they are preaching they concentrate on the twenty or thirty people behind them (the platform party) rather than the three thousand in front of them. So remembering his advice and forgetting the "Unseen witnesses" of the past I tried to concentrate on my present congregation. God helped me and He will do the very same for you, today.

D♦E♦C♦E♦M♦B♦E♦R 14TH

"The temple is not for man but for the Lord God". 1 Chronicles 29:1

David was proving at the end to be what he was at the beginning; a man after God's own heart. As he poured out the details of the blue print for the temple to his son, right down to the weight of gold for the very forks to be used in its service, he never forgot that what he was doing was for the glory of God.

It isn't easy to forget public opinion, is it? It is'nt easy to forget that the praise of men, the glory of men, is a fickle, impermanent thing. David, by long experience knew that what was done for the Lord would last. He reminded his son that the work he was doing was for God and that it demanded his very best. Someone described the future as " The time when you'll wish you had done what you are not doing now". Make up your mind that whether it be washing dishes, punching a word processor, driving a wedding car, teaching a school class, working on a hospital ward, ploughing a field, or, whatever, that you are going to do all to the glory of God. Such an attitude will give your work eternal significance.

D♦E♦C♦E♦M♦B♦E♦R 15TH

"Moreover, because I have set my affection on the house of my God, I have given to the house of my God, over and above all that I have prepared for the holy house, my own special treasure of gold and silver".
1 Chronicles 29:3

Did you notice that little phrase, "Over and above all that", in today's text? Sure, David was going to build a temple for God.

There were articles of silver to be prepared to be used in "Every kind of service", there were "Lamps of gold" and "Refined gold for the altar of incense". "All this", said David, "The Lord made me understand in writing by his hand upon me, all the works of these plans". But, "Over and above all that" David gave of his own special treasure of gold and silver.

I like "Over and above all that" kind of people, don't you? I know plenty who bloom on a Sunday morning only to fold up the rest of the week. I know plenty who have a token Christianity but not a penny more and not a penny less is given above their token. Give me the men of Nehemiah's day of whom it is said; "So we laboured in the work, and half the men held the spears from daybreak until the stars appeared". No quitting at 5.30 p.m. for them! They were "Over and above all that"; there was an emergency on and they gave it all they had. I'd like to start an "Over and above all that" movement. Care to join me? David was a founder member!

D✦E✦C✦E✦M✦B✦E✦R 16TH

"Then David spoke to the Lord the words of this song, on the day when the Lord had delivered him from the hand of all his enemies, and from the hand of Saul. And he said: 'The Lord is my rock, my fortress and my deliverer; the God of my strength, in him I will trust, my shield and the horn of my salvation, my stronghold and my refuge; my Saviour, you save me from violence". 2 Samuel 22:1-3

As David drew near the end he tries, in a lovely song, to express how he feels about the Lord's dealings with him. Let's concentrate on its details as we try to sum up all the lessons his life would teach us. From the very first day that David put his head up and talked to his antagonistic brothers about Goliath to the day Ashbi-Benob, the giant tried to kill him, David was hassled by enemies. No matter where he went, no matter what he tried to do, he was harassed by Satan. But he was delivered. Saul threw a javelin at him, but he escaped. Messengers were sent to watch David's house to kill him in the morning; his wife let him down through a window and he fled. Saul ordered that David be brought to him in his bed but the messengers found a dummy there instead. On and on went the relentless pursuit of David and again and again he was delivered.

Rest your mind on the images David chose to describe his God in today's text. "My rock". "My fortress". "My deliverer". "My strength". "My shield". "My stronghold". "My refuge". "My Saviour". With such a God you need fear nothing in your life for like David in so far as you are obedient to the Lord, you are immortal until your work is done.

D♦E♦C♦E♦M♦B♦E♦R 17TH

"I will call upon the Lord, who is worthy to be praised; so shall I be saved from my enemies". 2 Samuel 22:4

These inspiring words are sung all over the Western world as a chorus in churches and I happily confess it to be one of my favourites. But note that the armour of a soldier does him no service unless he puts it on. Even when the allies were protecting Singapore their huge guns were of no use for the simple reason that they were pointing the wrong way; they pointed out to sea and the Japanese army came on bicycles from the jungles behind.

Note the emphasis; if we want protection from God we must pray for it. Call on the Lord; so you shall be saved from your enemies. There is a touch here of victory before the event, isn't there? As W. A. Ward put it; "God wants us to be victors, not victims; to grow, not grovel; to soar, not sink; to overcome, not to be overwhelmed". So, pray, christian, pray.

D♦E♦C♦E♦M♦B♦E♦R 18TH

" Then the earth shook and trembled; the foundations of heaven moved and shook, because he was angry. Smoke went up from his nostrils, and devouring fire from his mouth; coals were kindled by it." 2 Samuel 22:8-9

The poet in David is certainly piling on the metaphors as he now describes the anger of God. He had seen it and known it and the subject of divine anger was certainly not the taboo subject with David that it has become in modern society. Unfortunately in our generation a lot of christians have accepted the taboo and conditioned themselves never to raise the subject. Why?

It seems to come from a suspicion that ideas of the anger of God are unworthy of God. You know, a slamming of doors, a stamping of feet, kind of anger. We tend to think of anger as plain bad temper. But, just as God's love never leads him to foolish and impulsive action so God's anger is never irritable, never self-indulgent, and never cruel. It is a righteous anger. It is an attribute of God. And we too are allowed to have God's kind of anger. That's why the Scripture says "Be angry and sin not". God is only angry where anger is called for. Let's pray that we behave in the same way.

D◆E◆C◆E◆M◆B◆E◆R 19TH

"He delivered me from my strong enemy, from those who hated me; for they were too strong for me. They confronted me in the day of my calamity, but the Lord was my support, he also brought me out into a broad place; he delivered me because he delighted in me". 2 Samuel 22:18-20

Our view of God is too narrow. Our vision of His purposes is too restricted. Standing one winter's night with some friends under a starry sky in New Zealand I asked the gentleman who was letting us use his powerful telescope if it was mist I saw in the sky. "Mist?", he replied with a smile, "They are galaxies of stars!" He soon showed me what was what. I felt so dumb!

People are so often content with the mundane. They are so like sheep. If left to themselves sheep will erode the landscape. They need good management which gets them out of their ruts and onto better pasture. David wrote of the good shepherd leading him up through the dark valley where death lurked to the table land. The good shepherd goes before his sheep and calls us after him. He wants to move us on to higher ground. "He brought me into a broad place", wrote David in today's text. Why, even Job tells us God created the oceans for the whale to sport in! Let God lead you into his greatness.

D◆E◆C◆E◆M◆B◆E◆R 20TH

"He delivered me because he delighted in me". 2 Samuel 22:20

We seldom think about the pleasure's of God because we are so bent on having our own. David knew that despite his sin God loved him and when he obeyed and followed him he brought great pleasure to God's heart. He knew that God delighted in him and this gave him impetus in all that he did.

Christian, be reminded once more that you are beloved of the Lord. I can hear you say "But I have sinned ..." Yes, I know. It's like a lady in Scotland who once said to me about her relationship with Christ that she "Dinna always treat him richt". None of us have. "Your father won't love you any more", said a childminder to a badly behaved child. When her father came home he found the child hysterical. Quietly he took her gently in his arms and said "When you are good I love you in a glad way and when you are bad, I love you in a sad way. But, whether you are good or bad I will always love you". Selah.

D♦E♦C♦E♦M♦B♦E♦R 21ST

"You will save the humble people; but your eyes are on the haughty, that you may bring them down". 2 Samuel 22:28

Humility. How can we define it? David's long experience had shown him that humility was something God prized. But "What is it? Let me quote two definitions I have come across. One is from Augustine who said "The sufficiency of my merit is to know that my merit is not sufficient". The other comes from that great christian leader of a recent generation, A. Lyndsay Glegg, the man who with others took Butlins at Filey and filled it with thousands of people for those great Filey weeks of christian teaching and praise that so many of us enjoyed. He said, "If there is one thing I would like to have said of me by those who are left behind when I have gone into the glory land, it would be just this - that the overflow hid the vessel". Now, that's humility.

D♦E♦C♦E♦M♦B♦E♦R 22ND

*"For you are my lamp, O Lord; the Lord shall enlighten my darkness".
2 Samuel 22:29*

Darkness constantly overwhelmed David. In his family, in his calling, in his marriage, with his children, in his nation; from his youth to his old age he must have often wondered just what on earth was going to happen to him next. The future constantly appeared to be dark.

Yet, there was always a light for David, no matter how dark. The Lord was a lamp for him. Just as the light in the tabernacle never went out so the Lord was the constant light in lightening David's darkness. So it is for the christian. We are not here to learn how to live in the dark but to walk in the light. As soon as a person comes to Christ they enter the light and continue to walk in that light and the blood of Jesus Christ His Son cleanses them from all sin. Notice that Scripture does not teach that the blood of Christ cleanses and then we walk in the light. It is the other way around. It is saying that when we repent of sin and trust Christ as Saviour we enter into the light which is Christ and we will walk in that light for ever and as we walk His shed blood will cleanse us from our sins, perpetually. Such truth will lighten any darkness.

D♦E♦C♦E♦M♦B♦E♦R 23RD

"For by you I can run against a troop; by my God I can leap over a wall".
2 Samuel 22:30

"David cannot come in here", said the Jebusites. The walls of Zion were no barrier to David and we read that "David dwelt in the stronghold and called it the City of David". So Jerusalem was founded. There is a joyful victory note that runs through this great story of David's as he recounts his life. Critics might say that he makes no mention of his sins in the song but such criticism won't wear. David had written of his failures and weaknesses as no other man in history has ever written, but, in this song he is emphasising his victories.

Don't you think the christian is allowed to sing a victory song from time to time? It isn't triumphalism to recount the triumphs the Lord has given you through your life as long as you give him the glory. There is a glorious spiritual chuckle in David's phrase "By you I can run against the troop and by my God I can leap over a wall"! It reminds me of the old lady who used to run the little christian tract shop by Yorkminister. I walked in one day with a friend and she looked at the pair of us; "Are you believers?", she asked. "We certainly are", we replied. "Well", she said, "It's worth a king's ransom to be able to shout Hallelujah!"

D✦E✦C✦E✦M✦B✦E✦R 24TH

"For who is God, except the Lord?" 2 Samuel 22:32

On this eve of Christmas we think of the Incarnation. When the Apollo mission took astronauts from earth to the moon, the astronauts never identified with the moon. If they had they would have been dead in seconds. Instead they took with them all the paraphernalia of earth. They took their own equipment, clothing, oxygen and food and established a sort of earth colony on the moon.

But see this little baby lying in a manger? He brought, reverently speaking, no paraphernalia with him. He identified with life on this planet to which he had come and brought nothing with him but Himself. The Eternal Son did not remain aloof from us in the safe immunity of Heaven, He came down to earth. He didn't shout the Gospel at us from the sky but He came down to us in person in great humility. The hinge of history was on the door of a Bethlehem stable. Come, let us adore Him.

D✦E✦C✦E✦M✦B✦E✦R 25TH

"You have also given me the shield of your salvation, and your gentleness has made me great". 2 Samuel 22:36

I often smile when I think of what Art Fettig said. "Some businessmen", said Art, "Are saying this could be the greatest Christmas ever. I always thought that the first one was". Indeed it was. As J. I. Packer put it "The Divine Son became a Jew; the Almighty appeared on earth as a helpless human baby, unable to do more than lie and wriggle and make noises, needing to be fed and changed and taught to talk like any other child ... the more you think about it, the more staggering it gets".

David looking back over his life speaks of the Lord acting to him like a tender parent; firm, wise, loving, patient. As we rejoice this Christmas Day in the birth of our Saviour we too can say that His gentleness has made us great. Where would we be without Him? David had been raised from the sheepfold to a throne by Him. We too have been set among princes. It was truly the best Christmas, ever.

D◆E◆C◆E◆M◆B◆E◆R 26TH

"He makes my way perfect. He makes my feet like the feet of deer, and sets me on my high places". 2 Samuel 22:34

God never calls anyone to do anything for him that he does not equip them for. Look back down your life to this Boxing Day. Can you not see a straight line? What God permits, He has foreseen. God's providence is much like the Hebrew Bible; you must begin at the end and read backwards in order to understand it. God has been in all your circumstances.

David's beautiful imagery sums it all up. He says God has made his feet like the feet of deer. Animals feet are specially designed to suit the circumstances and demands of their lives. For example, the oxen are suited for low land, the deer for high land. Watch the agility of the deer along a craggy precipice, they can handle it all with ease because they are suited and designed for it.

As David was trained and suited for his work as Israel's king, so you are suited to serve the Lord in your sphere of service. He will give you sureness of foot and keep you in dangerous places. "Do you know where you are going?", a little evacuee in London's blitz was asked as he boarded a train. "No", he replied, "But the King does". Selah.

D◆E◆C◆E◆M◆B◆E◆R 27TH

"You enlarged my path under me; so my feet did not slip". 2 Samuel 22:37

David is back, in this summing up of his life, to one of his favourite themes; it is the theme of God's desire to give us more, to widen our horizons, to lead us on into bigger, better, greater things. You get the same theme in Psalm 30:8 :"You", writes David "Have not shut me up into the hand of the enemy; you have set my feet in a wide place". You get it in Psalm 18:19 where David writes, "He also brought me out into a broad place". It occurs in Psalm 118 where David comments, "I called on the Lord in distress; the Lord answered me and set me in a broad place".

A friend of mine recently told me he reckoned I needed to understand again what the Gospel really is. He took me and taught me some things that took my spiritual breath away. Things to do with the future, of reigning with Christ, of christians judging angels, of helping in the running of God's vast future universe, of the redemption of the earth, of the redemption of the body. He showed me that Christ's death has effected more than getting us out of Hell, he emphasised how it will effect the very universe itself. Anyone can count the seeds in one apple, but only God can count the apples in one seed. You, christian, are only on the edge of a great and vast adventure.

D♦E♦C♦E♦M♦B♦E♦R 28TH

"For you armed me with strength for the battle". 2 Samuel 22:40

David found strength day after day for all that faced him and so can you. Do you remember the parable about the man who got out of bed to give food to his neighbour? Why did he get up? Because the man asking for it meant business! So, said Christ, ask and your Father will give the Holy Spirit to those who ask Him. This does not mean that he will give the gift of the Holy Spirit in a classical sense as given to the church once and for all at Pentecost. That's guaranteed to every believer but it does mean, as Paul put it, that you can ask, in prayer, to "Be strengthened with might through his Spirit in the inner man". And, just like in the parable, if you mean business, you will get what you ask for. Of course if you ask for it and in a week or in a month later you don't really care whether you have got it or not, you won't get it. Will you? Repeat; you must mean business!

D♦E♦C♦E♦M♦B♦E♦R 29TH

"You have also delivered me from the strivings of my people".
2 Samuel 22:44

It was, for David, from the very beginning, a long battle against a fickle people. The truth was that David faced more trouble in his life time from the divisions and contentions, warrings and grumblings of the Children of Israel than ever he did from his enemies. How did he survive? The Lord delivered him by giving him the right attitude. He looked beyond the people of God to their God and he put Him first; he knew that it really is true that life is 10 percent what happens to us and 90 percent how we react to it. The Lord gave him wisdom to have the right attitude.

Paul faced the very same problem. The divisions of the Corinthian Church were disgraceful and their criticism of Paul unrelenting. Why didn't he get out his apostolic guns and blow them out of the water? No. When they said he did not look good and that his speech was contemptible and that they preferred the sermons of Apollo's, Paul simply contended that if there was any spiritual blessing following his work then it must have come from God and not from him. He didn't let them drag him down to their level.

David's stickability as a leader of a fickle, moody, often divided people is an inspiration to all who would face the same problems today. For, the christian church seems to be the only group who shoot their own wounded. They, like the Children of Israel, may be the best spiritually taught people in the world but they are not by any means the best behaved.

D♦E♦C♦E♦M♦B♦E♦R 30TH

"Now these are the last words of David. Thus says David the son of Jesse; thus says the man raised up on high, the anointed of the God of Jacob, and the sweet psalmist of Israel; 'The Spirit of the Lord spoke by me, and his word was on my tongue. The God of Israel said, the Rock of Israel spoke to me; he who rules over men must be just, ruling in the fear of God. And he shall be like the light of the morning when the sun rises, a morning without clouds, like the tender grass springing out of the earth, by clear shining after rain"'. 2 Samuel 231-4

This is a perfect summary of it all, from David's own lips. He had been called by God to reign. He was, in his own words, a "Man raised up". His writing talent was certainly anointed of God. He gives the Son of God all the glory for the words given to him that have in turn inspired millions. He was the "Sweet psalmist of Israel" and we shall sing his psalms forever because they were the inspired Word of God which lives and abides forever.

It is, though, the final flourish of David's pen which perfectly captures the life of faith we have just studied over this year, together. David is not saying that he as a leader always faithfully discharged his obligations to God and his law but he is saying that the leader who does will be like "The light of the morning when the sun rises, a morning without clouds, like tender grass springing out of the earth, by clear shining after rain".

All of us are leaders in some way, as parents, or whatever, and as this year slips away from us and a new one looms, who would not like to be in their home, or business, or school, or college, or farm or factory like the clear new light of day, like the tender grass springing up and shining after a shower of rain? Have you ever stood in the sunshine after a shower of rain and looked upon everything as it glistens and sparkles? It is so clean, so refreshing, so inspiring. Make no mistake about it that true holiness of life and obedience to God is beautiful. So be what you are.

D٠E٠C٠E٠M٠B٠E٠R 31st

"So, David rested with his fathers, and he was buried in the City of David". 1 Kings 2:10

The evangelist, Mr. Bertie Johnston, a former officer in the Royal Ulster Constabulary was pressing his message home. My heart was deeply moved as I saw his gift flourish. But more than being moved, I was challenged by what he said. Looking at his congregation in the little town of Portrush on Northern Ireland's beautiful northern coastline he made three points and as they poured out of him I found them a perfect summary of this book and all that we have learned together.

The Scripture records that "David did what was right in the eyes of the Lord and had not turned aside from anything he commanded him all the days of his life, except in the matter of Uriah the Hittite". It is an incredible, yet ultimately sad epitaph. For, said Mr. Johnston, "Sin takes us further than we want to go". It did that for David. You don't mean to tell me that David wanted to see his baby die, Absalom rise in rebellion, the Children of Israel divide, his throne be threatened, Ahithophel commit suicide, and plagues sweep the land? David didn't want heartache and sorrow to dog all his final days. But sin takes us further than we want to go. "And", added the evangelist", "Sin keeps us longer than we want to stay". For a whole year not a single psalm came from David's pen and for the rest of his days the guilt of what he had done became the theme of most of the psalms he wrote. Purity is power but the wounded David found that sin kept him longer than he wanted to stay.

"And sin", said Mr. Johnston, finally, "Costs us more than we want to pay". In fact we couldn't pay the frightening debt it has cost us. Only David's greater Son did that at Calvary.

What have we learned, then, from the amazing life of this the greatest king Israel ever had? We have learned that sin takes us further than we want to go, keeps us longer than we want to stay and costs us more than we want to pay. David, shepherd, psalmist, and king stands as a warning light across the centuries.

Derick Bingham

Derick Bingham has a reputation for delivering a profound message with sharp wit, piercing logic, and complete honesty, he has authored many books, and is also a columnist with the *Christian Herald*.

Derick is a Bible Teacher with the Crescent Church, Belfast. His ministry has taken him throughout the United Kingdom, including the renowned Keswick Convention, and also to many other parts of the world.

Audio and video recordings of his messages are also available. For complete listings of books and recordings please write to the publishers.